The Heathen's Guide to
WORLD RELIGIONS

A secular history of the *One True Faiths*

"WICKEDLY FUN AND INFORMATIVE..."
~THE TORONTO STAR

"New World Order" Edition! Includes the Taliban, Bin Laden, and more!

William Hopper

Table of Contents

82

Printed in the United States of America

First Printing: August, 1997

Current Edition: 2011

ISBN-10: 097315084X

ISBN-13: 978-0973150841

PRAISE FOR THE HEATHEN

> "*The Heathen's Guide To World Religions is a masterfully written, wonderfully funny and deliciously snarky trip down religious lane as can only be written by an author the likes of William Hopper.*" ~Al Stefanelli/United Atheist Front

> "*Hopper has flair to kingdom come, and the grace to use humor instead of indignation. Highly recommended... easily one of the best places to invest your book buying dollar.*" ~The Georgia Straight

> "*Wickedly fun and informative.*" ~Toronto Star

> "*The serious side examines the precepts and contentions of various religions in the context of what history actually reveals. The other is to approach it all with biting satire and flat out humor.*" ~BlogCritics

> "*Hopper represents the most lethal of organized religions many opponents: a curious, well-educated individual with a sharp wit.*"~Queen's University Journal Review

READER REVIEWS

> In a nutshell: Buy it, Read it, Like it, Smile. ~John Taylor

> *The Heathen's Guide To World Religions* by William Hopper is awesome... Very highly recommended.~Dr. Craig S. Bruce

> Hopper's satiric wit and vast knowledge of religions is everywhere in evidence in the Heathen's Guide.This is easily one of my favorite books. ~Peter Jaworski

> Fodder for passionate discussion and book burning demonstrations alike. ~Stephanie Moore

The Heathen's Guide to World Religions

INTRODUCTION TO THE NEW WORLD ORDER EDITION

The Heathen's Guide to World Religion is an undeniably sarcastic (though accurate) look at the history of the world's religions. Because of this it's often been said that this book needlessly upsets kindly religious folks who would never hurt a fly. As the author I recognize that there really are many decent, kindly people involved in the religions of the world. While the upper echelons of religions have usually been involved in some treachery. deceit, or bloodshed, many people are still drawn to the churches because they see these faiths as a way to be decent and do some good. For this reason any view that opposes religion is seen by many as an attack on the decent, kindly people that strive to feed the poor and tend to the infirm.

These people are to be respected and admired. It's a hard world and anyone who strives to make it better should be commended. I also agree that decent and kindly folks are being victimized, but I don't believe that it's this book that victimizes them. The damage done eo them comes from the religious elite, and their promise that if you play the role of ignorant and submissive sheep long enough, you will achieve true peace, You see, no matter how conniving or power hungry the leaders of the world's faiths are, they can always hide behind the goodwill and decency of the sheep that trust them. So, when you attack the shepherd you, attack the sheep. And no one wants to hurt innocent sheep. Still, every day people are tortured and killed for various religious beliefs. Terrorists blow themselves up in restaurants and bus stops. Militant extremists commit rape and genocide in the name of their god while religious leaders bless them in their holy wars. All the while the sheep are donating their time at the soup kitchens and homeless shelters so the board of directors can make $85,000.00 a year telling the world how decent and kind they are.

I genuinely hope that sheep will be able to find their way to the solace and comfort they've been promised in religions. But the time has come to take the shepherds down.

William Hopper

HEATHEN, n. *A benighted creature who has the folly to worship something that he can see and feel.*

~ Ambrose Bierce, *The Devil's Dictionary*

THE EVOLUTION OF THE HEATHEN

In the beginning, we humans lived in the wild and ate whatever was slower or stupider than we were. At this time, we invented a thing called a "god." The god was made from the mightiest elements mankind could see: fire, thunder, lightning… all the big, scary stuff we didn't understand but knew was powerful.

As there were so damn many things we thought were powerful, we found we couldn't settle for just one god, so we made a whole slew of them, each god representing a different big, scary thing. We understood little about these gods, except for the simple fact that in their Infinite Wisdom they had decided they didn't need to eat us. As we found this good, we honoured and worshipped these gods.

As time passed and humans prospered on Earth, we learned much about the way the planet actually worked. Over and over again, we humans were put in the awkward position of looking at things like storm clouds and saying "Wait a minute...that's not a god. That's a high ridge of barometric pressure coming in from the cooler coastal region."

But there were still a lot of things we didn't understand. So, rather than waste more time and effort deifying every new enigma we ran across, we decided to simplify the whole mess by creating a single, omnipresent 'God' on whom we could throw all the mysteries of the universe until such time as our descendants could look at them and say, "Wait a minute...that's not God. That's..."

These days we've solved so many of life's mysteries that we're running out of things to call 'God.' Between mapping the human genome and cloning animals, we almost lack the ability to perceive anything as being more powerful than we are. This new mindset has opened the door to a broader contemporary theological search that requires a lot of time and dedicated effort on the part of religious leaders worldwide. Representatives from every faith are now struggling to place 'God' in our new, technologically advanced society. As a result, there's a very real crisis of faith in the world today, as leaders from the world's religions rise to meet this challenge through prayer, hard work, and a sincere scholastic inquiry. As all this keeps them the hell out of our way, the rest of us now have the chance to think for ourselves.

And so the era of the Heathen begins...

Chapter One: JUDAISM

Religion: *Judaism*

Prophet/Holy Guy: *Old Testament prophets/patriarchs from Adam to Malachi.*

Main Holy Book: *Torah, Mishnahs*

What to call the priest: *Rabbi, Rebbe*

What to Call an Adherent: Jew

Israel

To you I'm an atheist. To God, I'm the Loyal Opposition. ~Woody Allen

Okay, first off...forget *The Ten Commandments* movie. If you're going try using a Charlton Heston flick as historical reference, I suggest you use *Planet of the Apes*. It's no more accurate, but let's face it; a world run by apes is infinitely more interesting than a world run by Jewish patriarchs.

We can also forget about the "In the beginning God created..." bit from Genesis. I'm a little too pragmatic to bother getting into the whole creationism versus Big Bang versus "we-were-seeded-here-by-alien-life-forms" debate. Each position has its merits, but basically it really doesn't matter. We're studying religion here, and religion started a hell of a lot later than the universe did. What does matter is the history, inasmuch as we can separate it from the bullsh-... er, faith. Here's what we know...

Your average rabbi will tell you that this whole fiasco started in a mythical paradise called The Garden of Eden. As much as I love disagreeing with holy guys with long beards, I have to give them half a point on this one. I think it did start in a place called Eden. I just doubt it was the heavenly paradise we've been told about.

You see, according to the fable (sorry, "Bible") a guy named God created two humans, Adam and Eve, who were the progenitors of the whole human race. Supposedly Adam and Eve screwed up, got tossed from the garden, and God sent an angel with a fiery sword to guard the gates and make sure that no one got back in. This whole tale might just be written off as pure fable except for two small, niggling things that bug me about it. First, the Jews had to come from somewhere. It does little good to dismiss the Eden story if we have to replace it with a new creationism wherein the Jews just popped into being. They had to have had some ancestral origin before they went off and slaughtered the Canaanites and took over the Holy Land.

Second, the bible gives a pretty good description of where the place is geographically. Eden was not some mystic realm of winged faeries and giant dancing snakes. In Genesis, Eden had a clear physical locale identified by the rivers around it. There were four according to the tale. I hate to do this to you, but here's a bible reference for you—Genesis 2, verse 10-14. You'll need it when arguing with religious folks about this. It's really the only language they speak.

Genesis 2, verse 10-14[1] says:

"A river watering the garden flowed from Eden; from there it was separated into four headwaters. 11 The name of the first is the Pishon; it winds through the entire land of Havilah, where there is gold. 12 / 13 The name of the second river is the Gihon; it winds

through the entire land of Cush. 14 The name of the third river is the Tigris; it runs along the east side of Asshur. And the fourth river is the Euphrates."

We know the Tigris and the Euphrates. They're pretty famous rivers. It's this whole Pishon and Gihon thing that's been keeping the location of Eden a deep secret for millennia. Basically, if you found all four rivers, go to the root of them and there you have it— one Land O' Heaven on Earth.

As much as I'd like to take the credit for all of this, I have to admit that a British archaeologist named David Rohl has done a hell of a lot of excellent work on finding Eden while I've merely pondered the concept over cappuccino and cigarettes. In his book *Legend: The Genesis of Civilization*,[2] Rohl explains how he followed the known rivers, talked to the locals, did some research, and found the place. You can get right into this by reading his stuff, but to make a long story short Rohl figured out that Pishon is now Uizhun and Gihon is Araxes, which put the location of Eden in Iran, ten miles outside of a city named Tabriz.

In April, 1997, Rohl led an expedition to the site, found far more evidence than even he thought he would, and pretty much proved to the world that Eden was a physical place well known to many cultures. However, as he did not find a giant angel with a fiery sword guarding the place, most Christians and Jews tend to believe that Rohl is nuts. They figure that all of the silly facts, archaeology, and history Rohl presents falls apart in the absence of a giant angel with a fiery sword. There *has* to be a giant angel with a fiery sword. It doesn't matter if everything else fits. No Angel, no Eden. That's all there is to it. The Bible can *not* be wrong.

It astounds me that people who think like that actually rule a good portion of this planet.

THE HISTORY BOOKS

The people we now recognize as the Jews first enter popular history as a collection of nomadic tribes on the Northern Arabian Peninsula somewhere around 10,000 BC.[3]   Now, everyone you ever quote that date to is going to have a different opinion, so don't take that as, well, gospel. I settled on 10,000 BC because that's where carbon dating of artefacts found in the region puts the timeline. I don't really trust carbon dating but it's what we have to go with for now.

These folks basically wandered about the area going from oasis to oasis, trying to find grazing land for their goats, sheep, etc. Contrary to myth, they really weren't "desert dwellers." They lived mostly on the edges of the desert, keeping near the coastline and on the major routes. The area they were in was harsh, with small patches of green land, and they had to dig wells to find water.

The big surprise to most religious folks is that these guys were not monotheistic, meaning that they didn't worship just one god. That didn't come along for another, say, 5,000 years. Their gods (called collectively the *elohim*) were beings that inhabited nature. Special rocks or oases were considered to be filled with the entity of a god. There was nothing complex here. Basically it was just an extended version of a child looking up at the clouds when it's thundering and saying, "Hey-God must be bowling." The whole world was a mystery back then. As they didn't know about tectonic plates or barometric pressure, they just called them gods.

Now, you've got to figure it was a pretty harsh life back then, and there wasn't a lot of room in this society for deep thought and contemplation. If they found areas that seemed more "powerful" than others or seemed to have more food than others, they decided that there had to be a reason for it. Since they didn't know quite what the reason was, they said there were elohim, or gods there. (Actually, the modern idea of a "genie" is closer to their idea of the elohim than the Judeo-Christian concept of a god, but I figure if I kept saying "genie" we'd wind up losing the thread linking all this stuff to what JC was doing hanging on a cross several millennia later.)

Anyway, you get the idea. If it was a good god/genie, you'd sacrifice a goat and say, *"Hey, thanks. We really appreciate the help and please don't forget us in the future."* If it was a bad god/genie, you'd sacrifice a goat and say, *"Excuse me...Mr. God? Uh...we'll be passing by here this week and if you'd be kind enough not to fry us to little cinders just for fun of watching us melt like candle wax, we'd really appreciate it. To show you how much we'd appreciate it, I'm giving you this here goat and I hope you like it."* All in all, this entire theology boded very poorly for goats.

Okay, we have the concept. Rural nomads. No real cities. Gods/genies all over the place. Sacrifices to them. No churches. No ceremonies. Just kill something and hope the gods like it. Nothing could be simpler. Then along comes Abraham…

FATHER ABRAHAM

> *Almost anything is easier to get into than get out of.* ~Agnes Allen

Somewhere around 2,000 BC, these nomads made their way across the Red Sea. (No, this is not the big Red Sea thing. Heston's role is still several hundred years away at this point.) The tribes had basically run out of decent land in what's now Yemen and Saudi Arabia and had to push west to the Fertile Crescent.

Anyway…along comes Abraham. Anyone who ever had the horrid misfortune of having to go to church camp or Sunday school knows the song "Father Abraham had seven sons, oh, seven sons had Father Abraham…" (I get Roman Catholic flashbacks just thinking about it.) Abraham did, indeed, have seven sons. At least that's what his wife, Sarah, told him. The fact that he was way too old to be fathering children at the time didn't seem to hinder him. I figure he was either naive as hell about his wife's activities or had something in his diet that the Ovaltine people would love to get their hands on. But I digress. (A lot.)

Abraham came from Haran.[4] That's Syria to you and I. Before that, he was supposedly from Ur. That's Ur to you and I. (It's in Iraq, and it's still called Ur.) For whatever reason, he was the leader of a group of these nomads and he led them south from Haran down to Goshen-a small town in the aforementioned Nile Delta. As near as we can tell, they got there somewhere around 2000 BC and settled right in.

Understand, this wasn't some Stone Age culture. By the time Abraham was around, there were real cities, real trade, and real international wars going on. Egypt was run at the time by a group known as the Hyksos, a short-lived but delightfully bloodthirsty bunch of guys that had managed to take political power in Egypt.

Their reign only lasted about 200 years before they, in turn, met their gruesome demise, but at the time Abraham came on the scene he had alliances with them. (Note: The name *Hyksos* means Shepherd Kings. As the people under Abraham were shepherds this could well explain the alliance Abe had with them… a unity of sheep.)

THE GOD OF ABRAHAM

Man could not make a mite,

yet he makes gods by the dozen.

~ M. De Montaigne

Abraham had a working deal with a god, pretty much like any other leader of the day. Now remember, he comes from a group of these nomads who believe in the elohim, the god/genie beings. The one god/genie in particular that Abraham had a deal with was El-Shaddai. For those of you have an interest in such things, El-Shaddai means "god of the mountains." That would be opposed to the "*god of the sea*," "*god of the desert*," or the "*god of the purple-and-blue-flowers-growing-out-of-a-log-a-couple-miles-down-the-road.*" Abraham's people saw gods/genies pretty much everywhere. But it was with El-Shaddai that Abraham had struck a deal.

The deal was simple. With all the gods that could be sacrificed to, Abraham and his family were to worship and sacrifice to only El-Shaddai. In exchange for this, El-Shaddai was supposed to make Abraham and his descendants wealthy and prosperous. The fact that at the time Abraham made the deal he was 99 years old and had no kids didn't seem to bother El-Shaddai. Abraham agreed and mysteriously Sarah wound up pregnant with the first of seven sons. (That damned song again...)

Genesis 17 tells the story of El Shaddai's promise to Abraham. Read it for yourself. The Gideon's have put a Bible in every hotel room in North America. If you haven't yet managed to steal one from them, I'm sure you can steal one from someone. Ask a born-again Christian. They love giving them away.

For those who have some need to have all this set in bible perspective, Abraham arrives on the scene about 130 years after the Great Flood. If you haven't heard of the Great Flood or the whole Noah story, then you're probably in some small Swiss canton that has been isolated by mountainous terrain for the last two thousand years, in which case I'm amazed at the circulation this book is getting.

FIVE MINUTES MR. HESTON...

Only the good die young. ~Billy Joel

Abraham allegedly lives an insane length of time. We're talking 200 years here. That's twice as long as George Burns. His wife was still having children well into her 100s, and the family kept getting bigger and richer. By the time Abraham died, his offspring had "begat" so often they really were becoming their own nation. We're talking thousands of people, all related, and all living in the Nile Delta region. Lots of money. Lots of cattle. No problems. Life is good.

It really doesn't matter one iota what you think of Abraham or the whole idea of him living to 200. Personally, I think he probably lived to be eighty or ninety (which at the time was a miracle in itself) and the story of how old he was grew in the telling. But like I say, it doesn't matter. All you've really got to understand is that every true Jew on the planet is a direct descendant of old Abe. (Not counting those who converted to Judaism of course.) It sounds a little nuts, but it's true. They're all one huge family tree that's branched out around the whole world.

One of the weird things about this is that most pious Jews (called Hasidic Jews, which translated from the Hebrew means "pious".[5] Scary how deep these mysterious names are, isn't it?) can trace their lineage father-son, father-son right back to Abraham. I have trouble with my mother's maiden name.

Anyway... the bunch of them did well for themselves on the Nile Delta. So, you ask yourself, where does all this slavery stuff come in? If they're doing so well, how do things come to a head and wind up with Charlton Hest-er, Moses, freeing the enslaved nation of Israel and taking them to the Promised Land? The answer to this lies with an age-old proverb that for some reason never found its way into the Bible: "Life's a bitch."

THE BEST LAID PLANS

There are moments when everything goes well;

don't be frightened. It won't last ~Jules Renard

Now, I'm not saying there was or was not an El-Shaddai. That's an "article of faith" and as I haven't got any, it stands to reason that I'm not about to believe anything that depends on faith. But just for the sake of conversation, I'll say that if this El-Shaddai exists, he's a pretty damn fickle guy. Or god. Or whatever.

You see, the family became known as Israel. It's yet another of those deep mystic words. (You make a word deep and mystic by keeping it in your own language rather than translating it for people so they know what the hell you're talking about.) Israel literally translates as "one who has been strong against God." The "one" in question was Jacob, one of Abraham's many grandchildren who supposedly wrestled an angel on a mythical ladder and confronted God. When God was done berating him for it he gave Jacob a new name: Israel. In normal use the word Israel means "Jacob's children".

It's just a name hung on the descendants of Abraham/Jacob to say, "Yeah, we're the guys that made a deal with the god/genie/deity guy on the mountain." Since they were all related, the idea of a "last name" like Smith was redundant, so they just called themselves Israel. (Note: they kept track of their lineage by paternal name. As in Isaac ben Judah. The "ben" you so often see in Hebrew names means "son of." So Isaac would be the "son of" Judah. It would be like saying Bam Bam ben Barney.)

A few things went awry. First off, as in all families, there were those that didn't hold true to the values of their forefathers. El-Shaddai had set up some rigid ideas of what was demanded of his people and a lot of them kind of said, "Screw it." They went off and lived their lives and really didn't give a damn that their great grandfather Abraham had struck a deal with a god or whatever. Life's too short to waste on your great grandfather's ghosts, right? What, they supposed, could Abraham's god have to do with their lives being lived out hundreds of years later? Sure, they knew the story, but it was old hat.

Here the nation of Israel learned the first valuable lesson about striking up a deal with a god: Piss him off and you get natural disaster. Famine. The whole area of Goshen dried up— Lot, stock, and barrel. (Couldn't resist that one.)

So it happened that the entire nation of Israel wound up out of food and staring down a pretty bleak future. It would be the social equivalent of living in Detroit, Mich. when the auto industry closed up shop and left. The entire economy is simply gone...poof. Nothing. Nada. Not even UI or a welfare check to see you through. So what do you do?

Well, Israel did what many in Detroit did. They moved. In this case, to Thebes and other major Egyptian cities. Work was plentiful; Israel had contacts there. Lots of construction, farming, opportunities galore. Israel relocated and, for about 200 years, they never looked back. Things were good. For a while anyway.

The thing is, the Israelites were immigrants. Granted, they were well accepted and generally respected immigrants, but they were never quite "citizens" in spite of everything. In time, they kind of became like second-class citizens. Not disliked, but always sort of left out of major policy decisions.

So, you ask, how does this translate into being slavery? Well, you really have to understand what slavery was at this time. It wasn't like Roots by Alex Haley. That kind of slavery was cruel and inflicted. At first, the Egyptian brand was more like welfare. Land resources became the domain of either the monarchs (yeah... like Ramses from The Ten Commandments) or the elite. The Jews were kind of bounced around and left to their own devices, trying to get work here and there and hoping to keep their heads above water. One of the ways of doing this was for a Jewish father to go to a landowner and strike a bargain with him. (Suspiciously close to Abraham's deal with El-Shaddai). The father would promise the landowner that he, his family, and his offspring would be indentured (enslaved) to the wealthy family. This meant that the Jewish family would do the fieldwork, housework, and general chores for the wealthy family.

In exchange for this, the landowner would agree to feed, clothe, and house the Jewish family. Sure, the Jews lacked a few personal freedoms, but they were also cared for and would never have to worry about where their next meal was coming from. In a society where these things were becoming increasingly rare to anybody who didn't own land, the care of a landowner was a boon to their lives, not a cruel punishment.

The problems occurred two or three generations later. The landowners, now wealthier and more powerful, became opulent. Think of the monarchy in France just before the Revolution and you'll get the idea. The Jews became fodder to them. The class system that had arisen set the Jews far below their original office in the city, and they became mistreated and maligned by the Egyptians.

By the time Charlto...Moses arrives on the scene, the Jews were being treated like dirt by these guys- bullied and basically abused wherever they went. They're not liking it, but hey, tough. The laws are against them and they've been indentured into this situation by their own fathers or grandfathers. They're stuck, and as far as the Egyptians are concerned, they can suffer. The Egyptians are happy.

When the pharaohs decided to go out and start building huge monolithic structures (yeah...like the pyramids), they decided, *"Hey... why should we work? We've got these underpaid, under-appreciated Hebrews, most of who are already indentured to someone Egyptian. Why not just nationalize the indenture and make them wards of the state? Slaves, if you like. They build, we feed them. They don't build, we kill them. It sounds pretty harsh, but hey, think of the great postcards we'll be able to sell after these things are built!"*

Okay, the postcard line was mine. But otherwise that's more or less how it went. Israel was free labour. Or basically free. They were still housed and fed by the monarchy, but it's not hard to see how Israel got the short end of the stick on this one. They lived with and ate with the livestock. They had no hope, no future, and no real life to speak of. Things were pretty dire at this point in Judaic history.

So, life wasn't good for the descendants of old Abe. What they needed was a saviour, a being sent by El-Shaddai to end their misery and bring peace and love and prosperity to the nation of Israel. As JC was still a few millennia away, they had to settle for Moses.

THE SHEPHERD KING

Living well is the best revenge.

~George Herbert

Ah, Moses. He's actually one of my favourite characters in all this. Not because of his grand effect on the history of the Jews and on the human race in general.

No… I like the guy because he really knew how to get revenge.

You have to keep in mind that we're looking at a society where the descendants of Abraham (not yet called Jews) are basically low-life. If you're born into that caste, you're screwed for life. You have no hope of ever owning anything, no hope of ever doing anything that amounted to more than menial labour. Your best-case scenario is to be working for an Egyptian overseer that isn't going to kill you just for the fun of it. This is the kind of society that Moses was born into.

For those of you who missed the first ten minutes of the movie, Moses was adopted as a baby. And, for the rare person whose family hasn't owned a TV in several decades and has missed the Disney movie, he was secretly adopted by the pharaoh's wife. That would make him royalty. (Right up there with King Tut, Ramses, et al.) The guy had made it. By the adoption, he went from dreary life as one of the unwashed masses to being heir to the throne. It was a good stroke of luck.

If there's one thing to be learned in the history of Judaism, it's to beware good luck. It seems the better you do, the harder you fall. (For a really good example of this, read the book of Job.) Anyway, Moses was set to rule the nation of Egypt. He'd have lived a decent life and faded into history as a footnote in some archaeologist's text if it weren't for that one small issue that plagued his life-he wasn't Egyptian. It was a fact that his adoptive mother had neglected to tell anyone and, when the news broke, Moses was pretty much finished as an Egyptian royal. The pharaoh's real son Ramses (the bad guy in the movie) made for damn sure that Moses was stripped of all rank and privilege, thus ensuring that Ramses could take the throne when their father died. Furthermore, on the weight of this information regarding Moses' lineage, Ramses had Moses thrown out of the city just for the plain old fun of it. Sibling rivalry at its best.

Anyway, Moses wandered off in the direction of the Nile Delta. To cover a whole lot quickly, he meandered his way into a camp owned by a guy name Jethro (not Tull), married his eldest daughter, and settled in to being a nice shepherding nomad like the rest of Jethro's household.

Now, Jethro didn't appear out of nowhere. If you'll recall, Abraham led his people into Egypt. But not all of these nomadic tribes followed Abe. Some stayed out wandering around from oasis to oasis. This is where Jethro comes in. A few hundred years had passed since Moses' people and these people actually hung out together, but they knew of each other. More than this, they shared the same concept of elohim, the genie/god/barometric pressure deities that were so powerful out in the ol' desert.

Jethro wandered about finding grazing land for his sheep and goats. Among the places he would camp out was the foot of Mount Sinai where, presumably, there was fresh pasture for the animals. Now, it just so happened that Jethro was rather enamoured with "the God of the Mountain." We can assume that this was the same "God of the Mountain" that Abraham dealt with, but it really doesn't matter. It could have been a different mountain, different god. Who's to say? But the fact remains that there was a mountain and there was a god living on it and Jethro abided by this god's word. Since Moses was in Jethro's camp, he too had to honour this deity. The odd goat sacrificed, a few quick deals for better grasses or rain, that sort of thing. It was a working relationship.

Anyway, Moses does okay by all this. Sure, he's not exactly the ruler of Egypt, but hey, sheep can be good company too right? He spends all his time feeding sheep, fleecing sheep, cleaning up after sheep, slaughtering sheep, etc.. On his off days, when traders would come through to provide a distraction for him, he was able to spend his days buying and selling sheep. Then he'd lie down at night next to his wife on his soft sheepskin mattress and drift off, no doubt counting sheep. After settling into this routine and finding peace and contentment in the life of a simple shepherd, Moses did what any good urban prince-turned-shepherd would do. He snapped.

You see, Moses was aware of the contract "his" people had with El-Shaddai. I use "his" in quotations because he really wasn't raised to be one of "his" people. He was raised as a prince. This is important. Think about it-he's had his whole life turned upside down. He's gone from prince and heir to the throne to shepherd, and about all he's got left to hold on to is a weak affiliation with a people he's seen all his life but to whom he's never really felt connected. The Hebrews (those would be the descendants of Abraham) were beneath his station before. Now, sitting in the desert, they were all he had left.

So there he is, mulling his life over and sick to death of the smell of sheep, when it occurs to him that his people have a deal with this god. The deal was that the god would protect and care for them. Anyone who'd been through Egypt in the last few centuries could tell you these people were not exactly cared for and protected. His adoptive family were basically screwing them around left, right and center and getting away with it. You have a lot of time to think about this when all you're doing all day long is staring at sheep. You have a lot of time to consider things. A lot of time for resentment to grow.

"Why," thought Moses over his mutton stew, "should the Egyptians get away with this when they...er...we have a god right here that's supposed to be protecting them...er, us? Where the hell is he when we need him? What good is a deal with a god if he's not going to do a damn thing to help out when you're getting royally screwed?" (Pun intended.)

The story goes that a day came when Moses finally lost it. In what amounted to a mad frenzy of anger and resentment, he decided to take his bitching to the source. Since he'd already confronted Ramses and lost, he decided it was about time to go after El-Shaddai.[6] Basically Moses says, "Hey, what about these Hebrew people?" and El-Shaddai says, "Well, go free them. I'll help."

(Okay, it was a tad more dramatic than that. But hey, if you want deep character development, find Cecil B. DeMille. I'm a facts kind of guy.)

It was during this famous conversation that El-Shaddai got his new name: Yahweh. It's Hebrew for "I am." (The existential god of the mountain?) According to the story, when Moses asked for El-Shaddai's name the god said, "I am that I am." As it sounds a little silly saying "The Great I am that I am," Jews and Christians alike have kept to the Hebrew word for "I am": Yahweh.

(It should be noted here that the King James Version of the Bible translates "Yahweh" as being "Jehovah." Both words are translated from the same Hebrew characters, but the KJ guys decided to be different. No real reason there. They just plain decided they wanted to write it out in English characters in a different way than everyone else did. It's a small difference that at the time meant little but has since caused many poor innocent party-goers to get up at a ridiculously early hour on Sunday morning to brush off the Jehovah's Witness at the door. It could easily have been a Yahweh's Witness.)

Anyway, Moses gets the okay from Yahweh and goes off to Egypt where he demands that Ramses free the slaves. Ramses laughs. Moses turns his staff into a snake to prove the power of his god. Ramses' court magician does the same, evening out the power o' gods. Moses' snake eats the Pharaoh's snake and everyone agrees that either Moses' god is more powerful or his snake is hungrier. Either way, Ramses insists that the slaves stay.

The rest of the tale is basically a battling "my god's bigger than your god" contest that Moses wins. The only important thing to understand from all of this is that Moses did finally get the slaves out of Egypt and brought them all back to Mount Sinai, where Jethro and the sheep had been waiting patiently. The miraculous crap- locusts, firestorms, the parting of the Red Sea- all fall into that "faith" category. The fact of the matter is Moses won Israel's freedom from Egypt.

Okay, so they all wind up at Mount Sinai. Moses has managed to take away a huge chunk of the Egyptian labour force, thus undermining Ramses' ability to rule. Moses suddenly has this huge population living at the foot of the mountain that are totally under his control, and his life seems to have gotten itself together again. He's got the leadership and political power he'd been raised to expect, and he managed to get it by screwing over the very people that had banished him for being Hebrew. Ya got to like the guy's style.

Laws are an attempt to domesticate

the natural ferocity of the species.

~Seneca

You've read them. You've heard about them. You've even seen the movie. The Ten Commandments. They are the foundation of our Judeo-Christian ethics. The pillar of our society. The fundamental and unprecedented decree dispatched to Moses on Mount Sinai as a covenant between Yahweh and his Chosen People-the astounding "Law of God" sent to guide humanity, carved by His hand in solid rock and given on tablets to Moses for all the world to see.

Let's try my version of this…

Get yourself a copy of the Code of Hammurabi. There's a link to it in the endnote here:[7] (It's way too long to print out here or I would.) It was set down about a hundred years before Moses and was known to the Jews. According to the Catholic Encyclopaedia: *"The work of the Hebrew lawgiver consisted in codifying these ancient usages [Hammurabi's Code] as he found them, and promulgating them under Yahweh's authority."* That's a nice way of saying Moses stole the thing to make up the laws of Judaism, which is where I'm going with this whole story.

If you read the Code and tried to summarize it, you would come up with a synopsis that would sound an awful lot like the Ten Commandments, with the glaring omission of the first commandment that has nothing to do with Hammurabi Code. The other nine are simply a moron's version of a complex legal code that was in effect for hundreds of years. It basically says don't steal, kill, covet, sleep around, or have fun— that sort of thing. Only the first commandment doesn't fit. "I am the Lord, thy god. Thou shalt have no other god before me."

The Ten Commandments were the seal of a pact that supposedly went down between Moses and El-Shaddai, a.k.a. Yahweh. It worked like this:

The people of Israel, being the direct descendants of Abraham and heir to the promises of El-Shaddai made him, were to be given the land that El-Shaddai showed Abraham on his trip to the Nile

Delta. In exchange for this land (and the wealth and prosperity that go with it), the descendants of Abraham agreed to abide by the Ten Commandments (and a whole lot of other laws set out in Leviticus). Most importantly, they agreed to forsake all the other gods/genies/barometric pressure deities and support only El-Shaddai, a.k.a. Yahweh.

That's it in a nutshell. This "covenant" was (and, I suppose it still is) a contract-a legal, binding contract wherein both the deity and the nation of Israel had their rights and responsibilities, and if they both abided by the covenant/contract, everything would be fine.

Now, I'm not saying that Moses used his knowledge of Hammurabi code to scratch this out on two chunks of stone. Nor am I saying that Moses lied about seeing a god. Nor am I saying that the forty days he was up on the mountain alone allowed him more than enough time to think this up, scratch it out, and bring it down roughly hewn and say, "Yahweh gave it to me." I am implying the hell out of it, but I'm not actually saying it. It just strikes me that if I was sitting on the foot of a mountain and Moses (or anyone) walked up to me and said, "Hey, see these chunks of stone with words scratched into them? A god gave 'em to me," I'd probably nod and say "Yeah, right. And I'm Adonis." For the record, I'm not Adonis.

THE PENTATEUCH

It has been said that though God cannot alter the past, historians can. It is perhaps because they can be useful to Him in this respect that he tolerates their existence. ~Samuel Butler

I like the word Pentateuch.[8] It's just a cool-sounding word. It's actually the formal scholastic word that professors and theologians use to refer to the Torah. Torah is a lesser cool word used by the Jews to refer to the first five books of the Bible. (They would be Genesis, Exodus, Leviticus, Numbers, and Deuteronomy. Don't be impressed. I had to open the table of contents on my Bible to remember them in order.) They are the holiest books of the Bible, written by Moses while his people waited at the foot of Mount Sinai for the "wicked generation" (i.e. those who decided worshipping a cow was a lot more fun than worshipping Yahweh-read Exodus, or look up "Aaron" in the Glossary at the back of this book) to pass and a new generation to follow into the Promised Land. They're holy because they were written by Moses through inspiration given him by Yahweh. These five books chronicle everything from the Creation to the Great Flood to Abraham to the death of Moses (at 120 years old).

You'll notice that I've tended to avoid referring to these books an awful lot (less than your average book about the history of the Jews, anyway). It's kind of hard to tell the story of Judaism without using them, of course, but there are a few fundamental problems I have with the Torah. First off, you have to wade through a whole heap of myths and improbabilities before you get to anything you can begin to call fact. I generally forget about everything before Abraham, mainly because Abraham's era marks the beginning of interaction with other groups whose histories (independent of the Bible and through archaeological evidence) corroborate some of the Torah's narrative. We know guys like the Hyksos and Ramses existed because we have independent verification outside of the Torah. As for Noah or any of those characters, who the hell knows?

You'll also notice I've left out the grandiose stuff like the parting of the Red Sea. The reason is simple-it's unsubstantiated myth. Sure, the Torah is good for figuring out the comings and goings of Abraham and the Jewish nation, but you really have to wade through a lot of crap to get to what you want. The main problem I have here is the authenticity of the Torah. Its origins are extremely dubious, and the authorship is uncertain. (Yup...probably pissed a few people off with that comment...)

You see, the Torah was supposedly written by Moses. Well, first off, it's written in a second person narrative. Never does Moses (the supposed author) say "I did this" or "I saw that." Sure, you could say it was just his writing style, or that it was actually Yahweh speaking through him, but that doesn't really hold either. If you read the last three chapters of Deuteronomy, you'll see that it tells the story of Moses being told he was going to die, blessing the tribes, and then dying. Chapter 34 ends the Mosaic tale with the tribes wandering off from Moab toward the Promised Land with Moses dead on Mount Nebo. The question strikes me...if Moses is dead on Mount Nebo, how is it that he could still write about the fact that he was dead on Mount Nebo?

The whole thing seems dependant on faith. Jews and Christians have "faith" that these books are divinely inspired and protected. Moreover, they contend that the authors and those that have maintained control over these books were, in fact, honest. (See Constantine in the Christianity section.) The thing is, a lot of the stuff in the Bible is just plain wacky. It's presented pristinely in the churches, but the actual tales are truly weird. I'll cover two of the famous ones for you: Jonah and Jacob. Put into Will-ese, they're not quite as solemn as they're presented in Sunday school.

JONAH AND JACOB

Lord, what fools these mortals be! ~ *A Midsummer Night's Dream*

Jonah was swallowed by a whale (actually a "leviathan," a.k.a. sea monster). [9]We're all told about how God goads him over and over to go warn the Israelites and how, after being coughed up by said sea monster, he decides to do it. What we seldom hear about is when Jonah gets to the city he's supposed to preach to, God says, "Oh...never mind." Jonah goes through the whole thing for nothing. In the end, he wanders out to the desert, plunks himself down in the sun, and basically says, "What the hell was THAT all about?" Of course, Yahweh makes it all up to him by making a gourd magically grow above his head to protect him from the sun.

Yeah. There's real deep meaning in that story.

Or how about good old Jacob? He gets fed up because his people are being good and keeping up their end of the contract with Yahweh, but they still keep getting screwed around. He figured Yahweh owes his people an explanation, so he climbs up this mythical ladder, battles an archangel, wins (amazingly enough), and then makes it up to heaven where he confronts Yahweh with his above-mentioned bone of contention. Yahweh listens, then basically says, "Yeah, so? Israel's getting the shaft, and I'm not keeping up my end of the bargain. So what? I'm a god and you're just a piddly little human. Shut up, go home, and I'll damn well do what I want when I want. And by the way, forget your name. I'm gonna call you Israel from now on. You look more like an Israel to me."

Hmm...Nice god they got going' there.

These tales are characteristic of the Old Testament—fantastic yarns which are more likely to be rip-offs from older mythologies than valid historical data. That's the kind of stuff I've avoided, mainly because all this folklore and fantasy has very little to do with the actual history of the Jews. There's a theory that stories like Jonah and Jacob are actually just very old Hebrew jokes that were recorded for their humour value but got taken seriously after a lot of translations and time. If this theory is correct, then I figure it's only appropriate that I stick to the historical data and leave guys like Jerry Falwell and Robert Schuler to expound the intricacies of this biblical lore.

Personally, I figure these stories are just that: stories. To a Jew or a Christian they might be something worth perusing to see what this God guy's all about, but in general they amount to little more than myth and fantasy. That is, of course, unless you apply some faith here, in which case these tales are chock full of pithy, meaningful insights that only the enlightened could ever fathom because they are just too deep for the average person to comprehend. Naturally, for a percentage of your annual income, religions will explain these tales in simpler terms that our smaller brains actually can fathom. This book is considerably cheaper.

THE PROMISED LAND

I will give you every place where you set your foot, as I promised Moses. Your territory will extend from the desert of Lebanon, and from the great river, the Euphrates-all the Hittite country-to the great sea on the west. ~Joshua 1:3-7

Israel never owned all the land Yahweh promised them. At its height the Jews never conquered more than two-thirds of the Promised Land.

If you look it up on a map you'll see that the amount of territory promised to them was huge. The problem was that Yahweh seemed to feel free to give it away without really stopping to consult the other people who were actually living there before this promise was made.

Yup, you got it...Israel invaded.

At the end of *The Ten Commandments*, we're left with this romantic image of the nation of Israel wandering blissfully off into "the Promised Land". What we didn't see were the bloodthirsty battles that took place as the Israelites commandeered what their god had promised them. Aside from the fact that the indigenous people of Canaan had this insane idea that, hey, they *LIVED* there, they also had this small problem with the fact that they'd never heard of this Yahweh guy. The inhabitants had their own deals with their own gods.

So, once Moses was worm food on Mount Nebo, Israel is on the move. Twelve spies are dispatched to check out the Promised Land. Of these, only two return to say that the Amorites-Canaan's indigenous people-are ripe for the picking. Over the next six years, Israel defeats Sihon, Og and twenty-nine other Amorite kings, taking over huge territories. (This is where the story of the walls of Jericho comes in. Jericho was one of the cities the invading Israelite army took over.)

When it was over, Israel settled into the routine of being an actual landed nation, setting up judges, priests, bagelries, etc.. This was the foundation of much of what we now know as Judaism.

THE FIRST MESSIAH

It is impossible to reign innocently. ~Louis De Saint-Just

No...not Jesus. He's still a millennium away. We're talking about the line of messiahs. You see, messiah is yet another one of those deep, mystic words that causes all kinds of fuzzy notions about things. The word messiah means "anointed of God." (Christ, actually Christos, is merely the Greek form of the word messiah, meaning "anointed of God.") To get a handle on this, you have to go all the way back to the time of the prophet Samuel. (A prophet is a guy that can hear a god speak-usually a tortured soul who screams and yells at you because you're not keeping up your end of the contract with Yahweh. Aside from the noise, they played a significant political role as well.)

You see, Israel had defeated thirty-one kings. They'd done this as a "theocratic state"-that is, they had no king, only a prophet and a god at the helm. But the Jews weren't happy with this. Since everyone else had a king, and since Yahweh wasn't about to bodily sit on a throne for them, they demanded that their god anoint a real flesh-and-blood king to lead them. If you read 1 Samuel, verses 8-9, you get the story of how Yahweh basically didn't want to do it, but finally gave in and allowed a guy named Saul to be king of Israel (only because the people really wanted a king.) Saul had a relatively short and uneventful reign, then died. His death coincided with the dawn of what's known as the "First Temple Period." In a weird synchronicity, it's also the era wherein the most famous King of Israel, King David, designed the first Temple.

David was from Bethlehem, about eight miles south of Jerusalem. 1 Samuel 18:5-7 says that "All of Israel were lovers of David." This is basically true. The guy made Bill Clinton look celibate. He spent his youth skirting death and disaster while sleeping with anything that moved. Saul, the anointed King of Israel, had been about the only person who really hated David, and it was mutual. When Saul died, his son tried to take the throne, but the prophet recognized David as the rightful king. Ish-bosheth, Saul's son, died of natural causes shortly thereafter. (They chopped off his head, so, naturally, he died.)

So, David dreams up this concept of a temple. The idea here was to create a place for the Ark of The Covenant to rest. This gets to be a pretty important issue later on, so we better cover this whole Ark thing right off.

THIS WHOLE ARK THING

> *"Lightning, fire, the power of God...that sort of thing. The power to destroy whole nations. An army that carries the Ark before it is invincible."*
>
> *~Indiana Jones*

The Ark of the Covenant is a box. In Hebrew the word is *arohm*, which means either "coffin" or "chest." You decide which.

The Ark was 2 ½ cubits by 1½ cubits. Now I hear you mutter, "What the hell is a cubit?" It works out to 44" by 26" by 26". It was plated in thick gold. The lid was solid gold, with two kneeling solid gold angels on it. The space between the angels' wings was supposedly where a hazy face would appear and the voice of Yahweh would originate-kind of like a very expensive videophone to God.

Inside the Ark were kept the remnants of the Covenant. That would be the Ten Commandments (a new copy, since Moses had broken the first copy by throwing it at the people when he came down from Mount Sinai and found them begetting for all the wrong reasons), a golden jar containing manna from heaven (the fluffy wheat-like food that floated down when the Israelites were wandering from Egypt to Sinai and were hungry), and the Rod of Aaron. (That would be a rod. Owned by Aaron. It was like a magic wand, and did things like bring water up from solid rock when Israel was thirsty.) This latter piece was removed sometime before the building of the Temple. A copy of the Torah was included with all this, but was not to be kept inside the box. It was to be set in front of it.

Okay, that's basically what the Ark is. Anyone that's ever seen Raiders of the Lost Ark knows that this thing was supposedly really powerful. We're talking about something that would fry your enemies to crispy, crunchy bits in seconds. Think of it as Israel's answer to the atom bomb. Whether you believe in Yahweh and the whole Jewish tale or not, there does seem to be something about the tale of the Ark that's worth considering. It wasn't just the Jews that said it was capable of great destruction. Independent records from Canaanites, Babylonians, and Philistines confirm that pretty much everyone of the day believed this thing had power. Whether it actually did is inconsequential. Everyone believed it did, and that was the important part.

THE LOCATION OF THE ARK

Where your treasure is, there will your heart be also. ~Matthew 6:21

Indiana almost had it right. He was off by about 800 miles. In the movie, he finds the Ark in a tomb in Egypt, near the Valley of the Kings. Close, but no cigar. If you remember, the knights of the Middle Ages went on quests for things like the Ark and the Holy Grail (more on this in the Christianity section), which is how the myth of the "lost Ark" became popular.

The thing is, the Ark's not lost. Never has been. About the

only people who ever thought it lost were those that only looked to the Bible for information, ignoring the fact that there's a whole planet full of books out there that also recorded history.

You see, the last mention of the Ark of the Covenant in the Bible is at the time of Solomon. After that, it just disappears. A replacement Ark was built later to go into the Second Temple (circa 525 BC), but it was said to be "without power." The real Ark was lost. Or so we've been told.

Solomon had a lot of wives and concubines-we're talking in the hundreds here. To put it in perspective for you, the guy had more women in his lifetime than Gene Simmons and Magic Johnson put together. Of these women, the most famous of them was Queen Sheba. She ruled what is modern day Ethiopia. She was one of Solomon's wives but was not Hebrew. She worshipped Baalim, a word that translates as "Lords" or "Scary Barometric Pressure Deities". Basically she believed in the genie-type gods that need constant sacrifices so they don't fry you just for the fun of it. (Awfully fickle, these genie-type gods.)

Sol, being the good, loving husband that he was (when he had the energy left), was quite accommodating to Sheba. He even let her place her idols in the Temple of David. The Ark didn't like this and destroyed the icons. Solomon replaced them, and the Ark destroyed them again. "Oh well," thought Solomon, "I guess they don't make idolatrous icons the way they used to." Real quick, this Solomon guy.

The Bible doesn't record what finally happened in this dispute o' gods in the Temple. All we know is that the Ark up and disappeared. The question should immediately register-how does a solid gold chest disappear from the Temple of David without anyone noticing? Most people have figured that Sheba took it, since Solomon had given her permission to take "any of the wealth of Israel she desired." It's a nice theory and it's close to correct, but again no cigar. It wasn't Sheba.

Sol and Sheba had a son named Menyelek. He's not mentioned in the Bible. So how do we now about him? Well, you see, in 1957 there was a revolt in Ethiopia. The monarch, Emperor Salassie, was usurped and a military government took over. The fall of Salassie was the end of the oldest monarchy on Earth, dating back to before the time of Solomon. (Yup...Salassie was a direct descendant of Sheba. Kind of neat, ain't it?) Anyway, every generation of these monarchs has had a scribe, and every scribe has written down the major events of that generation. The collection of these writings is in a book called *The Kebra Nagast* - "The Glory of the Kings of Ethiopia." [10] The section that pertains to Sheba and Menyelek recounts the story of how Menyelek founded the "Solomonic Dynasty" in Ethiopia and adopted Judaism and the Law of Moses.

According to the legend of the Ethiopian Orthodox Church, the church of St. Mary of Zion in Aksum still has the original Ark of the Covenant. Ever since the Ethiopian monarch claimed to be a direct descendant from the biblical King Solomon and the Queen of Sheba, his descendants ruled Ethiopia in an unbroken line until the revolution broke out in 1974 ending the Ethiopian monarchy.

It seems that Menyelek was a pious Jew. He believed in the Covenant and Yahweh and the whole enchilada. Irate with his father Solomon for adding other gods to the Temple and defiling the sacred resting place of the Ark of the Covenant, Menyelekhired some Levite priests (the only guys that can touch the Ark without taking a dirt nap) and took the Ark back to Ethiopia, where he felt it would get the respect it deserved.

Back then, the capital of Ethiopia was Aksum. (Nowadays, the capital of Ethiopia is Addis Ababa. You don't need to know this, but it's a really cool name and I just like saying it... *Addis Ababa... Addis Ababa...*) Anyway, Menyelek built the Temple of Zion and put the Ark there for safekeeping. Somewhere around the sixth century (when the Muslims were on the march in the area), all of Ethiopia, including the Temple of Zion, became Christianized. The temple was renamed "The Temple of Mary of Zion" after Mary Magdalene that Constantine thought was irrelevant... more on that later. The Ark has stayed there, in Aksum, protected by a devout group of Christians who would literally skin you alive if you tried to screw with it.

As a footnote to all of this, rumour has it that the Jewish Hillel- the international Jewish league- allegedly applied to Lloyd's of London for insurance on the Ark of Covenant during the Second World War. Lloyd's just kind of laughed, idly wondering how much they'd have to pay if one of the most priceless pieces in existence had been destroyed by Hitler's armies. (Or stolen. Hitler was into this sort of thing.) Lloyd's didn't insure it. Read "Countdown to Armageddon" by Grant Jeffries for more on this. He's a nutbar born-again Xian, but he does do his research well. If you ignore the "give your heart to Jesus or burn in hell" aspect of the book it does have a lot of good info.

When Israel became a nation again, they asked Emperor Selassie for the Ark. Rightly enough, Selassie agreed that they could have it back only when the Temple was rebuilt and the Ark had its resting place again. So far, there's no new Temple, and Selassie isn't in power anymore so the whole plan is stalemated.

(For the apocalyptic born-again Christians out there, it may interest you to know that the rise of a new state of Israel and the return of the Ark to the Temple are both supposed to happen in "the end times." Israel's been a nation for fifty years now. The Ark is "found." The Temple stones have been cut and are ready to be placed on the mount to build a new Temple. It really is all happening. Even a poor, slovenly heathen like me can see that. I suggest you begin preparing for "the end times" by divesting yourself of all filthy, heathenous things like cash, gems, stock futures or negotiable bearer bonds. I'll be including an address at the back of the book where you can send it all.)

And that's the tale of the Ark of the Covenant. You now know one of the deepest, most prized secrets of all time: the location of the Ark of the Covenant. Kings and knights have killed and been killed for this secret for centuries. All it cost you was the price of this book. And I bet you thought it was too expensive when you got it, didn't you? As an added bonus, I'll tell you about the Holy Grail. But that's under the Christianity section. You're going to have to wait. Right now, I figure I should make some attempt to get this whole thing back on track.

For quite some time, the Israelites figured the Ark of the Covenant was safe enough carried around from battle to battle. Saul later decided-after the theft of the Ark by the Philistines-that it should be kept safely in a tent. David, having gone through a lot of shit to get the Ark back from the Philistines, figured the Ark needed a resting place that was a tad more secure.[11]

DAVID'S TEMPLE

A billion here, a billion there, and pretty soon you're talking big money.

~*Everett M. Dirksen*

David agreed that the Ark shouldn't just be carried around from battle to battle. He wanted a special place for it, where it would be protected and properly respected. To this end, he designed a temple. Unfortunately he was never able to build it. Apparently, Yahweh thought David had just plain killed too many people for no good reason to be allowed the honour of actually building the Temple, so it fell to his heir Solomon to do the actual building. The Temple was built in three distinct parts: the Copper Altar, the Holy, and the Most Holy.

The Copper Altar was used for sacrifices. This is the exact same idea as way back when they were wandering through the desert-kind of a "Hey, god, could you do me another favour and here, have another goat" sort of thing.

The Holy was the area (separated from the Most Holy by a blue cloth) where the Levite priests could see and read from the Torah that was laid near the Most Holy.

The Most Holy, The Holy of Holies, the original Sanctum Sanctorum, was where the Ark itself was kept. No one saw it but the king and the Levite priests. It was the most holy resting place of Yahweh on Earth.

That's it. That's the whole of the Temple (except for the courtyards and the King's house, which were peripheral to the main site.) It doesn't sound impressive, but figure this out. Solomon paid the following for this Temple:

100,000 talents of gold and 1,000,000 talents of silver from the treasury;

3,000 talents of gold and 7,000 talents of silver from his own money;

10,000 darics of gold and 10,000 talents of silver from his sons.

"Wow," you mutter. "This means a hell of a lot. What the hell's a 'talent' and why hasn't Madonna got any?"

Let me do the translation for you. At the current market

value (I actually checked the stock exchange for this one) the total amassed cash put into building David's Temple works out in today's money to $6,323,732,883.00.[12] Even counting the usual pay-offs and kickbacks, this is still one hell of a lot of money to spend on one building. We're talking solid gold statues. Walls and ceilings overlaid in gold. Copper pillars. You get the idea. It took seven-and-a-half years to build, from 1034 BC to 1027 BC.[13] When it was done it made the Taj Mahal look like a Wal-Mart in Las Vegas.

THE BABYLONIAN EXILE

> *There is no greater sorrow than to recall happiness in times of misery.*
>
> ~Dante, Inferno

The original temple stood until 607 BC, when it was sacked and looted by King Nebuchadnezzar. Various Jewish kings had diminished the opulence of the Temple over the years, so it wasn't quite as extravagant when it was destroyed. The thing is, the Temple was more than just a place to kill sacrifices. It was the symbol of the power and strength of Israel as a nation, kind of like Red Square is for Russia. When it fell, so did Israel. As a nation, it packed up its bags, folded its tents, and by all rights should have faded away into nothingness. They were beaten, then shanghaied to Babylon as servants of Nebuchadnezzar. All that remained was a shattered group led by the prophet Jeremiah (Not the bullfrog.)

What saved the Jewish culture was ritual. Say what you want about it being tedious, annoying, and inhuman-I'll agree with pretty much all of it. But without it, the Jews simply wouldn't exist today. You see, by the time the Jews were exiled in Babylon, the faith of Yahweh had taken a weird shift from its nomadic heritage. This is mainly because of a guy named King Josiah some eighty years before the invasion.

Josiah basically introduced the concept of worship.[14] This is pretty fundamental to the whole idea of Judaism and Christianity now, but at the time it was really unheard of. By Josiah's reign, Yahweh had become so ingrained as the deity of Israel that other gods (most notably the baal variety) were scorned and rebuked. Monotheism was drawing. For the Jews, the idea of there being other gods was irrelevant, since even if there were others, they wanted no part of them and refused to acknowledge them. This fundamentally changed the way people looked at the world and their place in it. Before this transition, gods were just more powerful beings that you could barter and deal with to improve your life. Josiah set the standard for not only rejecting other gods, but embracing Yahweh. The Covenant was no longer seen as a harsh contract, but rather as a loving and kind offer on the part of a god (now spelt God, since He's effectively the only one) who was deserving of people's admiration and supplication.

What this meant in the day-to-day life of the Jews was that they could go to the Temple, God's house on Earth, simply to praise and honour him. You didn't need to kill a goat every time you went there because you weren't always "looking" for something. Josiah took this step farther and basically told the people that they didn't have to go to the Temple itself to honour him. After all, the Temple was hundreds of miles away for some folks. Instead, he instituted the practice of "personal ritual"-the idea that your love for God could (and should) be shown throughout your daily life. Families could observe private rituals in the way they ate, slept, and worked that were designed to please and honour Yahweh. A family might then make a pilgrimage to Jerusalem once a year as a special event, but the day-to-day practice of serving God was in the home and the workplace.

Had this revolution not happened when it did, the destruction of the Temple would have been the destruction of Judaism. But by the time Nebuchadnezzar destroyed the Temple, its place as the focus of faith had shifted. The religion of Yahweh no longer depended on the actual building, but on the traditions of worship that were ingrained within the family and community. Israel brought this with them to Babylon in their exile, and it carried them through as a cohesive unit when many belief systems would have just fallen apart.

TEMPLE II: THE SEQUEL

Things that were hard to bear are sweet to remember. ~Seneca

In 583 BC, Babylon was conquered by the Persians. If it seems in this tale that everyone seems to be invading everyone else every time you turn around, it's only because that's about what was happening. Anyway, King Cyrus was the Persian king, Persia was modern-day Iran. He took over Babylon and basically didn't care what the Jews did with themselves. Most, though not all of them, went back to Israel.[15]

Unfortunately, Israel (and the Temple) were a wreck when they got there. To galvanize the Jews into rebuilding the Temple, Yahweh sent not one but *two* prophets, just to make sure the message got across. These two men, Zecheriah and Haggai, pushed the people to get a new Temple built. Despite their efforts, the people of Israel were more concerned about trying to re-establish their lives after years of captivity. The Temple, they thought, would just have to wait.

Haggai and Zecheriah spent most of their lives trying to convince these folks that the Temple should be the number one priority for the Jews, but the Jews weren't buying it. It took more money and effort than the newly repatriated Israelites had at the time. Cyrus had given orders that the new Temple be built, but apathy and depression hindered the work. Cyrus returned some of the money looted from the Temple and this, combined with the zeal of the prophets Haggai and Zecheriah, got things moving. The result of all of this was the creation of a poorer quality Temple, but a Temple nonetheless. No king. No Ark. Nothing in the way of the gold and silver of the original, but it did function as a place for worship and sacrifice, and for a while the people of Israel settled into their newly rebuilt nation under Persian rule.

Then, in totally unsurprising turn of events, the Persians were defeated by Alexander the Great. Just at the time when Judaism was settling into its newfound doctrine of monotheism, the entire area was overrun with Alexander the Great's Hellenism. About the only break the Jews caught here was that they were still allowed to be Jews. Alexander didn't care who they worshipped so long as the taxes were paid to him. From 500 BC through to 136 BC, the political control of Judea fell into the hands of the line of Herods.

Herod, you may recall, was the guy that killed hundreds of children because the three wise men told him that a new king had been born. But he wasn't the only Herod. The name was also a title, handed down through a single-family line. To understand this (and the dawn of the Christian era), you have to understand what went down with the Herods, and how the politics worked at the time.

HEROD THE GREAT

> *Politics has always been the systematic organization of hatreds.* ~Henry
> Adams

Yeah, I know, I know. This whole thing is getting kind of dreary and boring. Hang on. It gets pretty bloody real soon. We're coming up to the Herod the Great stuff with the story of him killing all the first born children. You can't get bloodier than baby killing.

Okay, back this up to 165 BC. The area of Judea is controlled by Syria, which was ruled by Antiochus III.[16] Antiochus III had taken the throne from his brother of Seleucus IV. Both Antiochus III and Seleucus IV were direct descendants of Alexander the Great. Yippy!

Anyway, this Antiochus guy got it in his head that he was going to convert the Jews and take what was left of the money and gold in the temple. Thing was, Alexander and the others who ruled the area hadn't cared about the religion. They just took their money off the top and didn't care who the Jews worshipped. This new guy got greedy, which is where the promised bloodshed comes in.

Enter Mattathias Maccabee, one pissed off pious Jew who hates Antiochus for leading the Jews away from Old Yahweh. After making a rather public display of killing a Jew who was taking part in a Greek sacrifice, Mattathias decides to up the ante by killing a royal guard. He then grabs his five sons and heads to the hills for some good old fashioned guerrilla warfare. [17]

He's joined in said hills by a bunch of apocalyptic nutbars— er, sorry, "Jewish enthusiasts"— who plot a Maccabee revolution against Syria. Antiochus basically says, "Okay, give us your best shot." They did. The Maccabees actually did pretty damned well for a bunch of hill dwellers. The long and short of it is this feud carries on for years. In time Simon Maccabee (one of the sons) actually managed to take political power in Jerusalem. This went well until Antiochus VII[18] launched an all-out attack on the Maccabees, who were now ruling Israel. Simon Maccabee proved himself to be an excellent ruler, defeating the superior army and winning the day. By succeeding against Syria Simon proved to the nation that his rule was strong enough to withstand any of the dark forces that were threatening the tenuous rule of the Maccabees. Everyone agreed that under Simon Israel would prosper, and no foreign power would be able to take him down. So, of course, Simon was assassinated by his own son-in-law.

This goes on and on. Various family members come and go over a relatively short period of time. The real nail in the coffin for this era was when two brothers, Hyrcanus II, a high priest, and Aristobulus II, both decided they should rule Israel. Flags waved, swords were drawn. Full scale civil war raged. It was all getting pretty damned bloody when, in 63 B.C., Rome kind of wandered in and took over. The Jews were basically too busy killing each other to put up a fight, so the whole region came under Roman rule.

Okay, I'm bouncing around here. What does all this have to do with Herod who I mentioned earlier? Well, I'll tell ya...

The Herod we all know and love from the nativity story was born 73 BCE. His father was one of the guys that backed Hyrcanus in the civil war that was going on when Rome showed up. Now, this gets to be a pretty cool story that you never hear about in the bible. Here goes...

Herod's dad, Antipater, won out when Rome settled the civil war and declared Hyrcanus to be ruler of Israel. Antipater goes on to a rich and prosperous career, having favored the winning side. He then gets another really big stroke of luck when he backs Julius Caesar in a civil war with Pompey. In 47 BC Antipater is made regent and given control of a lot of Israel. Being a good father he gives his son a lush post at the age of 16. Little Herod became the governor of Galilee. (It's good to have connections.)

Now, ya gotta follow this to catch how it all ties in with the Late Great JC and the nativity story we see on TV every damned December. Herod kills Hyrcanus' nephew (heir to the throne) and marries his daughter. (Yeah, that was a hot wedding night... "Hi, I killed your dad. Get in bed.") Anyway, he claims the right to kingship by becoming part of the family that Rome had appointed to rule after the civil war. The problem was the Jews never really had much of a say in any of this. It was all between Rome and Herod. For his part, Hyrcanus just manages to eke through all this. Herod steals all his power so Hyrcanus is just a figurehead. Herod is in charge.

Ok, more war and bloodshed. Rome goes to war with the Parthians (Iran and Iraq put together) and a bunch of Jews back the Parthians. Herods' face man Hyrcanus is taken prisoner by the Parthians, and Herod hightails it to Rome. There he meets with Octavian and the Senate, and whines that his cushy appointment had been stolen from him by the Parthians. The senate orders Mark Antony and his lieutenants to take two legions back to Jerusalem and reinstate Herod. There's nothing like two legions of battle hardened soldiers to show people who their real leader should be. So it was that Herod gained full and unquestioned power and control of Judea. It's a cool story.

So, here's what we wind up with around the time of Jesus. You've got the local politicians who are descendants of the guys that came back from Babylon and set up the new Temple. These guys are known collectively as the Sanhedrin— a local assembly of stuck-up legalistic guys called the Pharisees who made life hell for prostitutes, thieves, and blasphemers. (They were the local "law." You couldn't take a leak in the wrong place without these guys showing up ready to stone you for it.)

One step up the food chain, you have the Herod. He's claiming to be the new monarchy, but the Sanhedrin doesn't recognize him because he was appointed by Rome, and never anointed by a prophet as real monarch. Then, collecting taxes above all of these guys is Rome, whose military power was way too obvious for anyone to bother them.

And way beneath all of this is the poor average bastard living in Israel, paying way too much tax to three levels of government, none of which are generally considered to be legitimately representing the descendants of Abraham. You wouldn't be going out on a limb here to say that there was some unrest at the grassroots level.

JESUS, ANOINTED OF GOD

Well, we're covering Judaism right now, not Christianity. The best thing to do here is to skip over the life of Christ entirely and move on to 66 AD. You see, the sad truth is that the entire life of Jesus and his ministry really didn't affect the Jewish world at all, at least not at the time it happened.

Josh was one of many rabbis of the day who spoke up. Like a lot of other guys, he died for it. It was indicative of things to come for the Jews, but in and of itself the life of Jesus was a footnote-nothing more.

The depth and teachings and all that there stuff was the catalyst for a Christian movement, but you really have to get into the fourth century before it started affecting Jews in any real way. At this time (the first century) most Jews were far more concerned with the politics of the region. Josh and his teachings were a minor disturbance compared to what was happening to the nation.

Anyway, on with the Judaic stuff. I'll go into great detail about the Late Great JC in further chapters.

THE JEWISH REVOLT, 66-70 AD

There can be no real freedom to fail. ~Eric Hoffer

I've always found it funny that the Bible almost totally neglects the fact that the entire civilization of Israel was decimated thirty years after Jesus left. We're talking about the wholesale slaughter of the entire nation of Israel-men, women and children alike. The tales of the genocidal madness of W.W.II Germany are well foreshadowed here. What happened in Jerusalem and Masada at this time was the beginning of the real hell for Israel, and for the Jews born after its fall.

In 66 AD, the people revolted against Rome. The Pharisees (the legalistic Jews) tried to keep things in check, but as time went on, the people were just plain fed up of being overtaxed by a foreign government. They wanted their own nation and their own king again-their own "messiah." A group known as the Zealots rallied the people, urging them to put their faith in Yahweh. Faith grew as sanity and caution declined.

Essenes and Sadducees alike followed the Zealots' call-to-arms, and in 66 AD they all stormed the residence of Pompeii (then the Roman representative in the area, replacing the famous Pontius "I wash my hands of this" Pilate). Pompeii was set adrift in the Mediterranean and left for the dead. When this was done, the Pharisees-who worked side-by-side with the Romans and had never advocated outright rebellion-saw the writing on the wall and got the hell out of Dodge.

Unfortunately for the Zealots and their followers, Pompeii was made of sterner stuff than they figured. Wounded and on a makeshift raft, he survived the Mediterranean Sea and made his way back to Rome. His heroic story-complete with Pompeii's color commentary on how he "swam" the whole distance-so moved Caesar that the emperor gave Pompeii full access to whatever military resources he needed to exact his revenge on the Jews. Pompeii was not shy in taking up the offer.

This whole episode is chronicled by a guy named Pliny the Elder. This is opposed to Pliny the Younger, who also wrote but did so a few years later, presumably because he was, well, younger. You'll also find a neat smattering of it in stuff by Josephus. He's my favourite source of historical perspectives. The guy could really tell a story.

JOSEPHUS

Writers are always selling someone out. ~Joan Didion

The Bible doesn't talk much about this era. For any real information on all this, you have to turn to the works of Josephus. Don't let the imperial-sounding name get to you. He wasn't a general or a king or anything. He was basically just some poor slob who managed to get cash for recording everything he saw in Israel. He wandered around as a freelance writer, poking his nose into just about everything and sending the information off to Rome in quarterly reports.

A lot of Josephus's writings managed to remain intact over the years. Most of what we know of the battles comes from the fact that Josephus would wander around them (not taking any sides) and talk to Roman and Jew alike. He was the only person allowed to cross the battlefields, and even with the siege of Masada (another cool movie), where the Jews were holed up for moths without food or water, they still let Josephus past the barricades. This is where the famous story of the Jewish fathers killing their wives and children, then falling on their swords comes from. That was the final outcome of the Masada siege. When the Romans finally got through the barricades, all they found were corpses and the solitary figure of Josephus wandering around, taking notes.

Anyway, the information about the war comes mainly from him. Pliny the Elder also did some writing around the same time, but Josephus was much better. He had a knack for being right where the shit was about to hit and writing about it in great detail, which is how he came to be around Jerusalem in 66 AD.

The Jewish revolt ended in 70, when Titus came through the region. The nation of Israel was decimated. Jews literally ran for their lives, fleeing the country while their relatives died behind them. Rome was merciless in her pursuit of all things Jewish. The Temple priests were killed. The Temple (only just refurbished fifty years earlier by Herod) was burned, sacked, and looted. Israel was wiped off the face of the earth, and with it anything that might remind you that it had existed. In his record of the Jewish revolt of 66-70 AD, Josephus recounted how the Roman soldiers were complaining of the long, arduous hours they had to endure chopping heads off. The Jews had been corralled and were being systematically beheaded by the thousands in downtown Jerusalem. Resistance in outlying areas-most notably Masada-was short-lived. The Roman retribution for the Jewish was hands-on, wholesale slaughter of an entire nation.

In the aftermath the Roman province of Palestine was indisputably Roman. For the next few centuries (until the rise of Islam), Palestine was occupied by plain old Roman folk with their Hellenistic gods, gymnasiums, and the occasional orgy to keep things interesting. No Jew walked openly in the Promised Land for fear of death. The few Pharisees who remained in the area only quietly plotted the resurrection of the state of Israel. All in all, you could say that at this point in history, this whole Promised Land concept was not going very well.

The Diaspora

Another cool word, Diaspora. It means 'dispersion", specifically the dispersion of the Jews throughout the world. Basically the events in Israel (now Palestine) had brought an end of the Jewish homeland. Those that remained Jews which most of the survivors actually did) scattered throughout the Middle East and Europe. From there, they basically went everywhere. The thing to remember here is that the Jews did not spread out around world with any notion of conquest or assimilation. As had happened with the Babylonian exile, the dispersed Jews saw the fall of Israel as a temporary state of affairs. The Promised Land would, they were sure, be theirs again. They only needed to wait things out for a while, figuring that someone like Cyrus the Persian (who, you'll recall, freed them from Babylonian captivity a millennium earlier) would come along again and set their homeland flee from the Romans.

The problem was that, unlike the Babylonian exile the Diaspora was global dispersion rather than a collective indenture to another country. While the elite Pharisees struggled to maintain the idea of Jewish nationalism and a return to the homeland. The Jewish families that escaped Roman persecution in the first century traded in their ideas of Israelite nationalism for a new, more pragmatic philosophy consisting mainly of the credo: "I think I want to stay alive, thank you very much". While the Pharisee had no basic objection to this philosophy, they did feel that the average Jew should find a way to do this while still striving to reclaim the Promised Land. Most Jews weren't really buying this, seeing as how the vast majority of those that survived had seen their families and friends beheaded by Roman soldiers.

With the people getting further and further away from Israel and Jabna, the legalistic Pharisees that had held so much power over the people before the revolt felt their pull waning. The Jews in France and Spain were finding their own ways to observe Passover and Yam Kippur (the Jewish day of atonement-kind of like all of Christian Lent crammed into one day). The control of these things had always been in the hands of the Pharisees.

The Pharisaic elite needed to find a way to keep their control of Judaic thought alive while their people were in other countries so that when the state of Israel was rebuilt, there would be still be Yahweh followers to collect tithes from. Since they couldn't physically be there to chastise the people for breaking the Law, they came up with the next best thing-books.

THE HOLY BOOKS OF JUDAISM

> *It takes a great deal of history to produce a little literature. ~H. James*

The Pharisees decided they needed to get things straight. Most of the Jewish population was on the move and it occurred to them that they'd better get their version of things written down or it would get muddled over time. (With those pesky Essenes and Sadducees now out of the way, the Pharisees didn't have to worry a hell of a lot about anyone else's interpretation of what had been going on in Judaic history for the previous three thousand years.)

The Pharisees already had the Torah, but the Torah was only the books of the Law, and there was a lot of dissent as to how the Law was to be practiced or interpreted. It was the interpretation of the Law that had made the Pharisees famous (as opposed to the Sadducees, who abided instead by what the prophets had said, or the Essenes, who fused both the Law of the prophets and the Law of the Torah into one theology).

Anyway, the Pharisees in Jabna started collecting bits of folk tales and stories about how famous Pharisaic judges over time had interpreted the law. They added to this the day-to-day interpretation of the Law- things like how to prepare a proper Passover meal, what foods the Torah said were bad, how to eat, how to dress, etc. (It may interest the women out there to know that when it came right down to it, the rabbi's found they really didn't have a clue about most of these things. They knew about the debates on the law, but they had to turn to the women for the details on how the law was actually observed. The men were found to be great at abstract Judaism, but it was the women who knew the reality of the faith and the proper manner in which to abide by the Law. A lot of rabbis were pretty embarrassed by this.

Add to all this the folklore of gen eden (the Garden of Eden) and Gahanna ("the pit of fire"), toss in a few tractates on idolatry and a commentary on the new Israel to come and there you have it: the Talmud. One large volume encompassing everything one needed to know about Judaism. Think of it as "A Companion's Guide to the Torah."

What is now called the Hebrew Bible was compiled from a whole bunch of books by the Pharisees at the synod (council) at Jabna in 97 AD. It contained the Torah and the Pseudopigrapha, as well as the other books that are now standard Bible issue. (Bible, by the way, simply means "book." Ecclesiastics and the Song of Songs were actually left up in the air for a while, but were accepted as doctrine at another synod in 133 AD.

The "accepted" texts were those that did not obviously reflect the polytheism that had been part of Judaism up to this time (e.g. Abraham's ideas of "elohim", or god/genies/ barometric pressure deity. Only monotheistic texts were accepted in keeping with the Pharisees' beliefs, with the aforementioned exception of the Torah, which was "divine" and couldn't be rejected or altered.

KOSHER LAW

Good laws have their origins in bad morals. ~ *Ambrosius Macrobius*

The synod at Jabna was also the beginning of universal Kosher Law. The idea of kosher foods had existed before this, but Jabna was where the Rabbis set it in stone and made for damned sure that every generation of Jews from then to now were subjected to boiled dough and potato pancakes. (It's amazing what people will eat when you tell them it'll get them into Heaven.)

The word Kosher just means "fitting", meaning fit for pious Jews. There are kosher laws about everything from menstrual blood to underwear, but I'll use the example of kosher food to explain where the Pharisees got their idea of Kosher from. You probably know something about Kosher... like those meals that the Jewish passengers get on airplanes.

The entire concept was based on the idea that something

somewhere had gone horribly wrong with the Covenant between Jehovah and the Jews. The Pharisees, being legalistic, decided that it had to be a legal problem. They reasoned that the people of Israel must have been having fun somewhere along the line, which of course broke some if not all of the laws in Leviticus. The question was, which laws were being broken?

You see, the Pharisees in particular had been having absolutely no fun and so were abiding quite closely to the Laws of the Torah. Still, their country had been smashed to crumbly bits of marble by the Romans, so they figured that the laws must not be being abided by strictly enough. From there on in they applied a logic reserved only for devout clergyman and paranoid Schizophrenics. Here's how it went:

For example, The Torah says not to boil a calf in its mother's milk. Okay, said the Pharisees, we won't do that. (The reason, incidentally was that boiling the meat or a calf in its mother's milk was part of a baal sacrifice. Jews were not allowed to do this because, well, they were Jews, not baal worshippers.)

So the Pharisees didn't boil calves in milk from the calf's mother. But Israel still fell. So, thought the Pharisees, there's something we're doing wrong here. God, after all, could do no wrong. If there was a mistake, it had to be a human one. The Pharisees then looked at this whole dilemma and thought. "Aha! The problem is that there are so damn many cows and calves out there that we have no idea which milk comes from which cow! Why, we could accidentally boil the calf in its' mother's milk, and we'd never know it!"

(I suspect from the tale that the ancient Israelites considered meat boiled in milk to be something they might like to eat. Funny how times change...)

Anyway...

The Pharisees decided to call a moratorium on all meat boiled in any milk, just so they don't accidentally sin. Then they went a huge step further and thought, "Wait a minute...what if God's an imbecile that can't tell what we're doing and thinks we're boiling meat in milk when what we're really doing is putting cheese on a burger? Why, we could lose God's favour just because He saw milk products and meat products on the same plate! That's it. No cheeseburgers."

And so kosher food was invented. As they had with the food laws, the Pharisees proceeded to take every law in the Torah and made it as extreme as possible. The idea was not to reflect the spirit or intent of the laws of the Torah. Rather, it was supposed to set things up so that a Kosher Jew doesn't even seem to come anywhere near anything that might in some abstract way be seen as being close to sinning -- which is what the Kosher meals are about on the airplanes. You see, the last thing a kosher Jew wants should the plane go down is to be caught eating a cheeseburger and be accused at the Pearly Gates of boiling a calf in its mother's milk.

All of this stuff went into the Talmud as extra laws to make sure you kept the original Laws. Then the Pharisees wrote down the Mishnahs, which were commentaries on the extra laws which they had just set up to make sure you kept the original Laws. Then they gave all this to the Jewish world as sacred and authoritative text. This whole thing became known as The Talmudic code. It was basically a "How To Be A Good Pharisee-type Jew" handbook that kept the Pharisees' version of Judaism alive when Israel was defunct as a nation. You'll notice that I said "Pharisee-type Jew." The ethics and beliefs of the Essenes, Zealots, and Sadducees were lost for good by this point.

The few who survived couldn't recruit and were assimilated by the Pharisaic tradition. The legalistic Pharisee philosophy became the only Judaism that existed through to the Enlightenment era in 1700, mainly because the Pharisees were the only sect with the presence of mind (or presence of head if you prefer) to write their stuff down in time. Throughout the Middle Ages, all the Jews that lived in Europe were almost exclusively Pharisaic. This means they were Zionists, legalistic, and determined to maintain the Covenant (contract) with Yahweh come hell or high water.

THE MIDDLE AGES

Everyone's quick to blame the alien. ~Asclepius

The Middle Ages were not kind to the Jewish people. The crusades, which were designed to create a Christian fervour bent on ridding the world of Muslims, bled over onto the Jews in the form of pogroms. "Pogrom" is a Yiddish word meaning massacre, usually applied to the massacre of the Jews. Yiddish, for those who don't know, is a high German or "proper German" language. It's the type of German that next to no one spoke because it was too formal. Yiddish is generally written with Hebrew characters, mainly because most of the good scribes were Jews. As a result, most of the history of Europe was recorded at this time by Jews using Yiddish. It became the language spoken by a lot of Jews in Europe because it was their job, though the practical application of a written language meant a lot of French, Hebrew, and Italian words seeped into the vocabulary.

So, the Crusades led to pogroms. The Christians were so fired up to "save' the infidels in Jerusalem that they figured they'd get a head start on purging the world of non-Christians by sharing their newfound enthusiasm with the Jews in Europe (after all, charity begins at home), It may not surprise anyone to find out that Germany was a big fan of these slaughter fests. setting a standard for Hitler's pogroms some 1100 years later. The Jews that remained in Germany and central Europe were confined to "ghettos"— walled-up sections of the city that amounted to little more than jails. Generations of Jews lived and died in these ghettos with little if any change in the Pharisee-based Judaism they practiced.

The Jews that managed to get the hell away from the pogroms in Western Europe settled into Eastern Europe fairly well, which is where you have to look to see any changes that occurred in the religion.

KABBALAH

The best of seers is he who guesses well. ~Euripides

You'd never know it to read this but this subchapter was added after the bulk of this book was finished. I'd just started to relax and feel nicely complacent when the debate about Kabala reared its ugly head. I'd omitted it mainly because it's not a terribly important part of Judaic history but apparently it became popular when I wasn't looking. Most things do.

So, for the benefit of those people who looked at me in astonishment and said, "How can you write a whole book on religion and NOT mention Kabala?" Here we go, Kabala…

Kabala is the mystic branch of Judaism. Like the Muslim Sufi movement or the Christian Gnostic path Kabala involves an inner search. It's inherently an esoteric philosophy that deals with En Sof, which basically means the 'endless or "eternal" concept of the Divine. Kabala uses all the other books of Judaism (Talmud Mishnahs, etc.), but interprets them according to a book called the Zohar, written by a guy named Moses de Leon in Spain around 1300 AD. Zohar means *splendor*.

According to the Zohar, the En Sof had no personal attributes. It was basically like "the Force" from Star wars (You find the same ideas in Taoism and Buddhism). The only really deep and mystic surprise in all of this is that the philosophy found its way into Judaism without being called heretical.

The Zohar interprets the Judaic tale as being the interaction between the Shechinah (the Divine Presence) and humanity. Like George Lucas, the cabalists believe that all things are one, or at least should be. The fall of Adam was seen as the original rift between the Divine and humanity that allowed darkness and evil to enter the equation. Lucifer did not exist in this version of the Judaic tale. Both good and evil were characteristics of the Divine, and evil was interpreted as the Divine's judgments which were normally sound and pure, but had become disjointed because the fabric of En Sot, had been split Hell was the manifestation of the wise judgments of God that had become detached from the pure loving light and Divine mercy.

The goal of cabalists, then, was to reunify all of existence, re-incorporate all of the elements of the Divine (ourselves included, as were all made from the fabric of En Sof) and, by doing so, create an eternal and unchanging peace. One achieved this reunification by living a meek, peaceful life that surrendered all the elements of one's being to the oneness of En Sof and thus allowed at least that small part of the world to be unified again. It's all very Zen-esque.

One of the things that's become intricately linked to Kabala for no real reason is the idea of numerology, or the study of the secret and mystical meanings of numbers. This is mainly because the Zohar speaks about the ten Sefiroth. These are basically just the Judaic version of the Hindu yogic Chakra—power centers or levels or self-realization that you pass through on your way to unity with all things. Each Sefiroth is represented by a number, and since numerology had been popular around the same time as the Zohar was published, there was a misconception that numerology was an intrinsic part of it all. Add to this that Moses de Leon used a combination of Greek, Hebrew, and just plain invented symbolism in his book to make it deep and mystical, and you can readily see how it could be perceived as having something to do with numerology.

Oh...one thing I should add here; Moses de Leon didn't take credit for writing the Zohar. Until the book made it big, Moses de Leon (who was a nobody at the time) told people that had actually been written in the second century by someone way more important than he was. It wasn't until it started getting a following that he 'let it slip' that he may have written it. This technique is called "apocryphal writing." It basically means you put someone else's name on it that you think people will actually believe, because you know damn well they're not going to take your word for it. (I'm suddenly inspired to adopt a pen name.)

Okay that's the Kabala thing. There's not a hell of a lot to it, at least not as much as the New Agers seem to think. Having sufficiently met any obligations to the coffee shop mystics I now return you to tie regularly scheduled book, already in progress...

ANTI-SEMITISM

Bigotry may be roughly defined as the anger of men who have no opinions. ~G.K. Chesterton

Ok, even a slovenly anti-religious heathen like myself has to admit that anti-Semitism exists. We can talk about Hitler and Mussolini, but the truth is that anti-Semitism has run through pretty much every country. I would add that so has anti-gypsy, anti-gay, and anti-black. But as we are studying religion here and not gay black gypsies I figure we have to look at anti-Semitism. The question is, where did anti-Semitism come from?

Well, the Crusades were definitely part of it. Thousands of fanatical Christians bearing down on a bunch of Jews in, say, Berlin, is certainly a scenario that is conducive to anti-Semitism. But there's another side to it all. You see the Jews were at one point the scribes, and had done well at it. They made money and generally thought they'd fit in quite nicely. Unfortunately, Europe didn't see it that way.

To the Europeans the Jews were "different." Remember, the Jews always considered themselves "refugees" not immigrants. Because of this the Jews strove (in accordance with the Talmudic Code) to maintain their Israelite heritage no matter where they lived. As a result the Jews did not assimilate and tended to stand out like a sore thumb. This was fine by the Jews at the time, since as far as they were concerned this whole Diaspora thing was going to end shortly and it didn't matter one bit what other nations thought of them socially or personally. They felt they'd be home in Jerusalem some time soon, comparing notes on what kind of dolts the Europeans were. Well, the kind of dolts the Europeans were was a bloodthirsty, fanatical Christian brand of dolt led at the time by the hegemonic powers of the Holy Roman Catholic church. This (as the pogroms and ghettos show) was not good.

One other element that still adds to anti-Semitism to this day was Rome's ban on usury and money lending. Rome basically didn't like the idea of people other than themselves making money off their sheep's money. So the Church banned Christians from lending money. The Jews (who had made a good bit of money in the scribe biz) had this whole problem that they weren't allowed to own land or property in most of Europe. Any wealth they had, then, had to be readily portable on that off-chance that they'd have to run for their lives. This meant that the bulk of the wealth of the Jews was either in gems, gold, or hard cash. So, when the ban on Christian money lending was enacted, the Jews looked at their assets, looked at the money they could make from these assets, and basically said, *"Vat da hell I'm not Christian. Da people vant to borrow money, I'll lend it to them'."*

The Jews did well at this. They soon gained themselves a reputation for being thrifty, wise, and capable in all aspects of banking. As the money they made off these ventures came predominately from the Christians, the Roman Catholic Church and the people who owed the money were not happy with this arrangement. (I've always wondered how many of the devout Christians who started the pogroms were people that owed money to a Jew. After all, you don't have to pay money back to dead people.) Anyway, this era-before the ghetto-is where the Jews gained the reputation for being money-oriented and frugal.

Did this spawn some world-wide conspiracy of powerful Jewish banking elite that are bent on world domination? Probably. I don't know. They never let me come to their meetings.

HASIDISM

In Easter European countries like Yugoslavia and Poland, the Jews did much better, though it was still a couple hundred years before even these groups began to break away from the Pharisaic approach to Judaism. The first major step away from this was in 1700 by a guy named Israel Ball Shem. Strangely enough, the guy's reproach for Paradisiacal Judaism had nothing to do with hating all the laws and rules. His beef was about the application of these rules: i.e. with the rabbis.

Shem's new sect of Judaism, called Hasidism (nothing to do with the Hasidism of 525 BC), adopted a belief that was basically another case of religious plagiarism. He created the idea of the Zaddick, or perfect man. A Zaddick, according to Shem, was a pure and righteous man through whom the power of Yahweh could be channelled and experienced by those around him. Only a Zaddick was considered virtuous enough to interpret the Torah or tell people what to believe. I have no idea what credentials one needed to be a Zaddick, but (not surprisingly) Shem was one.

For those that haven't caught the theological coincidence (i.e. theft) in all this, I believe Shem stole the whole concept and a lot of myths of Hasidism from Eastern yogis. The whole idea that the Zaddick is the only pure man and that only a "pure man" can "channel" Divine peace is exactly mimicking the yogic concept of the guru. Like Kabala, this is merely Eastern mysticism translated into a Judaic construct.

In and of itself, Hasidism did little more than add some zing to a religion that was getting pretty stale at this point. But it did have one major effect: it opened the door for other Jewish thinkers to reinterpret the Judaic tale. The most important of these thinkers was Moses Mendelssohn, known as "the first modern Jew."

Moses Mendelssohn and Reform Judaism

> *BRAIN, n. An apparatus with which we think that we think.*
>
> *~Ambrose Beirce, The Devil's Dictionary*

Mendelssohn (1729-1786) was a pragmatic thinker from Westfalia. He basically looked at the old school Judaism (which, by this time was called Orthodox Judaism, because it hadn't changed much since 97 AD), Kabala, and Hasidism, and shrugged his shoulders. As a fan of Immanuel Kant, the philosopher, he followed Kant's lead by reducing the problem to its base elements. From there, thought Mendelssohn, you can build on it any way you want and still be Jewish.

The elements he brought Judaism down to were:

1. The existence of a god.

2. A belief in the providence and manifest power of that God, and

3. A belief in a personal, eternal soul that is subject to that God.

If you believed these three things, you were Jewish. It didn't matter what other elements you wanted to lay over top of these premises (say, like Jesus being the messiah). If you believed these three things at the root of your faith, then you were Jewish. This philosophy led to the formation of a whole new (and very popular) sect of Judaism known as Reform Judaism.

The first reformed temple opened its doors in 1810 in Westphalia, and was an immediate success—partly because it rejected the idea of Jewish nationalism as an integral part of worshipping Yahweh.

The Reform Jews are the most flexible and adaptive of the lot. In America, the vast majority of Jews are Reform, which works well within the pseudo-Judeo-Christian ethics of North America. Basically you can do want and believe what you want, so long as the three core elements of the faith are abided by and cherished—which, among other things, meant that was fine for Jews to eat cheeseburgers again. (Ronald McDonald rejoices.)

Just mentioning this is gonna piss both sides off. Take it from me, you can NOT discuss the Palestinian thing without being accused of being Zionist or anti-Semitic or both.

You'll get a lot more background on all this Palestinian stuff in the Islam chapter later on, but I have to toss in a bit of Islamic history here or the whole Israeli-Palestinian thing isn't going to make much sense.

Ok… there used to be this huge empire called the Ottomans. They were based in Turkey but controlled most of the Middle-East until the end of World War One. The guys in charge of said empire were the descendants of the Muslims who followed Mohammed in the seventh century, and they still controlled all the lands Mohammed had conquered. Up until 1917 the mid-east was controlled by this one big Muslim empire called the Ottomans.

The problem was, during the First World War the Ottomans backed Germany which, history shows, never really turns out to be a good thing. At the end of the WWI the allies kindly assisted the Ottoman Empire into an early grave, and the whole thing fell apart. Instead of one big empire we wound up with a bunch of independent regions, most of which went off to become real countries like Turkey, Iran, and Afghanistan. Of course the borders for these new countries were drawn up by England, so the people who lived there really had no idea where the hell they were. All they knew was that instead of being Ottomans they were now Turks, Iranians, etc. etc. It didn't go over well.

Palestine just kind of wandered in political limbo after the breakup of the empire. Because they didn't have much of a military or a real government, it was put under the administration of Great Britain under article 22 of the Mandates System adopted by the League of Nations, the forerunners of the United Nations. Now, watch closely and you will see the magic of bureaucracy at work.

According to the Mandate, Great Britain was supposed to limit its powers in the region to "the rendering of administrative assistance and advice". Yeah… like that was going to happen. Thing is, England went ahead and wrote this thing called the "Balfour Declaration" that expressly called for "the establishment in Palestine of a national home for the Jewish people". Jews from all over the world suddenly flooded into Palestine in the 1930's and 40's. The whole Hitler crap happened in this era, and every Jew who could get away from the Nazi dickheads headed straight for Palestine. Long before there ever was a state of Israel, Jews were already filling the streets of Palestine and trying to take the place back in the name of the ancestors who'd been booted out and slaughtered by Rome in 70 A.D.

The problem in all this is that there were already a bunch of Muslims (and Jews actually) already living in Palestine. These are the guys that had been part of the Ottoman Empire but of late had been living under English rule.

These guys were getting really pissed that all these Jewish immigrants were coming in and taking over the land they'd lived on their whole lives. They wanted things back the way they used to be or, at the very least, they wanted to be able to establish their own government the way Turkey had after the Ottomans fell.

This whole thing led to a rebellion in 1937 where the Palestinians tried to force both the Jews and the English out. To make a long story short it didn't work and everyone (including the British) just got more pissed off at the situation. The Jews thought the land was theirs because their ancestors had owned it. The British thought it was theirs because they were allowed to run it according to the League of Nations. The Palestinians thought they owned it because, well, they'd been living there for about 1500 years.

In 1947, Great Britain gave up on the whole argument and tossed it over to the new United Nations to deal with.

UNITED NATIONS

Like I said, no matter how I report on all this someone is going to get pissed somewhere along the line and say I am lying. To this end I have decided to use the word *"allegedly"* a lot. Trust me, there's a lot of hear-say evidence in all this, so reporting anything as truth is going to get you skinned somewhere along the line. As everyone involved in this has a lot more guns then I do, I figure I'll just keep using the word *allegedly* as often as possible to cover my ass.

In the interest of not boring the hell out of you I'm not going into great detail about every battle and suicide bomber in the last 80 years. This is just the highlights…

Ok…after looking at various alternatives, the UN passed Resolution 181[19], the partitioning of Palestine into two independent States, one Palestinian Arab and the other Jewish. This worked extremely well for those who are fans of bloodshed, mayhem, and all-out war. Generally speaking though, most folks seem to think it was a bad idea from the get go. A couple things happened right from the start…

In the interest of "maintaining peace," the Jews were *allegedly* forbidden to carry or own any weapons during the years of the British occupation. Then, literally overnight, the British withdrew and the Jews were left to defend themselves. With the British gone, the Palestinians *allegedly* saw their chance to reclaim their land from the *allegedly* defenceless Jews. It should have been a wholesale slaughter all over again, with the largest unarmed assembly of Jews since the Diaspora. Note that I said "*should have been*."

A funny thing happened on that faithful morning when the British packed up and left. It seems that the entire state of Israel had gone to sleep the night before totally unarmed and defenceless, and then miraculously woke up the next morning not only owning weapons, but being a very real contender for being the most heavily armed nation on the planet. As near as anyone could figure, the heavy munitions fairy visited every Jewish home in the night and left an AK-47 under every pillow and a grenade launcher in each living room.

Israel immediately went to war in 1948, and *allegedly* wiped out most of the Palestinian opposition, expanding its territory to occupy 77 per cent of the territory that had been Palestine. As a bonus, they also wound up controlling most of Jerusalem, all of which violated the basic idea set up by the United Nations for a peaceful and happy coexistence.

Over half the Palestinian population *allegedly* fled or was expelled in 1949, and the area that was supposed to become the Palestinian homeland was taken over by Jordan and Egypt. The

Palestinians were just kind of left out in the cold. Not to be outdone, Israel went to war again in 1967 and took over the last bits of what was *allegedly* supposed to be the Palestinian State (the area we now call the West Bank and Gaza Strip). They also managed to get the rest of Jerusalem, so for a short time in 1967 the Jews owned the entire area that was supposed to have been equally divided between the indigenous Palestinians and the new Israel. In 1974, the General Assembly told Israel that these Palestinians needed a place to live, and Israel gave in and ceded the West Bank and Gaza back to the Palestinians.[20]

This is where Yasser Arafat comes in. He was the head of the PLO… the Palestinian Liberation Organization. The PLO is an umbrella organization for a whole bunch of groups (some decent, some radical) that were living in Palestine before the Jewish immigration that started in the 1930s. They want their land back, they want the Jews gone, and they want to govern the area as an independent state called Palestine. For a while they *allegedly* hung out in Lebanon, *allegedly* planned terror attacks, and *allegedly* worked like hell to get the Jews out.

In June 1982, Israel invaded Lebanon and *allegedly* declared that they were going to kill every last PLO member.[21] After a bloody battle a cease-fire was arranged and the PLO troops agreed to withdraw if Israel promised not to harm the thousands of Palestinian refugees that were left behind. Everyone agreed, and the PLO backed down. But the PLO was *allegedly* well known for being sneaky, cruel, and bloodthirsty, and the Israelis *allegedly* didn't trust them. The Israeli brass figured that there were still militant PLO hiding in Lebanon that would not abide by the truce, so they went about *allegedly* massacring every man, woman, and child in the camps at Sabra and Shatila. The PLO were *allegedly* less than impressed and *allegedly* went about bombing, shooting, and otherwise bothering the Israelis in retaliation for the alleged massacre which was in retaliation for the alleged bombing which was in retaliation for the Jews allegedly taking the Palestinian land.

This whole thing goes on and on. Someone pisses someone off, they retaliate, then there's retaliation for the retaliation. It's a bunch of people fighting over who gets to live in a fertile stretch of land on the Mediterranean— the Palestinians who've occupied it for two millennia, or the Jews who were given it by the United Nations after two millennia of *Diaspora*. There really isn't an answer.

Personally, I think they should have set the whole damn thing aside years ago, had truly democratic elections, and voted in a secular government that doesn't give a damn about whose religion owns the turf. They're sitting on one of the most prized tourist traps in the world and they keep ruining it by fighting over who gets to control the damned thing. If they were secular, they could all be rich. History shows quite clearly that wealth sustains a people a hell of a lot better than a god does.

THE INTIFADA

> *"Believers, make war on the infidels who dwell around you."*
> ~*Koran, verses 109:1-6*

Intifada is an Arabic word that (as near as I can tell) means "to shake off", like a dog shakes off water to get dry. In practical application it's come to mean an uprising or rebellion, basically "shaking off" oppression or tyranny. Jews don't much like the word.

On December 6, 1987 an intifada or uprising started in the Palestinian refugee camps where a lot of the Palestinians have been living since they were chucked out by the Israelis decades before. Israel responded to this uprising with their trademark warmth, love, and kindness. The United Nations Security Council condemned Israel's warmth, love, and kindness as it seemed to involve slaughtering huge numbers of Palestinians and violating a lot of the Geneva Conventions. Israeli humanitarianism isn't exactly overwhelming.

Not to be outdone the Palestinians (in the form of the *Hamas*, who we will talk about in a second) were found to be fostering their own version of peace and love through *"dozens of Molotov cocktail attacks, over 100 hand grenade attacks and more than 500 attacks with guns or explosives."*[22] Hamas is also quite the humanitarian outfit.

Total official body count was 1,162 Palestinians and 160 Israelis.

This all gets settled by what they called *Declaration of Principles on Interim Self-Government Arrangements* or *Oslo Accords*.

INTIFADA 2: RETURN OF THE KING

Whoever thinks of stopping the uprising before it achieves its goals,
I will give him ten bullets in the chest.
~Yasser Arafat, Chairman of the PLO

On September 28 2000, soon-to-be Prime Minister Ariel Sharon visited in the Temple Mount which (you will learn in the Islam section of this book) is also one of the holiest sites for Muslims.

Sharon was a Zionist, which means he thought the Temple Mount was entirely owned by Israel and that the Muslim shrine there was just an annoying bit of mortar that should be brushed away to make room for all the glorious Jewish history hidden beneath. Thus began the second intifada, known as the *al-Aqsa Intifada*.

I'd love to tell you how that one ended, but as I write this (January 2006) it's still going on. The interesting thing about it all is that the Red Crescent Society (the Middle-east's version of the Red Cross) keep a running tally of the wounded and dead from the intifada. Currently, there's 3,808 dead, 8,520 injured, 6,526 people tear gassed, and 6,563 people hit with rubber bullets.[23]

HAMAS

"We plan to eliminate the state of Israel and establish
a purely Palestinian state. We will make life unbearable for
Jews by psychological warfare and population explosion… We
Palestinians will take over everything, including all of Jerusalem."
~Yasser Arafat

Looking at these numbers I want to reiterate that I do not support the Israeli or Palestinian side of this issue. If anyone thinks my facts are biased or one-sided let me make it absolutely clear here that I think BOTH SIDES act violently and irrationally to the detriment of their own people. In the last four years we've seen 3,308 people killed because these people can't have two religions on one hill without having to tear down the other guys' temple. It would be childish if there weren't so many lives being lost. As it is, it's just sad.

Having said that I am sure the *Hamas* will now accuse me of sympathizing with the Jews and vice versa. Paranoia runs deep in these groups.

HAMAS is actually an acronym for of *Harakat al-Muqawama al-Islamiyya*. Not surprisingly it's Arabic, not Hebrew. It literally translates as *"Islamic Resistance Movement"*. These are the Palestinians who are fighting the Jewish settlements and are trying to get back all land that the League of Nations gave to the Jews after World War II. Hamas does not recognize Israel as a sovereign state and refers to it as the "Zionist entity", which sounds vaguely like something out of Star Trek. These are the guys that blow shit up, do hit-and-run raids, and generally plot the destruction and downfall of the Israeli state.

In the West a lot of people ask why the hell a group so bent on destruction and killing would be getting so many followers. It's really important to understand that while Hamas tries really hard to kill or destroy all things Jewish, they also act as saviours to some pretty screwed-over people. Amid the bombings and shoot outs, Hamas also manages to make life more tolerable for the people living in squalor in the Palestinian refugee camps. They build hospitals and schools, bring food and medicine in, and generally do everything they can to help the people who live in these camps. Then they go back and blow shit up in Israel again.

Israel, for its part, doesn't like having its shit blown up so they take their revenge by blowing up the Hamas' shit… notably the hospitals, schools, and housing projects that Hamas builds. This then really pisses off the Hamas, who go back out and blow up something even bigger in Israel. Israel then goes back into Gaza or the West Bank and blows up more Hamas shit, and so it continues. Both sides keep fighting, and about the only ones that come out ahead in all of this are the network execs at CNN who get tons of ad revenues running pretty pictures of flaming cars and bombed out hospitals.

However, on January 26, 2004 Hamas offered Israel a 10-year truce in exchange for a complete withdrawal by Israel from the territories captured in the Six Day War, and the establishment of a Palestinian state. Amid all the bombings Hamas had come to the conclusion that it was *"difficult to liberate all our land at this stage, so we accept a phased liberation."*[24] They said the truce could last 10 years, though "not more than 10 years." In exchange, Hamas officials asked for the end of the "targeted killings" Israel had gotten so good at. On Sept. 12, 2005 Israel withdrew from the Gaza Strip and declared an official end to Israeli military rule in Gaza.

HAMAS AND PLO

For most of this tale the Hamas has been the militant wing of the Palestinians and the PLO have been the political wing. Things have gotten really weird lately though.

On January 26, 2006, the Palestinian Central Elections Committee announced that Hamas had won a majority of seats in the Palestinian Legislative Council, defeating the more moderate Fattah party and leaving Hamas to form a new government.

Western media and governments expressed shock and dismay that this radical group that had been listed as a "terrorist organization" by the U.S. could win in a democratic election. It should be noted, however, that three weeks before Hamas won the election Ariel Sharon, the Prime Minister of Israel, suffered a massive stroke that left him in a permanent coma. I suspect that Sharon was more in touch with the Palestinian demographics than CNN was.

In the month or so since then (it is Feb. 18 as I write) the whole world has been scrambling to find a way to deal with the Hamas as genuine elected government. So far, no luck.

Politically Hamas restates all its original goals… the destruction of Israel, the destruction of Israel, the destruction of Israel, and the destruction of Israel. Except now they have the legal backing of the parliament and the political powers to follow through. We're still covered by Hamas' 10-year truce deal so all should be fine and dandy.

My new career goal is to become a Kevlar salesman in Haifa.

JUDAISM: SUM UP

*We are so constituted that we believe that most incredible things and
, once they are engraved upon our memory, woe to him would endeavour to
change them!*

~*Goethe*

As I write, the new Palestinian leader Mahmoud Abbas has demanded that the Hamas recognize the existing peace deals with Israel and agree to negotiations with Israel. Hamas for its' part has pledged Israel's destruction and has said it is not moderating its ways, despite growing international pressure and threats of sanctions, including a blockade of the Gaza Strip.[25] Israel has decided to withhold $40 million in Palestinian aid money until Hamas is out of office, so we should be expecting some intense CNN coverage any day now.

Lest this whole history lesson dampen the main point of all this, I want to recap it here: modern Judaism is a construct of the Pharisees. The gods/genies/barometric pressure deities were replaced with "the one true God" Yahweh at the council in Jabna. Among the other things, this has left modern rabbis struggling hard to explain why it is that the Hebrew for their God is always in the plural form in the Torah, their holiest text.

What we see today as Judaism is an attempt to make a clean monotheism out of a bloodthirsty polytheistic heritage. It doesn't take much criticism to start rattling the foundations of this belief system. Your average heathen should be able to look at this with mild scepticism and nod politely. There are just too many obvious flaws in Judaism's religious doctrine to bother getting worked up about its explanation of our universe. Unless you live in Israel and your house keeps getting blown up over it all, in which case I offer you the same advice I offer all the Jews and Palestinians in the Holy Land: MOVE.

It ain't worth it.

Chapter Two: Christianity

For hundreds of years, theologians have contemplated the significance of Jesus' three days in the tomb.

Religion: *Christianity*

Prophet/Holy Guy: *Jesus, Peter, Pau, St. Augustine et al..*

Main Holy Book: *New Testament of the Bible, Canon Law*

What to call the priest: *Priest, Minister*

What to Call an Adherent: *Christian, Catholic, Protestant, etc.*

CHRISTIANITY

Time Wounds All Heels. ~Jane Ace

A note on the following gospel: This is ENTIRELY based on the synoptic gospels-Matthew, Mark, Luke, and John. If you're looking for footnotes, you won't find 'em. I'm following the story pretty closely from start to finish, so the only real footnote you'd need is to read the gospels concurrently. This text should NOT be seen as indicative of, well, anything. It's just a brief synopsis of what the Bible says, with a bunch of snide asides and a scathing critique of the Resurrection at the end. It can be seen as a brief study for those who are not familiar with the orthodox version of Christianity, but my intent here is not to address all the theology and depth Christians place on Jesus' sermons. It's merely an overview of the history as depicted in the Bible.

I should explain the name thing right off though. You see, in Aramaic, the language of the day way back in 1 AD, the guy we call Jesus would have been called Joshua. In Hebrew characters it's spelled yēšûā. You will notice that throughout this chapter I refer to the man, Josh, when discussing what went down and what he said and did. The guy's real name was Joshua, a common enough Judaic name. Then, as now, a short form for the name Joshua was Josh. Later you'll notice it changes to Jesus when we get into the religious crap. The different names used are meant to reflect the difference between the teacher who actually taught in Israel (Josh) and the icon that was created from his image (Jesus).

The name *Jesus* is actually Middle English. When the Hebrew name *Yesua* was translated into Greek it became *Iesous*. Just taking a look at that you can figure that, when English came along, most folks couldn't pronounce it properly. The "I" at the beginning became a "J" to make it easier to say. The hard "e" stayed the same, and the "sous" was shortened to "sus", making the name Jesus.

For our purposes Josh is the guy and Jesus is the religious figure. Alternately you'll see that I use the abbreviation "JC". There's no technical or linguistic reason for this. I just figure it sounds irreverent as hell and I like the idea of Christians shuddering in pious indignation as they read it

So, for those Christian readers who have not yet thrown this book in the garbage, here we go: the Gospel According to Will. The absolutely non-authoritative, non-inspired account of the life of the Late Great JC. (Gospel, by the way, is Greek for "good news." The original gospels were the "good news" given by the disciples to the Christians in places like Rome, Carthage, etc. My gospel is good news, too. It's just not good news for Christians.)

Ye shall know the truth, and the truth shall set you free. ~ John 8:32

And there was a virgin named Mary, or so the myth says. The Hebrew word *ulmah* is interpreted by Christian scholars as *virgin*. According to the Strong's Bible Concordance the word does not necessarily mean. Strong defines it as "Ulma: a young woman or virgin *1a)* of marriageable age *1b)* maid or newly married. [26] In Hebrew, if you're going to call someone a virgin, you usually use the word *bethulah* □, not *ulma*. Ulma is *occasionally* used to mean virgin. Bethulah is *always* used to mean virgin. I tend to side with the idea that this instance meant "young woman" as we are talking about a woman that had a child. Odds are she was not a virgin.

And the power of Yahweh did go into her and did make her pregnant outside of wedlock. Her fiancée at the time did see this and did think, "She did screw around on me, the stupid little trollop." But then an angel of God did come to him, saying, "Joseph, don't worry about it. It was God who made her pregnant." And Joseph accepted this, thinking, "Oh, great. I get to marry this woman and for the rest of our lives I have to live with the fact that her first lover was Yahweh. Even if I do really well in bed and I think she's really enjoying it, she's going to be screaming 'Oh God, oh God!' and I'll never know if it's me or Him that she's yelling about."

And this virgin gave birth in the city of David called Bethlehem. She rode on a donkey to the city with Joseph and found no inn or room to let, and did give birth in a barn while a star appeared overhead. Angels did announce the birth, and the whole world marvelled at the fact that this entire story had not happened since Simeramus (an Assyrian Queen) wound up childless after her husband died. The sun god Ra impregnated her, and she gives birth to the Son of God, whom she named Nimrod. Mary had about the same experience as Simeramus, right down to the donkey ride and the manger bit. Not that Christianity just stole the story or anything.

And there was sent to Earth a messenger named John the Baptist, who basically tried to be like one of the prophets in the Old Testament who were sent by Yahweh to point out the new king. He hung out in the middle of nowhere and what with no TV or movies to see, the people actually wandered out to listen to him preach, mainly because there wasn't a whole lot else to do. John the Baptist baptized people with water, stealing the practice from Egypt where the followers of Isis were dunked in the waters of the Nile. Since there was no Nile water readily available, John used the Jordan River, which worked just as well since he was baptizing Hellenistic Jews (i.e. Jews that had adopted a lot of Roman and Greek thought).

Like the prophets of old, John foretold of a new king that was to come and free Israel from the Roman bastards that had been taxing the hell out of them. People liked this idea and got baptized. Now, it seems that John himself was as close to a virgin birth as you can get while still being conjugal. His dad, Zechariah, isn't having a lot of luck in the begetting department, so an angel shows up at the synagogue while he's sacrificing and tells him that Elizabeth (his wife) would bear him a son that would go on to be another Elijah. Zeck gets all flipped out by this, wanders out of the synagogue totally agog and goes home to his wife. Pretty soon she's pregnant and little Johnny is born. All of this is a neat precursor to the JC tale, because Mary (the 'Immaculate Conceptee', being born without sin, ergo 'immaculate') was Liz and Zeck's cousin. When she winds up preggers, she heads over to their house and she and Liz compares notes on the holy and apparently virile nature of Yahweh.

Both women have kids, and these kids, Josh and John, are second cousins. Okay, so, little Johnny grows up to be John the Baptist who is supposed to be recognizing the new king when he comes along. One day he's out there preaching away at the river Jordan, converting the masses, that sort of thing, when Josh wanders up and volunteers himself for baptism. "No," says John in front of his followers. "It is you who should baptize me." "Suffer it be so for now," Josh says, and John baptizes him.

A lot of folks say that John was a prophet sent out into the wilderness to find the new king (messiah) and announce him to the world. The thing is, the two men involved here were cousins. It wouldn't have taken a hell of a lot for John to find Josh and announce him as the new king. All he had to do was wait until the next family dinner, say the Sabbath meal on Passover, and skip over to him after dessert and say, "Oh, hey, you're the new king." The passage as written in the synoptic gospels makes it sound like the two had never met and that this was a divine revelation given Mr. Baptist at the moment. But, hey, that's faith for ya.

Anyway, Josh wanders off for "forty days." Watch that "forty days" thing. It never really means "forty." It was just a number people had settled on to mean "a while." Sort of like people nowadays saying "a month of Sundays" or "forever and a day." Numerologists love to play with things like this.

Josh wanders off into the desert to prepare himself for his teaching, which was a common practice at the time. When he gets out there, he is "tempted by Satan"-who, by the way, is not a devil or Lucifer or whatever. You see, the Hebrew word "satan" was originally used to mean "intellect of man." Later about the time of the Babylonian exile-it also came to mean "enemy," meaning "enemy of God." (Like Nebuchadnezzar, the Babylonian guy that conquered them. He was referred to as a "satan.") However, the word generally meant Man's will or intellect: the thoughts and feelings that contradicted what old "I Am" wanted-such as temptation, which is what the whole desert incident was about. (Note: The Greek word for temptation, "periasmos," literally translates as "from evil." Since the word commonly used for evil is "baal," or "barometric pressure deity," temptation then comes to mean something from another religion or, more commonly, independent thought. Ergo, Satan. That's my take on it anyway.

Josh succeeded in purging himself of the temptations of the world and went out to the city to start teaching. Not on street corners. In synagogues. He traveled around for a while, giving his message in different towns, and then kind of wandering off. He was alone at first-no disciples, no crowds. He'd just show up and start teaching in the synagogue. The people liked what he had to say and he earned a reputation for himself as a pretty good teacher. From the nature of what he was saying, I guess it was hard for folks to figure out whether he was a prophet, a candidate for kingship, or just a damn good public speaker. Either way, most folks liked him. Things went well until he got to Nazareth, his hometown. There he stood up in the service, picked up the book of Isaiah, and read one of the prophecies out loud. It was a prophecy about the Icing that would be sent someday to reinstate Israel. He finished reading the prophesy, handed the book back to the guy he took it from, then proceeded to tell the whole congregation that he was the fulfillment of that prophesy.

This pissed everyone off. These were people he'd grown up with, peop1e that knew him. They basically thought he was being a fatuous, self-aggrandizing blasphemer. An argument immediately ensued and Josh did his best to tell them that he was destined to be king but that they just couldn't see it because they knew him too well. "A prophet is never accepted in his home town," he said in his own defence. The defence didn't hold. The congregation grabbed Josh and dragged him out of the synagogue. (Well, "grabbed him" is a little presumptuous. The word "krateo" is used as the verb. It generally means, "overpowered" but without a struggle.)[28]

Since what he said was blasphemous to them, they decided to kill him. They started dragging him to the city limits where there was a cliff from which they could throw him, but somewhere between the synagogue and the cliff Josh managed to get free of them and high-tailed it out of the city, never to return.

KING OF THE ROAD

> *I never give them hell. I just tell them the truth and they think it's hell.*
>
> *~Harry S. Truman*

About this time Josh gave up on organized religion. It's never said again that he taught in a synagogue as a regular teacher, though he did go to synagogues to argue with folks. He took to the road and taught in parks and marketplaces. There's no real explanation given for this, but that's apparently what he did.

Like John before him, he starts getting crowds. He starts healing lepers and curing blindness, etc., etc. Since Jim Bakker supposedly did the same thing, I'm reluctant to regard this as a testament to a divine nature. But the stories had it that Josh was doing miracles, and people flocked to him to see what it was all about.

One thing Josh did do consistently was piss people off. He started teaching against the orthodoxy, claiming he had the right to interpret or break the Mosaic Law as he wished. At one point he showed up at a synagogue where a bunch of Pharisees were watching to see if he'd heal on the Sabbath (which they figured was work and therefore illegal). He did, and when they confronted him Josh said he did it because he felt like it. He wandered around basically telling people that the Temple priests were idiots.

He had the wisdom not to attack Rome or the politics of the

time. He just pissed off the local guys. He taught about love and caring and a kind of anarchy under God. Along the way, he picked twelve of the guys with him to be apostles-sort of trainees. He taught them and eventually gave them the power to do all the stuff he'd been doing in the way of miracles. (Another reason not to rely on miracles as proofs of anything. Not only was the authenticity of miracles as dubious then as they are on the PTL, they're also performed by a lot of people then and now who never claim to be God Incarnate.)

One noteworthy event in particular happened about this time. While he was teaching his trainees, one of them asked how he should pray to Yahweh. Josh told him not to recite prayers or learn things by rote.[29] Instead (said Josh) you should just talk to Yahweh. He then went on to give an example of how a person should speak respectfully with a divine being. His example is what is now called "The Lord's Prayer" and is learned by rote in most churches and is recited daily around the globe. Talk about missing the point.

He said, "The first will be last and the last first" in about thirty different ways at different times. The concept was pivotal to the guy's theology. Basically it meant that the poor and suffering would get the better of the rich guys sooner or later His advice for the rich was to give everything to the poor so that they'd be as poor as anyone else when the tables got turned. Then, as now, there were more poor than rich, so this philosophy was widely liked, especially by the poor. Go figure.

Time goes by and Josh hits the city: Jerusalem. It was like traveling around America and finally hitting New York City. This was the big time-the center for religious and political debates in Israel. With the crowds he was getting, Josh was recognized as being something big. As all the prophecies had it that the new king would come from Bethlehem and reign in Jerusalem, Josh's appearance was an intriguing one. People came out in droves to see if this would be the new king that would reinstate Israel as an independent nation and get rid of all the foreign taxation. The Sanhedrin (the local council of Jewish elders) watched dubiously, checking him out and cross-examining him. Like he had everywhere else, Josh slammed the orthodox beliefs and offended the religious elite, which made him popular with most people but hated by the officials. Hmmm. Something vaguely familiar in that. Can't quite place what, but something...

While I maintain Josh had some formal indoctrination in the Essenic sect of Judaism (more on that later), he never really explained in any of the gospels where he got his authority from (i.e. the right to put his opinions forward in a legalistic region that demanded a person have some credentials). The closest Josh ever came to explaining himself on that was when he was asked by the Pharisees, "Tell us by what authority you do these things." Josh answered with a question (a common practice for the guy). He said, "I will tell you by what authority I speak if you tell me from where John the Baptist received his authority." [30]

Well, John had by this time met his demise, being served on a platter (sans torso), and had become a martyr. The people loved him, and Josh knew it. The Pharisees knew that if they said John's power was "from man" (that is, not divine) then the crowd would stone them. (They just loved stoning folks back then. Just pick up a couple of rocks and start chucking. It's simpler than crucifixion and gives a real sense of hands-on, community- based righteousness).

Anyway, the Pharisees say they don't know where John got his power and Josh says, "Oh. Well then, I'm not going to tell you where I'm getting mine." All this and one stunning Sermon on the Mount, happen in and around Jerusalem. The public is loving it. The priests are being publicly humiliated by this Josh guy and it's all taking on the flavour of a WWF main event. Any hope Josh had at getting the priests on his side was entirely gone by this point, but the people loved him. I mean, REALLY loved him. They thought he was the best damn thing since leaven bread. (Sliced bread hadn't been invented yet.)

This whole scenario got bigger and bigger, and as the annual Passover feast drew closer, the priests were getting worried. Passover was their cash cow-the time of year when they raked in the most in offering and donations. It was also the time when their power over the people was reaffirmed in the feasts, even to those that didn't attend regular services. (Think about Midnight Mass in a Catholic Church on Christmas Eve and you've pretty much got the idea.) The last thing these priests needed was everyone showing up for Josh's gig instead of theirs. Something had to be done, and quick.

Here we get around to Judas Iscariot, well known traitor and popular candidate for eternal damnation. The official story is that he sold out Josh for 30 pieces of silver The Pharisees paid him off to point out Josh in the garden of Gethsemane, at which point they'd come in and arrest him. Yeah, like the Pharisees wouldn't have recognized Josh, the guy that's been making their life a living hell for months. Judas was the closest of all the apostles. If you read the gospels, you'll see that Josh spent a hell of a lot time alone with Judas-arguably more than any of the other guys. I figure the "betrayal" was a planned thing. There have been a lot of books written on the topic (like The Passover Plot or The Judas Factor). The idea is that Josh believed he had to be arrested sooner or later and it might as well have happened while he had the public backing of thousands of followers. That's just theory, though. The fact of the matter is that Josh was arrested.

This gets a little tricky to follow. The Sanhedrin issued a warrant for Josh's arrest on the charge of heresy. Normally, all the members of the Sanhedrin would have to issue such a warrant, but in Josh's case they waited until the evening and only a fraction of the council was there to sign the warrant. The warrant went to the Romans (who are the real law of the area) and Judas led them to Josh. They arrested him and carted him off at, say, eight in the evening. Josh was brought before Pontius Pilate, the local Roman governor. If Pilate were to condemn Josh, then it would free the Sanhedrin from any culpability, seeing as how it would then be a Roman decision to kill him. This would stave off the public revolt that might have happened if the Sanhedrin had Josh killed.

The problem was that Pilate read the charges and decided that heresy wasn't a crime punishable by death. It was a mild annoyance to him, and only mattered in that it might disrupt the peaceful flow of things in this backwater area of the empire that Pilate had been condemned to govern. So, after speaking to Josh and deciding he was probably a little nuts but basically an okay guy, Pilate sentenced him to forty lashes and sent him on his way. The Sanhedrin was not happy. While Josh was being whipped, the Pharisees were busily working to come up with something that would stick and force Pilate to issue a death warrant. By the time the whipping was over (say, 10:30 PM), Pilate was just settling in for the night when the Sanhedrin showed up yet again with Josh in tow.

This time they charged Josh with wilfully opposing Rome and inciting the masses to revolt. This would fall squarely into the "we got to kill this guy" category of Roman law.

So Pilate finds himself back in the fray. It's pretty obvious to him what's going on and why the Sanhedrin want Josh dead, but it really doesn't matter to him politically or personally. Having actually kind of liked Josh the first time they met, he really didn't want to have him killed, but the charges had to be answered. It was the answering part that Josh had a problem with. He wouldn't say anything. Nothing. Zip. Pilate tried to do everything he could to get Josh to defend himself, but he just stood there. The governor actually said, *"Look, I don't want to kill you. Just say something. Anything. It doesn't matter what. Just talk."* Josh said nothing.

Finally Pilate reads him the charges, and says, *"This is your last chance. You've been charged with inciting the people to revolt against Rome. Did you do it, or what?"* (Actually the "charge" was saying he was the King of the Jews, a political position. By making this claim, the Sanhedrin was accusing Josh of claiming the power of a monarch in Rome's territory, which, of course, is what he was doing.) Here Josh signs his own death warrant with the words: *"My home is not of this Earth. Were it of this Earth, I would call down armies of angels to destroy you and all your people if that's what I wanted to do."*

Pilate is now SURE that this guy's nuts, but there's nothing he can do. The charge sticks and Josh is condemned to death by crucifixion. That's at about 4:00 am. At 6:00 am, or the sixth hour of the Day of Preparation, (meaning preparation for the Passover celebration) Pilate gave Josh one more chance. Sure the charges stuck, but this was Passover. The Jews had this clause in the Law that allowed one convicted criminal to go free on Passover Figuring this is a good out, Pilate puts Josh up as a candidate for this Get-Out-of Crucifixion-Free card. The people are supposed to vote on which convict should be freed, and Pilate selected a guy named Barabbas, a convicted thug and general asshole, and let the people choose between him and Josh-figuring the people would definitely pick Josh over an asshole and that would settle the matter.

The problem was that the Sanhedrin knew all this was going down. They stacked the crowd with their own people and made sure Josh's followers weren't aware of what was going down. When the vote was taken, Barabbas won and Josh was finally condemned to die.

At this point, Pilate was exasperated. Having done everything he could possibly do to save Josh, he turns from the crowd, looks at the crazy guy, and says his famous "I wash my hands of this" line. Thereafter Pilate is not mentioned in the scriptures. He sinks back into historical oblivion, probably spending the rest of his days wondering at the sheer lunacy of Judaic ethics.

I have no idea if Barabbas was a repeat offender.

GOLGOTHA (OR "WHERE TO HANG IN JERUSALEM")

The reports of my death are greatly exaggerated. ~Mark Twain

Okay, so Josh is crucified. There's nothing spectacular about this. He was crucified just like a bunch of other guys that day. They nailed him to a chunk of wood and suspended it on a crossbeam and left him there. Now, normally speaking, you stay hung up there for days and die of asphyxiation. The way you're hung up there maces it hard to breathe, and you have to keep pulling yourself up with impaled wrists (while bracing with impaled feet) to catch a breath of air. Eventually you just give up on it all and suffocate.

Now, I say normally that's the way it was done. But this was Passover they weren't allowed to have half-dead criminals lolling about on a holy day (it would be like sending someone to the electric chair on Christmas). So the guards wandered around breaking legs. With their legs broken, the people hanging up there couldn't support themselves, so they'd die quite quickly- hopefully before sundown, the official start of Passover

They broke the legs of the guys on either side of Josh-but not his. When they got to him, he was already "dead.' Just hanging there limp. Instead of going to all the trouble of breaking the legs, the guard took his spear and stabbed Josh in the right side of the chest, just below the rib cage. A mixture of water and blood came out and the guard decided Josh had it.

The body was taken down and handed off to Joseph of Arimathea, one of the Sanhedrin who secretly supported Josh but wasn't around for the late-night vote to have him arrested. Joseph took Josh's body and stuffed it in his own tomb.

So Josh is "dead." They'd whipped him, beaten him, nailed him to a chunk of wood, then hung him up for, oh, eight hours or so.

That's the Crucifixion. Pretty harsh, no doubt about it. The question is; could he have survived it? Eight hours isn't long enough to have died of exposure (especially with friends giving him water and "a bitter mixture"-a potion?). The wounds were bad, but hey, people have lived through a hell of a lot worse. A guy in Wisconsin had his leg chewed right off by a bear and managed to walk for three days to get help. [31]

Then there's the question of whether he could have gone without breathing long enough to appear dead when the soldiers came by. Yogic mystics have been doing this sort of thing for millennia. They just bring their heart rate down and meditated their way through it. This would also help considerably with blood loss and possible punctured lung had the spear pierced that far in the chest.

Okay. You figured me out. I think the guy was still alive. He was hurting -no doubt about it. But I don't think he was dead. They took him down, stuffed him in the tomb, and tended to him. Pilate's guards watched over the tomb, but that doesn't mean a hell of a lot. Pilate didn't want to kill the guy in the first place. Three days later, Mary and Martha (more on them later) go to the tomb and are greeted by a living Josh and "two men dressed in white." A note here: the Essenes were the healers of the day. They spent a lot of their time learning about herbs and healing and stuff like that there. They also wore (you guessed it) white clothing. [32]

Josh wandered around for a time after this. He showed up once while the apostles were at dinner and again when they were fishing. He came and went and continued teaching for a bit. Two gospels say Josh was taken bodily up into Heaven awhile later. The other two just say he left them. Either way, the guy disappears.

A note to the born-again Christians out there who may be reading this: Please allow me to save you the trouble. Yes, I know that if you're right, I am going to hell. I'm perfectly fine with this. As a matter of fact, I've made special arrangements to be buried with a whole box of marshmallows that I intend to roast along with my evil, godforsaken self. But I'm dealing in fact here. I'm not terribly concerned with articles of faith, like the resurrection thing.

We have ample information regarding the era we're talking about here. Rome kept records. The Jews kept records. The Phoenicians kept records. (Phoenicia was Israel's trading partner-

Israel grew barley, wheat, etc., and the Phoenicians shipped it out. They were famous for their seafaring skills.) Anyway, there's a lot of stuff out there besides the Bible. The point is, there's no record of people rising from the dead anywhere in Israel but in the Christian tale.

Now, I figure if Pontius Pilate had ordered Josh's death, watched him die, then seen him wandering down the street the next week chatting it up with Peter, he might have mentioned this somewhere, or his scribe might have. Either way, there would be some record. I haven't found any. It may have been overlooked, but it strikes me that incidental things like convicted criminals rising from the grave and wandering about the streets would bear some sort of attention. The Sanhedrin should at least have had something to say about it all. But, what the hell... It's all about faith, right?

And that is the tale of Josh as recorded here by your lecherous, irreverent, and utterly heathenous not-even-close-to-witness, William of Hopper.

THE NICENE CREED

> *No man with a sense of humor has ever founded a religion. ~R. G.*
> *Ingersoll*

If you're working from the Bible, there's really only one thing you need to know about the life of JC: the Apostles Creed (also called the Nicene Creed). It's what they used to put the Bible together. Read it through...

> *We believe in our God, the Father, and the Almighty, Maker of heaven and earth, of all that is seen and unseen.*
>
> *We believe in one Lord, Jesus Christ, the only Son of God, eternally begotten of the Father, God from God, Light from Light, true God from true God, begotten, not made, one in Being with the Father. Through Him all things are made. For our sake and for our salvation He came down from Heaven: by the power of the Holy Spirit was born of the Virgin Mary and became man.*

For- our sake He was crucified under Pontius Pilate; He suffered, died and was buried. On the third day He rose in fulfillment of the Scriptures; He ascended into Heaven and is seated at the right hand of the Father: He will come again in glory to judge the living and the dead, and his kingdom will have no end. We believe in the Holy Spirit, the Lord, and the giver of life, who proceeds from the Father and the Son he is worshipped and glorified. He has spoken through the Prophets. We believe in one holy catholic and apostolic Church. We acknowledge the baptism for the forgiveness of sins. We look for the resurrection of the dead, and the life of the world to come.

Amen to that.

Okay, that's the creed. It was originally written by a guy named Hippolayatus in the third century. It's undergone a few very minor revisions since then, but it is essentially exactly the same today as it was when it was written. Those readers who have had Catholic indoctrination will recognize it as being the first words said in a mass. Anglicans usually say it just before the communion service. Basically, this creed is supposed to sum up the entire Christian faith in one short statement that any zombie can recite. [33]

JESUS THE KING

Okay-was Jesus the Messiah? It's a major debate in Christian circles. I figure it's only a major debate because the Christians have what they want to believe and they've got to work hard to defend it in the face of reality. Whatever you may think JC was, he was NOT the messiah. (I can just hear the Christians grow1ing at this.)

It's true. Messiah and Christos are both transliterations of the term "anointed of God." Ask any rabbi. In the Judaic tradition, a person cannot be called a king (a messiah) until he has been properly (and legally) anointed on the forehead with the Holy Oil of anointing (a.k.a. The Perpetual Oil of Anointing)[34]. Josh never was. This oil was kept safe by the Pharisees at the time of Jesus. No other oil was allowed, and a stringent process (involving the blood of a pure red bull and the remains of the old oil) was needed to create more Holy Oil of Anointing. The "no-name" version wouldn't cut it. Nor would John the Baptist's Holy Water of Baptism (as some Christians contend).

Legally, Josh was never king. He never had a throne or any of the stuff David and Solomon before had as king. The cold, hard reality is that as far as the Jews were and are concerned, Josh was just a rabbi and teacher He was not in the line of kings that ruled Israel.

JESUS, SON OF GOD

Have we not all one father? ~ Malachi 2:10

Christians call Jesus "God incarnate." Quick question...didn't God the Father "walk in the morning" with Adam and Eve (Genesis 2)? If he were walking and talking with Adam, that pretty much means he's got legs, right? I mean, it didn't say, "floating around like a spirit." No, Yahweh was walking. On legs. With arms and a torso, presumably. A head in there somewhere for good measure. Wouldn't that make God incarnate? I mean, the spirit made flesh, etc., etc.? If there's one thing to be figured out from all this, it's that the Judeo-Christian god in all his forms-Yahweh, Elohim, Shaddai, etc.: is anthropomorphized.[35]

The histories are full of stories of the Judeo-Christian god talking and wandering and doing pretty much everything else humans do. Remember, we're dealing with mythos that originates with rural polytheists like Abraham. There's nothing unusual about this anthropomorphic construct; it's the same in every religion on the planet. It's just that modern-day Christians seem to want to forget that their god was originally envisioned as a physical being that walked and talked not unlike Apollo, Zeus, Mithra, or Harvey the Rabbit. Christians have always wanted to look at every other religion in the world and say how backward they are because their gods are blue or animal-like, or just plain different from their Christian concept.

The thing is, there's not a hell of a lot of difference here. Yahweh is divine, yes. But he is (in the mythos and in the Bible) as divinely fallible and human-like as Apollo or Zeus. Sure, he's omnipotent, but so was Zeus. Like Zeus, Yahweh threw tantrums and declared him to be "a jealous god." Yahweh, like all other gods, was originally a physical being who interacted with the Jews in a very human way.

So, what's all this about Jesus being "God Incarnate" if we already had an incarnate god? It sounds a little redundant, doesn't it? That's one of the fine blessings of faith. You just don't have to stop to consider stuff like this.

It all gets pretty silly from here on in, and if you want to have even half a hope of figuring all this out you've got to get a grasp of the whole Roman influence here. Now, understand that this is going to sound a lot like a dreary history lesson, but I've got to cover Rome, Greece, and Hellenism before we go much further. If you want to understand how this rabbi named Josh became the divine Jesus Christ of Christian mythos, you have to understand all the crap that went into inventing the myth of Christianity. There was a lot going on back then, and the people that created Christianity did their best to adopt most of it into the faith.

HELLENISM

If triangles made a god, they would give him three sides. ~Baron De Montesquieu

Rome, like every other ancient city, started out with a few nomadic people stopping one day and saying, "Fuck it. I'm fed up with wandering around. We're staying right here and that's that." (Folklore says that Rome was actually built by Romulus and Remus, two twin brothers who were abandoned at birth and raised by wolves until they were old enough to build the city. How one learns basic architecture from wolves is beyond me, but that's the story.)

Anyway, Rome did well for itself (mainly in the salt trade) until about the fourth century when its citizens got too greedy for foreign taxes and everything went to hell. Like the Jews, other parts of the empire revolted or refused to pay the tax and eventually Rome just gave up trying to hold it all together. Without the cash, the military dwindled and the people just kind of got discouraged and wandered away. There. Now that I've covered the entire rise and fall of Rome in two short paragraphs, let's deal with the religion.

In early Rome what we call "religion" was a lot like the beliefs of Abraham's nomadic tribes. The Roman belief system worked on the ideas of *religio* and *pietas*. The astute reader will notice that *religio* is the word religion without the "n." For the etymologists out there, the answer is yes, this is where the word religion comes from. It's actually two words: re (as in *"Ra"* or god/genie/barometric pressure deity) and *ligio*. Think of words like *"ligament"* and *"link."* They both have the same origins.

Ligio basically means *contract* or *bond*. So religio, and therefore religion, means a contract or bond with a god. Pietas, you may have guessed basically means piety. You see, in Rome the deals or contracts you struck up with a god were the framework for the relationship. The pietas, or piety, were the respect and honour you gave to the god. And other humans, for that matter, but it applied mainly to respecting the gods.

The gods were called the numen (numina in the plural). This was roughly the same as the nomadics' version of the elohim Like the Canaanites; the Romans didn't concern themselves with any sense of the afterlife or a heaven/hell concept. The numina were basically more powerful barometric pressure gods who could and should be consulted about major things, like "Should we go off and conquer the Gauls or not?" Gods weren't the only form of worship in Rome.

About the time Jeremiah was in Israel, the idea of mane worship became popular. Manes were the spirits of dead relatives who walked unseen among the living-ancestral worship, basically it was a minor part of it all and you can feel free to forget you've ever heard about the manes. I just figured 1'd throw it in just so nobody walks up to me and says, "Hey...you didn't mention the manes when you were talking about Roman religions."

GREECE

I'm thinking that any decent historian reading this must be pulling their hair out about now. You see normally one would go on and on about the intricacies of the many aspects of the numina before covering the Greek influences. The thing is, it's irrelevant. I'm trying to get across the ideas and the history of the religions.

I'm not trying to convert anybody to them. If you really want to know the ins and outs of the rituals and the names of each of the gods involved, you can look them up. I'll be providing a bibliography at the end of this book that you can feel free to follow up on.

So... with both Rome and Greece thriving, it didn't take long before the two cultures overlapped. Greece had the same basic concepts of the numina, which they called the gods/goddesses/barometric pressure deities. The only real difference was that Greece had anthropomorphized the deities to a greater extent. The Romans already had a list of deities. The Greeks had created the faces. Basically, Rome used the Greek myths to update their own numina and make them more "user-friendly"

For example, to the Romans; Jupiter was the greatest god-basically because Jupiter was also the biggest thing in the sky. The Romans acknowledged that Jupiter was an entity, but it took the Greek influence to identify Jupiter as a man-like being. Jupiter meshed with Zeus, the all-powerful god. Neptune fused with Poseidon, Juno with Hera. You get the idea. That's not to say that the Romans hadn't had any human-like gods. It's just that Greece did a far better job of making them real. They brought in the whole story of the interaction of the gods. For example, if Jupiter was aligning with Saturn in such a way as to blot Saturn out from view, the Greeks saw this as a "battle" or a "conflict" between the two gods that Jupiter had won. The Romans heard this view and basically thought, "Hey Neat. The gods think like us. Tell us more..."

And thus the Roman pantheon was born. All the stories you've heard about Venus, Neptune and friends started here. They came from the stargazers and the naturalists who looked at the world, saw phenomena they didn't understand and made up stories that fit the events. This is what we call Hellenism, and it was this belief system that came to Judea with Alexander the Great. It was also this belief system that the Pharisees and the Zealots were working hard to get rid of.

You see, by the time Jesus was teaching in Judea, the Jews had settled into the idea that Yahweh was the only real god. These gods of Hellenism were either "bad gods" (meaning they weren't their god, Yahweh) or they weren't gods at all. They were seen as beings that were stronger than humans but less than "the one true God." They were considered to be other creations of Yahweh that were trying to convince humans that they were gods. This particular interpretation led to the Judeo-Christian invention of the daemonic sphere: the realm where these other beings lived that wasn't heaven and wasn't Earth. The gods were called daemons.

In the Middle Ages, the daemonic sphere became hell and the daemons became "demons." This has no bearing at all on Hellenism at the time of Josh, but I was just thinking about it as I was writing and I figured I'd throw it in since it's a neat piece of information. (It's my professionalism that really makes this all worthwhile, isn't it?)

PHILOSOPHICAL HELLENISM

> *There is nothing so absurd that some philosopher hasn't said it.*
>
> ~Cicero

At the time of JC there was also a philosophical branch of A Hellenism that had become popular. It was basically the same Hellenism with a lot more thought. People like Plato and Aristotle had had their influences here. (No need to nod off at this point. I promise this isn't as boring as it sounds like it's going to be.)

Basically the philosophers[36] got the idea that there was a macrocosm, a cosm, and a microcosm. The macrocosm was the big, wide universe that we can't begin to understand. The microcosm was the world of what we now know as microbes and bacteria, too small for us to understand. Then there's the cosm, our place. The cosmos where we live and eat and exist. Religion was viewed as the interplay between these three levels of existence-gods in the macrocosm interacting with humans in the cosm. Hera and Zeus and Apollo were all seen as residents of the macrocosm, who would look down into our world the same way we'd look into the world of bugs or fish or any smaller life form.

A later addition to all this was the metacosm, the place where there is only Ultimate Expression. It was a place that even the gods could not understand because it defied the comprehension of anyone who was within time and space, including gods. Anyway, you get the idea. Gods and goddesses, three levels of existence and above it all was the metacosm. Congratulations. You've passed Philosophy 101.

ZOROASTRIANISM AND MITHRA

A man hath no better thing under the sun

than to eat, drink, and be merry.~Eccl.s 8:15

By this point you should be figuring out that it's basically impossible to talk about Christianity without dragging up pretty much every major religion that was at the time. They all kind of mingled and interbred during the first three centuries, and it's too hard to decipher what came from where so you have to cover them all. Churches like to give this image of early Christianity (and Judaism) as being this monolithic faith that was sturdy and solemn and carried on unaffected by the evil influences around it. This, of course, is bullshit.

All you have to do is look at Acts and you'll see that there was enough dissension between the apostles alone to found twelve different churches. The common Church (the one true faith of Christianity) didn't come into being until 325 AD. But we'll get to that. I want to cover Mithras first.

Mithras was a god. Think of him as Darth Vader's good twin. He was a being who was constantly locked in a battle against the forces of evil. To secure his victory, Mithras sacrificed a bull (why a bull I do not know). Anyway, he sacrificed the bull to Ahura Mazda (the supreme god of a religion called Zoroastrianism) and won the day. To commemorate this, his devotees sacrifice a bull in their ceremonies. They then have a ritual meal wherein the devotees eat beef, drink wine, and celebrate. I can handle a religion like this.

Mithra (the faith) was originally a Babylonian religion. Mithras (the god) was known as *Sol Invictus*, or "the unconquerable sun." He was also known as "The Eye of Mazda." Not the car, the god. It was a warrior's religion. It was also known as one of Rome's "mystery religions." Christianity became another "mystery religion".

By "mystery" they don't mean mysterious in the modern sense. They mean it was a religion that offered something beyond a simple contract that made life worth living. It offered the warriors a chance at a better life after death and, through the ceremony, it promised the adherents the chance to touch and know the Divine while still on Earth. Like the Catholic Eucharist, the Mithran services offered a physical, tangible touch of the Divine by eating the consecrated sacrifice of the bull and by drinking the holy blood of that sacrifice. Eat of my body, drink of my blood. Josh, the "ultimate sacrifice"... Sound familiar yet?

It should. This would be where the whole "transubstantiation"[37] concept came from when they were putting Christianity together in the fourth century. Like baptism, which was stolen from Isis worship, the transubstantiation of bread and wine into the body and blood of Jesus was a "borrowed" concept. It's taken directly from Mithra/ Zoroastrianism.

The average Christian might be sitting there right now saying, "Yeah, right. Why would the Church fathers steal from other religions when Christianity was fine just as it was?"

Well, the truth is, it wasn't. When all this went down, Christianity was just a bunch of rumours and legends of a dead or missing rabbi. No one knew what it was all about. All they knew was that it was a new religion. The people wanted this new religion to be "religious"-that is, they wanted it to meet the standards of what a "religion" was in their day. So the Church fathers stole a whole bunch of stuff from the religions that people knew and served it up to them as something different called Christianity.

Did it work? Well, I'm writing this book, aren't I?

The Late Great JC

It is convenient to believe there are gods. ~Ovid

You've read the book and you've probably seen at least one of the movies. The Greatest Story Ever Told was one of my favourites. Of course, I also liked Steven King's Salem's Lot. It doesn't mean I believe it. Well, now that I've happily trashed the holy, sanctified version of "the one true Son of God," let's try to infuse a bit of reality into the tale. (Pentecostals hate it when you do that.)

Having removed some of the chaff from the story, the question now becomes; "Who the hell was this Josh guy before all the crap and mythos built up around him?" Well, The Gospel According to Will is a good intro, but there's a lot more out there than gospel. Josh was a rabbi from the line of David. Since prophesy has it that the next king had to be a direct descendant of David (see Isaiah: the whole damn book), this means that Josh qualified as a candidate for kingship (as chronicled at the beginning of Matthew)-unless, of course, you believe in the immaculate conception, in which case Josh wasn't in any way related to David at all. The Immaculate Conception would make Yahweh his father, who— as near as we know— [38] was not a blood relative of David. If this were the case, he would not be a candidate for kingship because the king HAD to be from the line of David. Granted the Son of God would make a pretty decent king, but it would definitely conflict with the prophecy. I find Christians don't tend to appreciate the fine irony of this.

JESUS AND CHRISTIANITY

I have to follow them... I'm their leader. ~Alexandre-Auguste Ledru-Rollin

Don't kid yourself... they're two entirely different things. If you've read the section on Judaism, you'll have a fairly good idea of the political environment that JC was born into. Israel was a volatile place at the turn of the millennium from BC to AD (it's now BCE for Before Common Era and CE for Common Era, but I'll stick with BC and AD). All the sentiments that finally erupted into the Jewish Revolt of 66-70 AD were widespread. The Jews were overtaxed. Herod had set himself up as a makeshift king (AKA messiah, AKA Christos). The local government was run by a group called the Sanhedrin: a combination of Pharisees and Sadducees that judged religious crimes (adultery, fornication-all the fun stuff).

At the time, there were four distinct sects of Judaism. I'll give you the lowdown on each so you have an idea of who we're dealing with here:

Sadducees: These guys controlled the Sanhedrin for the most part. They were religious conservatives who stuck to Jeremiah's theology— the "Law of the Prophets," as it was called. Their big thing was the rejection of Roman Hellenism (polytheism) that had become the "in" thing at the time. Since their local powers were recognized by Rome, they weren't about to go screwing around with revolution. They pretty much liked things just as they were, though ideologically they wanted Rome and Herod gone.

Zealots: Simon-Peter was one of these guys. They also rejected Rome and Herod, but unlike the Sadducees, the Zealots pushed for an all-out rebellion to kick out any foreign powers (along with Herod, who they didn't recognize as king). They were led at the time by a man named Judas of Galilee (no relation to JC of Galilee). They were the messianics, which basically means they wanted a real messiah (king) to take over

Pharisees: Less political than the Sadducees, but way more. They believed in exact obedience to every word recorded in the Torah, no matter what. These guys are the rabbis and scribes, the ones you hear about who came out to chastise Jesus for not following "the Law."

Essenes: These guys are my personal favourites. They're the nutbar, genuinely certifiable Jews, the ones who would have been in Waco, Texas if they'd lived today. Instead of Waco, they found a place even more desolate: Qumran. It's on the northwest shore of the Dead Sea, about a mile and a half inland. The closest inhabited spot was Angali, about an hour's walk. This was also the closest place to find fresh water The Essenes were "apocalyptic." This means they'd hidden themselves away from the world (i.e. the Jews in Jerusalem) because it had become corrupt and evil. Hellenism had run rampant and was infiltrating the Judaic lifestyle. Unlike the Zealots-who actively looked for a revolution-the Essenes stayed in virtual hiding, waiting for Yahweh to send a prophet who would lead them into the final battle between good and evil. They, of course, were supposed to win. Nobody bothered to tell Rome this.

Amid all this crap arrives Josh.

The Bible never says what sect of Judaism Josh belonged to, but I'm going to go out on a limb here and say it's pretty obvious he was Essenic. (Yup...the nutbar guys that lived in Qumran and hid from the world waiting for Har Maggio, the final call to arms.)

What, I hear you ponder, would an Essene be doing in the city if they were all hermits? Well, I'm glad you asked.

The answer lies in the Dead Sea Scrolls...

God is dead: but considering the state Man is in, there will perhaps

be coves` for ages yet, in which his shadow wilt be shown.

~*Friedrich Nietzsche*

In the spring of 1957, a Bedouin named Mohammed ad Dib I was chasing his sheep; a common enough practice for a Bedouin. He was just up from the Dead Sea, wandering about like his forefathers trying to find decent land to feed his flock. [39]

Now, Mohammed (not THE Mohammed) was one of your basic polytheistic genie/barometric pressure deity worshippers. (Yes, they still exist today, relatively unchanged from Abraham's era.) Anyway, one of the sheep wanders down a hole and Mohammed decides to follow it down, what with the cost of sheep these days.

I have no idea if he ever actually got the sheep. I'll look it up, but no one seems terribly interested in recording ovine history. What he did find were jars-clay jars, to be exact. Kind of reddish clay, sealed with wax. In true human style, he sees this and thinks, "Wow! How much can I make off these things?"

With the sheep forgotten, he decides he needs to know what's in them. He gets himself a rock-readily available in any cave-and smashes one of them. The effect was instantaneous. The jar, being as old as it was, was immediately pulverized. Gone. Poof. Magically disappeared. The bits of clay that had been the jar were caught up in the breeze coming in from the outside and were blown aloft. The sun caught the glassy motes of clay and, in the darkness of the cave; they glistened all around him.

Mohammed screamed- being the good polytheistic Bedouin that he was, Mohammed thought he had loosed a genie. He ran screaming from the cave (presumably forsaking said sheep) and down the hillside to where his buddies were. After he carefully explained the divine nature of the threat, they decided to go check it out. Armed to the teeth, the men re- entered the cave and found the eight clay jars, several scrolls lying on the floor, bits of clay from the broken jar, but no genie.

There's no record of whether the sheep was still there.

What they'd found (and what archaeologists were to unearth

more of later) were the famous Dead Sea Scrolls. They're scrolls. Found near the Dead Sea. (Amazing the depth of interpretation I put into this, isn't it?)

"Okay, so what the hell were they really?" you ask.

Well, they're actually pretty important in understanding the history of Judaism and Christianity.

You see, when the Zealots went against Rome, they initially did okay. A few minor battles; a usurping here and there. Nothing major happened until Titus takes over and decides to slaughter them all wholesale. The thing is, the Jews weren't stupid. Least of all the Pharisees. It was getting obvious that Rome would retaliate sooner or later, and nobody was taking odds that Israel would win. But the Jews had seen all this before. They'd been invaded and taken over, and they'd lost a hell of a lot over the years. This time they figured out a way to prevent the invasion from taking away the holiest of their stuff. They started out by taking the most sacred artefacts (like the original Menorah, the Holy Oil of Anointing, etc.) and hiding them all in walls and burial places around Jerusalem. Then they recorded the hiding places on a copper scroll for safekeeping.

Then they gathered up their most important letters, scriptures, and other documents (from all the sects-Pharisee, Sadducee, Zealot, and Essene) and shipped them off with the copper scroll to the safest place they could think of...Qumran. It was a Jewish monastery, and therefore in danger from Rome, but it was also so damned remote they figured (rightly) that it would be the last place the Romans would attack. Well, as you know, Rome did attack Jerusalem. But it was only after the siege of Masada that the Romans, as an afterthought, got around to killing everyone in Qur'an.

By the time they got there, the monks had had more than enough time to take the documents (their own and those belonging to the other sects) and seal them inside clay jars, which they buried in the hills above the monastery. The Romans killed the monks and took over the spot, making it into a garrison, unaware of the copper scroll or any of the other documents that were buried right behind them. The scrolls stayed there intact from 70 AD (the fall of Israel) until 1957, when Mohammed's sheep got away from him and slipped down a hole. (If you want a much better account of this, read anything by Elaine Pagels on the subject. I highly recommend

Adam, Eve, and the Serpent.) Okay, that's what the scrolls are. Now, back to JC...

JC THE ESSENE

Tell me the company you keep, and I'll tell you what you are.

~Miguel De Cervantes

Josh was a rabbi, a teacher. At the time (actually, all through Judaic history) you couldn't just stand up and decide you were going to be a teacher. If you did, they either stoned you or called you a prophet, depending on what you were saying. To be a rabbi or teacher you had to have been taught-you had to have some credentials that showed the people that you deserved the title "rabbi." Even the Pharisees, who obviously didn't like Josh, called him teacher or rabbi. So you have to figure that somewhere along the line, JC had to have gotten some formal indoctrination:

Unfortunately, the Bible doesn't mention it, so Christians tend to say that Josh just lived an ordinary carpenter's life until he went off to become God. Knowing the people of the day and the beliefs of the society, this just doesn't make sense. Josh wouldn't have been afforded the esteem he was given if this had been the case. The Jews respected education and knowledge. Even if you think JC was the Almighty Son of God, he was dealing with a human society with standards that he obviously met. He was a rabbi. We can safely assume he wasn't Pharisee or Sadducee, since he spent a lot of time pissing these guys off in the synoptic gospels. We know from his conversations with Peter that Josh didn't advocate bloodshed or open war, so he didn't fit in with the Zealots. So that leaves the Essenes. Except the Essenes were also waiting for the Apocalypse, so they would seem to be warlike. Right?

Well, almost right. Among the scrolls found at Qur'an, there are two in particular that are definitely from the Essenes and not from the other sects. They are the War Scroll and The Doctrine of Peace. The War Scroll is well, a scroll about war. It chronicles the final battle of Har Mageddio, complete with angel warriors and demons fighting on behalf of the evil "enemy." It's really bloody and cruel and full of painfully masochistic stuff that the "good" soldiers were to do to keep themselves pure for battle. On the other side of this equation was the Doctrine of Peace. It's a warm-fuzzy that basically says "Love everybody and let Yahweh lead us into a new age of peace, love, and universal brotherhood," the type of stuff JC would have been proud to call his own. Now, knowing that Josh didn't fit the other sects of Judaism very well, this scroll allows for his philosophies to fit into Essenic Judaism, providing it can be reconciled with the War Scroll. It doesn't seem a difficult task.

You see, even Josh talked about "the end times" and the "armies of angels" he could have at his command. The idea of the Apocalypse is compatible with Josh's teachings and certainly with Essenism in general. If you'll recall from the Judaism section, the Essenes were founded by the Teacher of Righteousness, whose theology was full of love, peace, and severed body parts. Both the scrolls in question here would have been written by (or possibly under the tutelage of) the Teacher, who had extreme views on both love and war.

Josephus actually lends a hand here in getting more information on all of this. Before the revolt in 66 AD, Josephus spent some time in Qur'an. He recorded for Rome that the Essenes were "a peaceful people." He basically said they were easy-going hippie-types who wouldn't hurt a fly. Granted, his report to Rome would have been tempered by a pro Judaic bias (he liked the Jews) that would prevent him from saying, "Hey, Caesar, these Essene guys are just waiting for the chance to kill every living Roman in Israel." But even so, Josephus didn't say the same peaceful things about the other Jewish groups he saw, so you've got to figure there must have been something to it.

So Josh was most likely an Essene. The Manual of Discipline (another scroll) tells how an initiate into the Essenic order progresses through to the highest order of the monastery during his cloister. The apex of this life (if one lived long enough) was to become a teacher (and, of course, a recruiter). You see, the Essenes were also celibate. No sex, no women. Period. Aside from the inherent problems this brings about in Essenic dating circles, it also meant no children and no way to increase or sustain the number of Essenic adherents. To this end the most educated, the wisest, and the ones that just plain lived long enough were sent out into the world to teach and recruit.

People generally accept that Josh started teaching in his early thirties. In a civilization without medicine, clean water, or basic toiletries, living to your thirties would have been considered a feat. I submit, then, that this is what JC was-an Essenic monk who had lived long enough and had learned enough to be sent from Qumran to the cities to teach. It's just a theory, but it makes a whole lot of sense to me.

ROME AND EARLY CHRISTIANITY

It is unfortunate that so few enthusiasts can be trusted to speak
the truth. ~Arthur James Balfour, Letter (1891)

I know what you're thinking. You're thinking about the Roman coliseum and the Christians being thrown to the lions, right? That's the idea everyone gets when you talk about early Rome and Christianity in the same breath. The answer is yes, the Christians were fed to the lions at the coliseum. Let me give you an idea of how this came about...

When Christianity first came to Rome, it was accepted as just another part of Judaism. As this was well before Judaism was illegal, the Romans had no real problem with adding Jesus (along with Yahweh) to the ranks of the Roman pantheon. The problem was that the Christians were not content to remain a mere Jewish sect. They felt they were really onto something with this idea of grace and an eternal life. They also knew that the Romans were wrong with their hedonistic attitudes and their polytheistic Hellenism. And they weren't quiet about it. At all. This would fall squarely into the "not good" category.

What the early Christians did to piss off the Romans so badly was to proselytize. Rome had fully allowed them to be Christians-no problem there. The problems began when the Christians would show up at other temples and scream and yell about their worship being a slight to "the one true God." This was a polytheistic city. The Christians managed to piss off every other religion in Rome, so much so that the Senate had to pass a law banning Christianity from being practiced.

This wasn't done to destroy the faith. It was done to preserve the peace. Rome simply couldn't have these fanatical Christians showing up everywhere and telling people they would suffer an eternal death if they continued worshipping their gods. With all the religions that came and went in Rome, Christianity was only one of two that were ever banned. The other prohibition was Bacchus worship, which celebrated the god of wine and fertility. Apparently, they had some sort of social problem as well, but it had more to do with rowdy parties than proselytizing. (Hey, if you're going to get your god banned from a city, this is the way to do it.)

As you can read in Acts, Christianity went underground. For about a century it was illegal. The "secret meetings" you've heard about in church, where the devout gathered in catacombs to worship, all happened during this era. Unfortunately, this did more harm than good for the Christian reputation. The bread and wine service ("eat of my body, drink of my blood") was generally interpreted as cannibalism by the Romans who heard about it.

Christianity became known as a weird and psychotic faith practiced by the emotionally disturbed. (There's some validity to this. There were some nutbars around at the time. Apparently a philosophy grew that was mentioned in Acts wherein some Christians rationalized that since they were saved by grace, and since grace can't be earned but had been given freely by God at the moment Christ died on the cross, then nothing they could do would affect this. Grace, as given by God-an eternal being-could not be revoked. Ergo, they were free to do anything they wanted, since they were already saved and couldn't die an eternal death. Neat logic, anyway.)

This is why public sentiment went so harshly against the early Christians. They were seen as lunatics and criminals who met secretly to drink blood and plant vile things in the catacombs. (For those who don't know, the catacombs were also graves, which really added to the motif.) Moreover, Christians refused to serve in the Roman military or fight to protect Rome because of their faith. This is why Christianity was a crime punishable by death. The whole lions-at-the-coliseum thing was Nero's answer to the dilemma. A bit later, in the third century under Decius, the rounding up and slaughtering of Christians really took off. (Note: they weren't ALL thrown to lions. Some were still crucified or hung. Capital punishment was as eclectic a pastime in Rome as orgies. This wasn't specifically an anti-Christian thing. Thieves, murderers, and basically anyone who screwed up at the wrong time were also executed. For instance, if you were a sentry in the military who was caught drinking on duty, they'd remove your shoelaces. The first lace bound your hands. The second was tied around the end of your penis so you couldn't piss. Then they'd force as much wine down your throat as they could. This would go on for hours. When you were bloated and in agony they'd slit your belly, allowing the wine to sluice out through the gash. With the alcohol in your system and the belly wound you'd bleed to death, but very slowly and painfully.)

Now, on the topic of slow, agonizing pain, let's talk about Saul of Tarsus…

SAUL, OR "WHO TO HATE IN CHRISTIAN HISTORY"

> *If you talk to God, you are praying; if God talks to you, you have schizophrenia. ~Thomas Szasz, The Second Sin*

Tarsus was the capital city of the Roman province of Cilicia. It was about ten miles in from where the Cydnus River empties into the Mediterranean, roughly eighty miles north of the eastern tip of Cyprus. It was about as popular as Winnipeg, and it was Saul's hometown.

He lived there until he got himself a pretty good job with the Roman military, when he was given the chore of killing off all those pesky Christians that had been causing so much trouble in Rome about that time. Saul the Christian-killer did okay at this, right up to the point where he went clinically insane, changed his name to Paul, and went on a "messenger from God" trip that made David Koresh look tame. Not that I have a bias here or anything...

Now, I fully admit that my opinions of Paul are purely interpretive and are therefore open to debate. But since I'm the guy writing the book and you're the one reading it, I get to pass off my opinions first. I'm sure more than a few people will take the opportunity to either write me their opinions or accost me on the street to share them. Probably very loudly, with Bibles in hand. Hey, it's fun.

Anyway… Paul. Er, Saul. Whoever. Saul of Tarsus is riding along with his buddies on the road to Damascus, off to kill a few more Christians. This is in the era when Rome had outlawed Christianity and it had gone underground (literally). While they're riding along, Saul sees this bright light explode in front of him. He falls off his horse and a voice comes from the light, saying, "Saul... Saul...why do you persecute me?"[40] This would be JC speaking the same JC whose followers Saul was on his way to kill.

Now, this whole story might carry a tad more validity if the other guys with Paul had seen and heard the same thing. But that's not what happened. His buddies just kind of sat there on their horses, staring down at their boss thinking "What the hell's wrong with him?" Paul then proceeds to curl up in a foetal position for three days, during which he doesn't eat or drink. When he snaps out of it, he's fundamentally changed. He's no longer Saul the Christian-killer. He's now the newfound leader of the Christian Church on a mission from god (er, sorry...God) to convert the whole world. (Just to explain the whole Paul Saul thing... in Hebrew his name is Saul, the same name as the first King of Israel. The Latin version of this name is Paul, which is what he went by when dealing with Romans and Greeks.

If this Saul/Paul guy said and did the exact same stuff today, he'd be referred to a nice mental health ward at a local hospital, where qualified psychiatrists would diagnose him as some form of schizophrenic and pump him full of Librium or Prozac until he felt better. But these were simpler times. Back then, if someone flipped, they either tossed them out of the city to wander in the wilderness mad as a hatter or (as in Paul's case) they took them seriously. The fact that Paul was a respectable person before all this added to the idea. "If Saul says a god spoke to him then I got to believe him," his friends would say. "I've known him most of my life and he's always seemed sane and honest to me."

Today, one in ten people suffer from some form of schizophrenia. Many of their families deny the fact, consoling themselves with lines very much like this one.

PAUL'S INFLUENCE

A precedent embalms a principle. ~Benjamin Disraeli

If you've ever read the Bible, you'll see that the vast majority of the New Testament is written by Paul. Like a good psychotic, he took rigid control and ordered everyone around, insisting that his visions were purer and holier than the mere plebes that had walked and talked with Josh. The guy had the balls to try to excommunicate Peter over the issue of circumcision. (Paul was Roman. Peter was Jewish. Think about it a second. Who's going to know more about circumcision?)

Aside from his anti-woman, anti-Jew, anti-anything-that-disagreed-with-him stance, the guy was "afflicted." Three times in the Paulinian texts, Paul refers to a "vexation."[41] He implores God to take it away, but God decides that Paul should live with the burden. For once, I agree with God.

People have theorized that this vexation may have been sexual (homo or hetero). Other, more kindly Christians feel it may have been an ailment of some kind, like emphysema or asthma. Personally I think it was probably something more akin to a large, talking pomegranate that would appear when no one was looking and tell him to do nasty things to small furry animals, but I do tend to be more creative with this sort of thing than your average theologian.

Anyway, Paul took the reins of Christianity and basically denounced anyone that disagreed with him. He spent most of his life in Greece until the Greeks eventually got so fed up with him that they finally killed him, Roman reprisal or no. Christians were dropping like flies in the Roman Empire at this time, what with the Christians crawling through the catacombs and being seen as weird cannibals. While he was alive, Paul had spent a lot of his time writing letters to the Romans, Ephesians and others, telling them all how to be good Christians. This letter thing went over so well that long after Paul was dead people in these cities kept the letters as some sort of homage to the guy, reading them over and over again to grasp the intricacies of Paul's theology. As you may have realized by now, it's these letters that make up the vast majority of the New Testament.

POST-PAUL TO CONSTANTINE

> *The last temptation is the greatest treason:*
>
> *to do the right deed for the wrong reason.*
>
> *~TS. Eliot*

So the Christians were still being fed to the lions, crucified, etc., etc. Things were not going well. Even with their foremost Christian-killer Saul out of it, the Roman legions did a good job of rounding up and offing Christians everywhere in the empire. Each of the apostles meet their gruesome demise (er, martyrdom) during this era. If there was one thing Rome was good at it was killing, and this particular aptitude was demonstrated quite admirably throughout the first two centuries.

Christians fled through all of Europe, trying to get as far away as they could from the Holy Land, the Roman Empire, and pretty much anything else that they might have called home. For the Celtic buffs out there, this explains why it is that there are so many ancient Christian emblems interlaced with the indigenous Celtic symbols in places like Ireland and Scotland. Long before the Inquisition "Christianized" these countries, small bands of Christians had retreated to these backwater areas to get away from Rome.

The Roman persecution of Christianity was increased several fold when in 250 AD Emperor Decius demanded that every Roman citizen recognize him as divine and sacrifice to him. If you were caught on the street without a paper saying you'd appropriately sacrificed to him, you were subject to arrest. This, more than anything, made the Christians stand out like a sore thumb. At this time, there were some happy Heathens that made a good profit by selling fake forms saying you'd sacrificed to Decius. Those Christians that were loyal and true but were not above lying to stay healthy bought them and lived. Those that couldn't afford these papers, or those who were too honest and true and couldn't bring themselves to sacrifice to a false god, invariably wound up under arrest. This of course made the lion population in Rome that much happier.

For the next fifty years, under Valerian (the emperor, not the root) and Diocletian, the persecutions continued. The, in 311, Emperor Galerius issued his Edict of Toleration which Christianity legal in the Eastern part of the Empire. Damn that Galerius.

Anyway, the persecution of Christians came to an abrupt end under throughout the empire a few years later under the reign of Constantine, when what we know of as "the Christian Church" really began.

THE FIRST COUNCIL AT NICAEA

Important principles may and must be flexible. ~Abraham Lincoln

Anyone who knows anything about religion will be wondering how it is that I've gotten so far into this book without mentioning the word Gnostic. The truth is I've been saving it. Gnosticism was a popular polytheistic Christian philosophy that's vaguely mentioned in the Bible in Paul's letters. He only alludes to it, calling it "the Gnostic heresy," basically saying you should avoid it or perish in flames. It comes from the Greek word gnosis meaning "divine knowledge." [42]

Let me introduce you to Constantine. Constantine was a Caesar, or emperor of Rome, from 306 to 337 AD. He was what could be considered the last of the great emperors of Rome. For a change, the people actually liked him. Sure, he kept the idea of the emperor being divine, but for a pompous ass he was much better than his predecessors. The important thing was that he listened to his military and his people, and whatever he did was done to fit their needs as well as his own.

Constantine himself was a worshipper of Apollo. You probably know Apollo, at least from the Hercules cartoons or Shazam. Apollo was the Greek god also known as Phoebus, the carrier of light. (Interesting that Lucifer means "carrier of light" too, isn't it?) Anyway, Phoebus Apollo was also into medicine, healing, and music. You see a lot of him in Greco-Roman art. Constantine was the head of a military that was predominantly Mithran. You remember Mithra. If not, go back a few pages. It was the military religion with the god Mithras locked in battle with the evil forces of darkness. Mithras (you will recall) was known as the Eye of Mazda— Mazda being the one true and good god of Zoroastrianism. Constantine had no problem with Mithras. He just figured they'd gotten the names wrong. Mithras was (in his mind) Apollo. Mazda was obviously Zeus, the father of all the gods. This worked well.

Now, Constantine had a mother named Helena, who was a Christian. This made it awfully hard for Constantine to persecute or kill the Christians, since his mother would either be dead or hate him for it. Over the years, Constantine came to accept this religion in spite of its legal history and backed off from the persecutions. More than this, he actually used the Christian symbol (the Labarum, or cross, and JC's monogram) when he went into battle. Constantine attributed his success at the battle of Milvian Bridge to the Christian insignia— so much so that after he won the battle, he built a palace for himself on the battlefield and placed an inscription on the archway saying that Josh had helped him win the day. Understand though, this was not a "Christian" act. It was Constantine, a Hellenist; paying appropriate honour to a god he thought had helped him out. That's the way you did things. This whole idea of pietus, remember? You have to have piety and goodwill between yourself and the gods. Part of that was to give credit where credit was due, which is what Constantine did. Christians tend to interpret this whole episode as indicative of a Christian conversion that just never happened. Constantine lived and died as a Hellenist. He was never a Christian.

Look This Up

> *It is amazing how complete is the delusion that beauty is goodness.* ~
> *Tolstoy*

In almost every picture you've ever seen of JC, he's portrayed as a beautiful male figure wrapped in white robes and looking very loving and wise. Unfortunately for the Christians out there, these images have nothing to do with the man Josh. They're adopted visages of Apollo, Constantine's god, who was always portrayed as the perfect male. Josh was no such thing. The average person would say that it's impossible to know what JC looked like because the Bible never told us. Well, the Bible never did lot of things. Again, we turn to Josephus the scribe to fill in the blanks. Here's what he had to say about Josh:

At this time, too, there appeared a certain man of magical power, if it is permissible to call him man, whom certain Greeks called a son of God, but his disciples the true prophet, said to raise the dead and heal all diseases. His nature and form were human; a man of simple appearance, mature age, dark skin, small stature, three cubits high (about five feet), hunchbacked, with a long face, long nose and meeting eyebrows, so that they who see him might be affrighted, with scanty hair with a parting in the middle of his head, after the manner of the Nairites, and an undeveloped beard.[43]

According to Robert Eisler, this description was supposedly edited by Christians in the fourth century to read as follows:

...Ruddy skin, medium stature, six feet high, well grown, with a venerable face, handsome nose, goodly black eyebrows with good eyes so that the spectators could love him, with curly hair the color of unripe hazelnuts, with a smooth and unruffled, unmarked and unwrinkled forehead, a lovely red, blue eyes, beautiful mouth, with a copious beard the same color as the hair, not long, parted in the middle, arms and hands full of grace...[44]

You'll find a really good translation of this description in a book titled *The Messiah Jesus and John the Baptist*, by Robert Eisler. Also, read the original Josephus. Any copy will do, but as Eisler explains in his book, the early Christians doctored some (though not all) of the copies of Josephus's works. The original text is still readily available. You'll know you have the un-doctored version if Josh's description reads more like someone you'd see at Halloween than at Christmas. [Note that this Josephus quote comes from a disputed source, so I reference Eisler rather than the original Josephus so you can get an idea of where this comes from]

The Prelude to Nicaea

> *Most people sell their souls and live*
> *with a good conscience on the proceeds.*
> *~Logan Pearsall Smith*

There was no such thing as "the Church" at this time. What you had was a bunch of sects that had arisen around the Mediterranean and Europe. Each of the apostles had wandered off three hundred years earlier and founded churches that had, over time, kind of drifted away from one another. It was in this era that they started to overlap again and interaction between the sects could occur (seeing as how you weren't going to be fed to the lions for being Christian anymore).

This interaction didn't turn out to be a happy one. It seems that each of these groups had come up with a different idea of what Josh was all about. To this point, only the Roman and Greek churches had been pivotal in the development of Christianity. Now the Egyptian, the Sicilian, and other churches stepped forward, presenting documents and philosophies that really contradicted some of the things Roman Christians had come to believe as tenets of the faith-like the whole "Josh is divine" thing. In Hellenistic Rome, the idea was quite common and accepted. However, most of the lesser groups stood up and said, "What, are you nuts? He was a rabbi and a prophet. What the hell's all this divinity stuff?"

Now, Constantine didn't have much of a problem here. Like he had done with Mithras, he easily accepted Christianity as mistaken identity. Josh was obviously Apollo. Yahweh was obviously Zeus. So (he figured) where's the problem? The problem was that the Christians were about ready to kill each other over these differences. Since Constantine liked the idea of using JC as a battle standard and religion for his reign (hey, it worked at Milvian Bridge), he needed a clear mandate on what Christianity was.

Finally, and probably because his mother told him to, Constantine decided to put an end to the bickering so he could get on with the business of ruling the biggest empire on the planet. To this end, he put out a summons around the inhabited world, calling for every Christian bishop to come to Nicaea to settle things once and for all. The scary thing is he almost did just that.

CONSTANTINE AND THE ECUMENICAL COUNCIL

> *Men will wrangle for religion, write for it,*
> *and die for it; anything but live for it.*
> *~Charles Cales*

Ecumenical is another deep, mysterious word used to make things sound more important than they are. It comes from the Greek word *oikoumene* and it simply means "the inhabited world." Okay, so Constantine sends out his summons and a total of 318 Christian bishops show up in Nicaea. Remember, Constantine is footing the bill here. He's paying for the travel, the accommodations, the wine, food, and hookers--whatever. Although Constantine wasn't actually in the council room for the debates, everyone pretty much knew what he expected as an outcome. He wanted a Christianity that wouldn't interfere with Mithras or Apollo worship or (more importantly) his role as an emperor and leader of his people.

The reigning Pope at the time of Constantine was Sylvester. He doesn't bare much on the outcome of the council, but I just had to throw his name in so you'd go through the next three pages with this mental image of a black-and-white cartoon cat with a pope's hat on. I gotta be me.

The data we have on this council mainly comes from St. Athanasius' letter *Ad Afros*,[45] though other sources exist as well. It's a lame retelling of how great everyone there was. Athanasius' lists the big names that were there, most of whom were Greek. The only non-Greeks mentioned are Hosius of Cordova, Cecilian of Carthage, Mark of Calabria, Nicasius of Dijon, Donnus of Stridon in Pannonia, and the two Roman priests, Victor and Vincentius, representing Pope Sylvestor. Sylvester didn't make it there himself. Seems he had other business. (Sorry... I tried. I couldn't find a Tweety joke that wasn't lame.)

The most famous members of this council were Alexander of Alexandria, Eustathius of Antioch, Macarius of Jerusalem, Eusebius of Nicomedia, Eusebius of Caesarea, and Nicholas of Myra. One has to take special notice of Nicholas of Myna.[46] He is St. Nicholas... Old Santa Claus himself. That's right... Santa Claus helped put the Bible together. You always suspected as much, didn't you?

Ok, we have the list of suspects. Let's review the crime...

The first question to be posed to the council was whether Josh was divine or not. This was a biggie, since a lot of Romans believed he was and Constantine had a vested interest in making sure of it. After all, he couldn't very well adopt a faith that was started by a mortal rabbi in a backwater region of the empire who was executed by Rome three hundred years earlier. There had to be more to it— and even if there wasn't, there would be. Constantine was to make sure of this.

When the call for the conference went out, the bishops scurried around packing up their notes and sacred texts (some of which would later become the books of the Christian Bible) and headed off to Nicaea. Since the bishops were made acutely aware of what Constantine thought Christianity should be, most but not all of them made sure to present stuff that wouldn't ruffle too many imperial feathers. By the time the council got under way, everyone had had the chance to selectively assemble the documents they figured were holy enough and safe enough to present to Constantine as sacred doctrine.

When asked if Josh was divine, Arius and Marcius voted no, making a 316-2 in favour vote. The problem was it had to be unanimous. The debate raged on. Arius basically contended that Josh was "of the essence of God but was a creation of God," and that "there was a time when Josh was not." But that would mean that Josh was not truly divine, and they just couldn't have that. So another vote was taken. This time it was on Arius and Marcius, and they weren't allowed to vote. The result was 316-0 in favor of declaring Arius and Marcius to be heretics. The judgment was made against them and both men were summarily excommunicated.

Now, there are two versions of what happened next. Some say Arius was summarily beheaded n the council floor, others say he died a horrible gruesome death some years later. Either way we can assume the council didn't like him much after this. According to the Catholics, Arius left the council after being excommunicated, went to Palestine, then Syria and Asia Minor. He gained followers wherever he went and these followers later reaped horrible havoc throughout the Christian Empire. I can't figure out which version of this story I like better, but either way Arius is ok in my books.

The end result of all of this was that no further objections, the now unanimous vote of 316-0 in favour of the divinity of Josh went through unhindered and Josh became a god. Er, God. Whatever.

The Gnostic Heresy

Religion is to mysticism what popularization is to science.

~Henri Bergson

It's difficult to know where to fit the Gnostic tale in here because it kind of pervades the whole history of Judaism and Christianity. It's basically Hellenism, which we talked about in the Judaism section, but it's adopted Judeo-Christian myths. It becomes relevant to the making of the Jesus myth soon, so I figure I'll cover it here.

The Gnostics believe in Yahweh, but they call him "Ialdaboath" or "the God of the Deaf". They think He was an immature, childish god who did things like throw tantrums and kill everybody because they wouldn't love him. (The whole Noah thing.) The Garden of Eden was seen as a prison, a place where Ialdaboath could keep his creations as stupid, ignorant pets that would worship him blindly.

Genesis backs this belief up, noting that Adam and Eve weren't thrown out because they disobeyed their god by eating of the tree of the knowledge (gnosis) of good and evil, but because... ah, hell, I'll quote it to you. Here's the scripture, Genesis 2:22-24

And the Lord God said, "The man has now become like one of us knowing good and evil. He must not be allowed to reach out his hand and take also from the tree of life and eat and live forever."

This is taken from the New International Version of the Bible, but the verse is the same in the King James and the Thompson Chain. Note the plural form, *us*. Let us cast them out. This is because the Torah (of which Genesis is the first book) was written by Moses at a time when Israel was polytheistic, when El-Shaddai had other gods to talk to. Because it's considered holy it couldn't be changed, so there are a lot of polytheistic references that make no sense in modern Judaism. Of course, Christians say it was JC he was talking to, but what the hey. They also give money to the PTL. (Note: Most people believe Adam and Eve were thrown out of Eden because they sinned. Read the tale. They were thrown out so they couldn't live forever.

The Gnostics are basically Christians who reverted back to the polytheistic era. Remember, Hellenism had lived side-by-side with Judaism for almost a millennium now, and the monotheistic beliefs hadn't really caught on well to begin with. This is where the Gnostic movement came in. It incorporated Greco-Roman myths and astrology (including characters like Sophia, the goddess of wisdom) into Christian lore. It was quite popular, and the Nicene crew hated it.

You see, one of the main tenets of Gnosticism was that every man and woman had a divine spark. No human was better than another (say, like an emperor or something). Each person had it in him or her to achieve a level of personal godhood, or independent evolution of the soul. While the Gnostic texts are rife with mythical tales of divinities dropping by to casually mess with humanity, the philosophy of Gnosticism was about the individual and his or her claim to spiritual power (which, the Gnostics believed, was the true quest for any mortal). In Gnosticism, there was no need for emperors or hierarchies or sacrifices (financial or otherwise) to a temple or church. Gnosticism was about humanity's quest for divinity. Since Constantine had set himself up as a "divine emperor" already, a bunch of Gnostic walking around saying, "Yeah, okay, you're divine but so am I" just didn't work.[47]

The Gnostics met their end at Nicaea with the Arians. The views of the Gnostics didn't agree with the political tide that was forming; the Gnostic ideals of self-revelation and an inner search fundamentally undermined the Christianity that Constantine wanted, so they wound up out of the loop. The main reason for this can be traced to the essence of Gnosticism. Gnostics didn't have a hierarchy. Gnostics just "were." They had teachers, but as the Gnostic scriptures explained, a teacher was only a signpost. The path was the individual's to take alone. Since they were on a private path, most Gnostics would just shrug at a summons to Constantine's council and go back to personal meditation. Because the Gnostics didn't have rank, there were no "bishops" or leaders to accept Constantine's summons. The result was that the Gnostics were way outnumbered by those who were sucking up to Constantine. Nicaea was doom to this philosophy. It's not that having any other representatives there wouldn't have saved the philosophy from being banned, but the ideas may have stood a chance if they'd been around

All the religions we call false were once true.

~Ralph Waldo Emerson

A lot of cool stuff has come to the surface in Christianity in the last century. The discovery of the Dead Sea Scrolls was a major boon for the curious. Vatican, the Roman Catholic ecumenical council of the 1960s, shook a few things up as well. But for me none of this compares to the implications of the Gnostic Texts.

You see, there were a lot of books out there in 325 AD. Gospels and such. Holy Books written by the apostles about the life and times of JC. What you and I know of as the New Testament is Matthew, Mark, Luke, John, Acts, then a whole heap of stuff from Paul, a couple short letters from minor guys, then the enigmatic Revelation of John.

Still, a good 70 per cent of it was written by Paul, who came into the picture after Josh was gone and just sort of took over. Did you ever stop to wonder why Timothy or Bartholomew or the rest of the apostles never bothered to write their own synoptic gospels? Why only Matthew, Mark, Luke, and John? I mean, if these guys had lived and been taught by Jesus, and had then gone out and taught throughout the known world, you'd figure that at some point they'd each sit down and write out what happened. Surely after all the crap they'd gone through to teach this stuff, they must have had something they felt was worth writing down and preserving.

Well, they did. The Nicene council had access to a whole lot of literature that for the most part no one ever saw after that council-other gospels, other ideas of Josh recorded by the people closest to him, books that the people at Nicaea declared heretical and outlawed. They disappeared until the 1800s when a guy was...

Hell, I'll just cover the whole story. The Reader's Digest version of this tale is as follows:

The Nicene guys banned the other texts. Someone-we don't know who-decided this wasn't right, so, like the Essenes two hundred years earlier, they took complete copies of all the rejected texts (and a few other things, like Plato's Republic) and buried them just outside of a nowhere town called Nag Hammadi. It's in Egypt (Arius's territory). They would have stayed buried forever if it weren't for a Bedouin with a weak bladder. (Yeah, I know...another Bedouin. They keep finding these things. That's probably because they're the only ones wandering around the desert on a regular basis.) So this fellow's off to settle some kind of family feud (more blood, for those who've missed it in the last few sections).

He's going off to kill a bunch of other Bedouins for some kind of vendetta, when he has to take a piss. He gets off his horse and sneaks around behind a big rock and is busily pissing away when he notices the ground he's pissing on is loam, a rich soil that's rare in the desert. Shaking himself off, he sets to the task of packing some of this stuff in his saddlebags when he hits upon (you guessed it) the jars. It took a while before the pages-bound in leather, not done as scrolls-made their way from his hands to Oxford University, where they were quickly copied and distributed to keep them safe from the Roman Catholic monopoly on them. (The Vatican didn't know the texts existed until the story showed up in the newspaper.) Beyond these bits of information, the story's actually pretty boring.

Okay, on with the really cool stuff, what was in them:

WHAT WAS IN THEM

Here's a list of the books found, in no particular order. The ones marked with an asterisk have names given to them because they either had no title or the title was unreadable. [48]

> The Gospel of Mary
>
> The Prayer of Paul
>
> The Apocryphon of James
>
> The Gospel of Truth
>
> The Treatise on Resurrection *
>
> The Tripartite Tractate *
>
> The Apocrypha of John
>
> The Gospel of Thomas
>
> The Gospel of Philip

The Hypostasis of the Archons *

The Origin of the World

The Exegesis of the Soul

The Book of Thomas the Contender- (Doubting Thomas)

The Gospel of the Egyptians

Eugnosis the Blessed

The Sophia (*WISDOM*) of Jesus

Dialogue of the Saviour

The Apocalypse of Adam (Yeah, the Genesis Adam. Apparently he could write.)

The Acts of Peter and the Twelve Apostles

The Thunder Perfect Mind (Very cool. Find it. Read it.)

Authoritative Teaching

The Concept of Our Great Power

Plato's Republic (I suspect the Gnostics didn't write this.)

A Discourse on the Eighth and Ninth Powers

Asclepius

The Interpretation of Knowledge (Gnosis)

The Thought of Norea

The Testimony of Truth

The Act of Peter

The Sentences of Sextus

A Prayer of Thanksgiving

On Anointing

On Baptism

On Eucharist

On Donner and Dasher (Sorry. Couldn't resist it.)

That's the list. (Except the Donner and Dasher part. You get bored typing all this out.) "So," I hear you ask yet again (You talk a lot for someone who's supposed to be reading quietly), "What's so different about all these gospels? What do they say that's any different from the orthodox stuff?" Well, I'm glad you asked.

THE GNOSTIC DIFFERENCE

There is no female mind. The brain is not an organ of sex. As well speak of a female liver. ~Charlotte Perkins Gilman

The coolest line in all these texts is probably from The Apocalypse of Peter, where Peter records a conversation with Jesus about the orthodoxy and what it's going to do when he's gone. I have to quote this to you. It really says something about the divinity concept. (Remember as you read this that The Apocalypse of Peter dates to the second century but was a copy of an older script, so we're talking about a document that is closer to the time of Jesus than the oldest copy we have of the synoptic gospels.)

Jesus said, "They will cleave to the name of a dead man and consider themselves pure. But they will fall into a name of error- and into the hand of an evil, cunning man and a manifold dogma, and they will be ruled heretically. They will do business in my word. And there shall be others who are outside our numbers (meaning not the apostles) who name themselves bishops and deacons as if they have received their authority from God. They will bend themselves under the judgments of the leaders. These people are dry canals."[49]

Well, gee, I can't think of a single reason why Constantine and the Nicene group wouldn't want this stuff out there. Awfully nice of them to protect us from these evil influences, isn't it? This is kind of the way of things in Nicaea, and in the millennium and a half since then. Nicaea cut out a huge section of what was the recorded history of Josh and his followers-like the rivalry between Peter and Mary Magdalene.

As far as the synoptic gospels (and the orthodoxies) are concerned, Mary Magdalene was a footnote in Josh's life, a harlot that Josh saved with his famous "Let you who is without sin cast the first stone" line. In the Gnostic tale, she's pretty damned important. She and Josh were...uh...close. Yeah. That's it. Close. She is referred to as "the companion of the Saviour" in several texts. Just so I fall short of anything that'll get me killed here, I'll leave this to you to interpret as you will. In one text (The Gospel of Thomas) it's put plainly, saying, "The companion of the master was Mary, whom he did love and did often kiss on the lips." Peter gets ticked at this, figuring the master was spending altogether too much time with the fairer sex, so he challenges him, saying, "Master, why do you love her more than us?" Josh (in good Josh form) replies cryptically, "Why do I not love you as much?" You have to give him credit. He really had a way with words.

Anyway, enough of the "Mary and Josh as lovers thing." If you want more on it, read The Holy Blood and the Holy Grail. I don't recommend it all that highly, but it's a good jaunt through the Mary-Josh connection.

The one important aspect of this female character in the Gnostic texts is that she was NOT a subservient little kitten as she's been portrayed in the Bible. Do you remember the story from the synoptic gospels where Josh was staying at Mary's house with her and her sister Martha? In the Bible version, Martha gets pissed off because Mary is sitting at Jesus' feet, listening to him teach when she should be helping with dinner. Jesus tells Martha not to worry about it since "The son of man is here for only a short time and she has chosen the wiser path."

Yeah. Nice tale. The same story is told in the Gnostic texts, except it's a wee bit divergent. See if you can catch the subtle differences.

In the Gnostic text, Mary is not sitting adoringly at Josh's feet. She's arguing with him about religious issues. She, Josh, and the apostles are getting right into it, debating the ins and outs of some deep topics. Martha, who's making the meal, gets pissed off and tells Josh to send Mary into the kitchen since she didn't belong in a man's debate. Josh answers her by saying, *"Not until the male is female and the female male can you enter the kingdom of Heaven. Mary has chosen the better path."*[50]

Gloria Steinem fans unite.

The difference in gender roles in these gospels is enough to make any pope sit up and stop wearing dresses. You see, in the Gnostic tale Mary wasn't just the "companion" of the master". She was a well-respected disciple. So much so, in fact, that when JC ascended/died/moved to Taiwan, Josh appointed Mary to be the new head of the early Church. (You just don't find this in the orthodox Bible.)

Each of the Gnostic texts talks about Mary's role as leader of the Church, and of Peter's growing jealousy. According to the tale, they finally have it out in an open forum, wherein Peter challenges her for the leadership. Aside from the fact that she was a woman (and therefore inadequate to lead), Peter adds that at the Last Supper, "when the master said, 'This is my body that will be given up for you, you laughed." Mary acknowledges that she did think it funny at the time but says she didn't understand then what she does now. Peter says that laughing at Josh was bad form and obviously she shouldn't lead. Peter wins and Mary becomes a footnote.

Now, for all the women out there. Have you ever wondered how it is that your gender wound up being considered dirty, evil, slimy beings that shouldn't be allowed to speak in church lest they insult the Almighty with their ignorant female voices? Thank Constantine. And Paul. He had a lot to do with it too. Quotes like "Better to marry than burn in hell,"[51] or Timothy's "suffer not a woman to teach, nor to usurp authority over the man, but to be in silence" did little for equal rights.

There's no doubt that Paul and company had no real love for women, but that's only half the story. The question is, 'Why did anyone listen to him?' Why was what he said considered doctrine? What happened to the Mary thing? Josh obviously respected her. So how did she wind up a footnote? Again, this lands on Constantine.

You see, the vast majority of the New Testament is written (or accredited to) the apostle Paul. This is rather odd when you stop to consider that Paul (a.k.a. Saul) never met JC. Sure, there was the whole conversion story wherein he met the divine JC on the road to Damascus, but you gotta figure he lived and worked around people who actually knew Josh. They'd spent years wandering around the countryside with him, swapping stories and listening to his views on everything. Sure Paul claimed to have had his divine experience, but the others had years of watching Josh eat, sleep, preach, shit and piss-the day-to-day stuff. Then along comes Paul and he takes over and starts telling them all what to do and what it means to be a follower of Josh. It all sounds a little off, doesn't it?

The thing is, Paul was a major force in the early Church, particularly in Greece. This was mainly because he was a Roman citizen and the Greeks didn't want to screw around with a Roman citizen. It's like being American in, say, Libya. You might be hated as an individual, but there's no way the government would summarily execute you for no good reason. The Americans would be down on them in a second, and they wouldn't risk it. The same was true of the Romans. Whatever they thought of Paul, he was Roman and you didn't want to mess with the Romans.

So okay, what's the deal with him being the leader of the Church, and why did his stuff make it past the Nicene Council when the disciples' stuff was thrown out? Think about it. Paul was Roman. Constantine was Roman. Paul remade Christianity in the first century into something that would "sell" in first century Rome. Constantine bought it three hundred years later-a patriarchal religion created by a male god incarnate that promised eternal rewards for being a subservient peon who would obey the emperor. Yeah...Constantine liked it.

The results of this council became the canon, or religious law, of the Holy Roman Empire. It is still the law of Roman Catholics today. The sacred texts that agreed with the Nicene Creed became the basis of all Christian dogma to follow. The process basically went like this: all the books were measured against the Nicene Creed. Those that fit it were accepted. Those that didn't were chucked out. The "good books" were assembled into one collection called "the Codex." (The *Codex Vaticanus* is a copy of this original Codex and is the authoritative "bible" in the Vatican.) The Codex, in time, became known as the Bible. The New Testament is, for the most part, the Paulinian Bible. Remember this. The skew of the thing is entirely Paul's, as adopted in Nicaea. If it sounds like I'm going on a bit here about this whole Nicaea thing, it's only because I am.

325 AD was a pivotal epoch in the history of Christianity. After this point, every ecumenical council becomes farcical, debating small details of a faith that had its guts chopped out. I see it as kind of like trying to decide what color you want to dye your hair when your skull's been destroyed. Sure it's important to have nice hair, but beneath it all there's still something missing.

Nicaea took out a lot. For those of you out there who want to claim that God had a hand in all this, I'd like to say that nowhere in the records did he mention that anyone felt particularly divinely inspired here. Eusebius Pamphili, Bishop of Cæsarea in Palestine did say that everyone felt the influence of the Emperor, but nothing of God. This was political. From the word go, Nicaea was a politically motivated, politically funded endeavor that was overseen and monitored by Emperor Constantine. Not God. Constantine. (For those of you who have difficulty distinguishing between the two, Constantine was the shorter guy with the red robe.)

Now, for the Christians who persist in claiming that the Bible is a holy book that's been protected and guided by the hand of God from its conception in Nicaea to its misconception by Jerry Falwell, I pose this question concerning the Gnostic texts: What sounds more like divine intervention? That the Bible and its books were decided upon by a group of politically motivated bishops who then used it to launch bloody inquisitions in the name of their "truth," or that the full texts (including the Gnostic and Qumran texts) survived buried in sand for almost two millennia while the Christian monopoly on truth played out? These texts have now resurfaced, when the power of the Roman Catholic Church and its offshoots are waning enough for the people to decide for themselves what's right and wrong. How's that for divine intervention? Had these books been found even a few decades earlier than they were, they would have been confiscated by the Church and consigned to some dusty shelf in the Vatican, with a small note on the cover-"Heretical Literature: Do Not Open."

I don't believe in divine providence, but if I had to, I'd have to say the survival of the Gnostic texts and the Dead Sea Scrolls is strikingly more dramatic and indicative of divine intervention than the orthodox Bible. The Bible was (and is) a book that's been in the hands of the political and religious elite since it was deliberately manufactured in Nicaea as the Codex.

This book, adopted by Constantine's council, has been the foundation of all subsequent Christian dogma. Each ecumenical council since that time- e.g. Constantinople in 381 AD, Toledo (not Ohio) also in 381, Chalcedon in 451, and Trent in 1545-all used "the Holy Bible" as the authoritative text, ignoring the heretical (and much cooler) Gnostic texts.

These councils served to set up the mandates by which Christianity could inflict itself on every aspect of human existence in its bid to dominate thought, action, and intent for the next 1600 years.

FOR THE LOVE OF GOD...

Is sex dirty? Only if it's done right. ~Woody Allen

There is nothing more special, sacred, and powerful in a human life than the intimacy and closeness one feels when in bed with a lover. It is an inherently personal and private exchange of warmth and tenderness to which no social institution could compare. So, of course, this became an aspect of human existence that Christianity felt it absolutely HAD to control.

To the Christian hierarchy, sexuality became a theological void that needed filling. Since sex was integral to people's day-to-day life (especially in a post-Hellenistic society where it used to be a customary religious practice), if Rome wanted to control people, it had to control sexuality. The problem was that even their own Bible didn't give the priests the mandate to deny or regulate a person's sexuality to the degree they desired.

Don't believe me? I'll show you. Let's go back to Genesis—chapter six, verses one through ten, for those of you who are sitting there anxiously waiting to turn to your Scriptures and begin with today's Bible study. (I'm really disappointed if even one person reading my book falls into this category.)

Anyway, you've had a chapter or two to prepare for this, so I'm assuming those of you who didn't have a Bible before have managed to steal one somewhere. Genesis, chapter six says,

"When men began to increase on the Earth and daughters were born to them, the sons of God saw that the daughters of man were beautiful and they laid with any they chose."

Okay, sounds good so far...

"The Nephilim (children of angels and humans mating) were on the Earth at this time and also afterwards, and the sons of God mated with the daughters of men and had children by them. These were the Heroes of old, men of renown"

So, God allowed angels to have sex with human women. We mere mortal men are then supposed to have more self-control and prudence than angels? It kind of makes John Travolta's portrayal of the archangel Michael seem more plausible, doesn't it?

So it was fine for angels to lie with the daughters of men.

One might infer, then, that it was also fine for men to lie with the daughters of men. (Not your own daughter, mind you, but other people's daughters were fine to lie with.) Either that or the angels were the only ones able to lie with the daughters of men, which would make for more than a few drunken brawls between angels and jealous mortals. I think we can safely assume that men laid with the daughters of other men. David and Solomon certainly did— and they did so with impunity. As they were kings (and God's voice on Earth), I'm sure their example was followed. Zealously.

But in modern Christianity, there's this whole idea that the Ten Commandments tell you not to engage in casual sex (presumably, angels have more pull with God than men). Of course, this is crap. Like most of the rules regarding sex in the Old Testament, the Ten Commandments tell you not to break the oath of marriage. "Thou shalt not commit adultery" is what it says. That means if you've promised to stay with one man or woman, then you should damn well stay with one man or woman. (Actually, it could have been more than "one." Polygamy was accepted and practiced until the Jews figured out that one spouse was enough for anyone to handle.[52]) However, the Old Testament says nothing about having sex outside of marriage between two unattached heterosexuals. Neither does most of the New Testament until we get to Paul's letters. I'll deal with Paul in a sec. But overall, the Bible is really not concerned with consensual sex between two unattached people.

It's true. Look it up. Leviticus outlines in great detail all the forbidden sexual acts.[53] (I'll deal with homosexuality in a minute.) No animals. No relatives. No kinky moonlight encounters with twelve of your closest friends and a pentagram. But I defy anyone to show me anything in the New or Old Testaments that prohibits two heterosexuals from having casual intercourse when neither partner is promised to or married to anyone else. (Trust me, I've looked.) It talks about bestiality, incest, rape, ritual sex, adultery and contemplating adultery, but nowhere does it say that two consenting heterosexuals can't have casual sex. To further complicate matters, in all the gospels, Gnostic or Orthodox, Josh never really discussed sexuality. It could be argued that it was actually this ambiguity toward sexual issues that left a vacuum for later theologians to create the dogma that controlled sexual activity, even within marriage.

Now, I'm not saying that controlling sexual desire as a function of religion did not already exist as a concept. It's true, for example, that by the third century, celibacy was ingrained in monastic fringe elements of Christianity; but these groups (like the Essenes 300 years earlier) only abstained so that their denial of all things carnal (i.e. their sexual frustration) could somehow further glorify God— but not because it was required by any canonical law. Until the fourth century, there had never really been any formal Christian dogma that "governed" sex in a universal, institutionalized fashion.

Homosexuality

...and his heart was going like mad and yes I said yes

~James Joyce

By now you'll have figured out I'm not Christian or Jewish, so what I'm about to say has no moral judgments attached. Personally I feel that people's concepts of sexual intimacy and fun are meant to be explored and enjoyed. Not always by me, but hey, do what you want to.

What gets me, though, are the nouveau-Christians (particularly the Anglicans) who somehow manage to believe that homosexuality can be included within the Judeo-Christian morality. Let me put this to you as succinctly as I can: *You cannot be both Christian and gay without living your whole life in the belief that you're going to roast in hell for all eternity!* I'm not being interpretive here. Back to the Bible again...Leviticus 18 to start: *"Do not lie with a man as one does a woman. That is detestable."*

Okay, you say, we're detecting some "homophobic vibes" here. "Detestable" is a pretty harsh word, but you can work around it, right? Jump ahead to Leviticus 20:13. *"If a man lies with another man as one lies with a woman, both of them have done what is detestable. They must be put to death, and their blood will be on their own hands."*

Now, like I say, I have no personal skew here against homosexuality, or any form of sexuality. I'm generally a fan of most of them. Trust me on this one. But I really can't see how you can take stuff like this and still embrace the faith of Christianity if you're gay. Sure, this is Old Testament stuff, but the Law was never changed. This sentiment has been reflected in all Jewish and Christian and it has always been enforced.

Here's a bit of Christian history about homosexuality for you: Have you ever wondered why gays are called "faggots" by rednecks? A faggot is actually a bundle of kindling used to start fires. (This is why a cigarette is called a "fag" in England...it's a small burning stick.) Gays have been called fags because of the witch burnings. A little-known fact was that while the witches were burned at the stake (a wholly unpleasant experience); the gays were bound and thrown into the actual fire at their feet. The witches usually died of smoke inhalation. The gays were literally burned to death since they were in the actual heat of the fire. Ergo, they're called faggots. They were kindling.

So, to recap: there was a time when sex was basically okay, unless you were a monk or gay. Then, just after the Nicaea mess, we saw the dawn of a new age of sexual stupidity, heralded by a sleazy, two-bit despotic hypocrite who single-handedly ruined puberty for generations of Christians. (Get the feeling I don't like this guy?)

THE PATRON SAINT OF SEXUAL REPRESSION

Give me chastity and continence, but not yet. ~St. Augustine

Augustine was born in 354 AD in Tagaste in North Africa. He was raised as a Christian but gave it up when he moved to Cartage and became a Neo-Platonist. (This basically means he believed that everything on Earth is an imperfect version of something that is perfect in another sphere, and that we're all working to achieve that perfect sphere of existence. He then jumped ship on the Neo-Platonists to become Manichean. Manichaeism is basically a mystic mesh of Christianity, Zoroastrianism, Buddhism, and Judaism. It's a lot like Kabala but came along a lot earlier.

He stays a Manichean until he wanders down to Milan, where he meets Ambrose, the bishop who replaced Hosius of Nicene fame.

Now that he's had all his fun (which he chronicled in a book called Confessions), he finds Christianity again and is baptized on Easter in 387, whereupon he promptly forsakes his mistress and goes back to Tagaste to found a monastery. In 396, he is appointed

Bishop of Hippo by Rome, making him the modern equivalent of a pope, with all the commensurate political power. He spends the rest of his life advocating asceticism, abstinence, a strict moral code, and an adherence to order and discipline. He dies in 430CE when a troop of meandering Vandals invades his town, rapes the livestock, kills the women, and loots everything in sight.

So it was that the holy and chaste 'St. Augustine' died amid a bloody and debauched sacking of the celibate monastery he held dear.

I like the Vandals.

Augustine's Theology

> *"The truth is that, in view of the purity of the body of Christ, all sexual intercourse is unclean".* ~St. Jerome, Augustine's mentor

There's an old joke where God looks at Adam and decides he needs a penis. Poof, it appears. Adam is enthralled. He marvels at all the wonderful things it can do. He watches it go from soft to hard. He does tricks with it, making it bounce around happily. Then he touches it and is amazed that it can make him feel so good. Totally elated by this gift given by a just and loving God, Adam thanks him profusely for this wonderful addition to his life. "There's only one condition I place on this new thing," says God. "What?" says Adam. "Anything. You name it. I'm so happy with this, I'll do anything to show my appreciation."

"You can't use it." says God.

That about sums up 90 per cent of Christian sexuality. If it's fun and it feels good, don't do it. It's bad. You'll go blind. You'll grow hair on you palms. There are teeth down there. You'll get pregnant every time. It hurts. You'll catch something and your penis will drop off. And, of course, the famous:

GOD IS WATCHING YOU!!!

If a god really is watching me, he's a twisted, voyeuristic god with a bent for handcuffs and candle wax. But that's another book. The thing is, these sentiments are not scriptural. They're theocratic-that is, they're the "accepted doctrine." This basically means that someone people thought was saintly and pious said it, and ever since it's been accepted as holy and right. The saintly, pious person in question was Augustine. Let me give you an idea that this Augustine guy really was...

After spending most of his life with a mistress, our hero decided that this was bad-not only for him, but for all humanity. You see, at the time there were four words that meant "love." These were amore, *philia*, *agape* and *eros*. Amore was romantic love. *Philia* was brotherly love. *Agape* was the love for God. *Eros*, of course, was erotic or sexual love. Augustine reasoned that all of these forms of love constantly vied with each other for your attention. All four were very intense and had a tendency to displace each other—especially (thought Augustine) *eros* and *agape*. Since agape was the single most important love, Augustine wanted to make sure nothing interfered with it. Basically, what this meant was that at the point where you're at the height of passion, sweating and totally into the sexual act, there was no room in your mind for the love you have for your God, even though that may be whose name you're shouting at the time. According to Augustine, love for a sexual partner and love for your God could not exist in the same mind at the same time. The simple answer: get rid of sex. (Note: Jerome, Augustine's mentor, once said)

This is the reason why sex has been considered bad and evil for so long. It puts God totally out of your mind. The same was said by Augustine to be true of philia and amore, but not to the same extent. Sex was the one occasion when a human would find it impossible to pray or have any meaningful adoration for God, because sex is too much of a distraction. If he'd had his way, sex would be totally banned. However, this would mean no children and the death of Christianity in a generation's time. Provisions had to be made.

The "provisions" were contained in marriage. If you were married by the Church, it was basically a license to have sex, providing you don't enjoy it. You were just doing your duty to keep the faith alive-a necessary evil, as it were. To have sex outside of marriage (as in with a mistress, like Augustine had for years) was seen as a frivolous encounter meant for pleasure, not procreation. And you couldn't have pleasure. If you actually enjoyed sex, you were ignoring your God, and that was evil. Only through a marriage which was designed to create baby Christians could the sex act be justified. This is where premarital sex became taboo and any sexual practice that involved contraceptives or ejaculation in places that couldn't possibly bring about children became considered evil. It all took you away from "the Divine."

As a theological spearhead of the new post-Nicene Christianity (with the Roman military to back his ideas), Augustine became very powerful and so did his beliefs. His notions of sex and marriage, along with the new Codex, became the foundation of Christian ethics-not because what he said reflected the scriptures (he made no real attempt to justify his philosophy with scriptural references), but because he said it all at a time when the Church was forming itself into a legal and political body. Augustine's beliefs are as intrinsic to Christian dogma now as Constantine's, or Hippolayatus' Apostles' Creed, and were a fundamental contribution to the dominance of Christianity in the western world. All of which, you may have noticed, seems to be getting further and further away from the late great JC and anything he may have had to say about life. At this point in history, the majority of what was recorded of Josh's conversations is buried in Nag Hammadi in clay jars waiting to be found in a millennium or so.

Of course, the orthodoxy sees this as a good thing.

THE ORIGIN OF THE PAPACY

We'd all like to vote for the best man,

but he's never a candidate.

~Kin Hubbard

Okay, quick synopsis. The Roman Empire wanes. The people are either leaving for better cities, like Constantinople/Byzantium, or trying to eke out an existence in the vestiges of the empire. Those that remain become undereducated serfs, for the most part. The Church (after Constantine) maintains the political power and, not surprisingly, the wealth. With this wealth come the books and all the knowledge of Roman (history, architecture, that sort of thing). The only people who are allowed to learn to read at this time are the monks or priests who are properly initiated into "the Church."

Everyone else is just sort of left to learn how to milk cows for a living.

This is where the recurrent myth of "magic books" comes from. At this time, books were the only source of basic information. Since only the holy guys got to read books, and since they were all seen as powerful, myths grew up among the peasantry about what was written in these books that could make these men so formidable.

In 800 AD, the Holy Roman Empire was established-as opposed to the Roman Empire, which was much bigger but had of late fallen flat on its face. Political power in this "new" regime was officially held by an emperor, but that kind of faded out by 900 or so when the people realized that most of the power was actually held by a person called the Pope, "*pope*" meaning "father". The position of pope evolved from that of a bishop— the Bishop of Rome. There had always been a bishop of Rome, just as there had always been a bishop of every city. But when the Holy Roman Empire was established, the Bishop of Rome was declared to be the "father" of all bishops. Like a father, he had the final say in the "household." Appropriate books were written to back this idea up, and a few people were canonized as saints for having the divine insight to recognize the wisdom in this.

Not everyone agreed that the Bishop of Rome should be the father of all bishops. This is where the Greek Orthodox Church comes from. At the time, they basically went against Rome and said, "Screw you guys. We have a bishop right here. Why should we listen to your bishop over our own?" A lot of groups tried this, but only the Greeks were financially and militarily strong enough to resist Rome's theological rationale for pre-eminence. (That and they were far enough out of reach that it would have cost Rome too much to send an army that far to bring them back into their loving fold.)

The Pope exploited Augustine's ideas thoroughly, managing to use his religious role to achieve and secure his political power. Basically what happened was that the "religious" issues settled at Nicaea, combined with the canon set down by people like Augustine, led the masses to believe that the Bishop of Rome was divinely led. While the emperor (who held the political power) was able to kill or imprison people, the pope was seen as having "the keys to the Kingdom of God." He could eternally damn you, whereas the emperor could only physically damn you. This scared the shit out of people. Scared people do desperate things. The Pope desperately wanted money. Getting the picture?

The papacy not only insinuated itself into all sexual activity as discussed earlier, but into every other aspect of human life. Europe was living in a feudal system at this time. The entire structure bound the people to the land and kept the Church as a divine "lord." The hallowed nature of the ministry from priest to pope gave all Church representatives an autonomous veto over any dispute. The Church was judge, jury, and executioner (see the Inquisition). What education the people got, they got from the Church. Through weekly masses, the Christian canon was bred into these people. It's all they were ever allowed to know, from cradle to grave. When the Pope said something, the people blindly and blissfully agreed. At this point in history, Rome had a whole empire of the insipid, pliable sheep they have always unabashedly striven for.

The Church used the consecrated graft it milked from these people to build its power militarily and politically, and quite soon the role of the emperor became redundant. The popes and the emperors quarrelled back and forth for a while, but basically it was no contest. The popes had as much money as the emperors, and they also had the people's souls. You just can't beat someone who's holding onto your money and your soul.

In time, the emperors were basically bought out and/or retired, leaving Rome and the Vatican to God's appointed representative on Earth-the Pope, father of all bishops and the richest man alive. Okay, that's the papacy in a nutshell. Meanwhile, back in the desert...

PILGRIM'S PROGRESS

Travel is glamorous only in retrospect. ~Theroux

In 637 AD, the Muslims took control of Jerusalem, the holy city of David and home to lots and lots of priceless Judeo-Christian antiquities.[54] This really pissed off the Christians in that they couldn't make their pilgrimages. A "pilgrimage" is a long, arduous journey to some famous place that's considered holier than where you were when you started out. The idea here was to get closer to God by going to places where he had supposedly been and then debasing you. Starvation, self-mutilation, and caking you in shit were not uncommon elements of pilgrimages in any religion. (It's basically exactly like your last vacation, but on purpose and without the margaritas.)

More importantly, the Islamic victory in Jerusalem really pissed off the Pope, because he couldn't find a way of making a profit off the Christians' inability to make pilgrimages. There were, however, huge sums to be made out of freeing the passage up, so that the people could pay Rome lots of dough for the privilege of starving themselves on the way to Jerusalem. Since the vast majority of the population was kept happily ignorant, the only people who had any clue where the Holy Land really was were the priests, bishops, etc. Without a guide from the Church, you weren't considered to have a hope in hell of actually making it to Jerusalem. So people paid lots of cash to be led there by a duly appointed representative of the Church who could make sure you got there with an appropriate amount of awe and pain.

Sure, Catholics could go to Rome for a pilgrimage, but Rome was relatively close and Jerusalem offered the Pope the chance to charge huge sums of money for people to travel to "the Promised Land"—not to mention the fact that there were rumors of fantastic wealth there, including the legendary gold and diamond mines that had belonged to King Solomon.

Despite all this, the Church didn't manage to muster any kind of real response to the Muslim occupation until a guy named Peter the Hermit riled up everyone in France and had them insisting that the Holy Roman Empire reclaim "the Promised Land." That was in 1096. Between 637 and 1096, the Church in Rome really didn't do a hell of a lot except gain money in Europe and lose power in the Middle East. They gained money in that they refined many new and exciting ways to fleece the peasantry (see indulgences in the Martin Luther section); they lost power in that Islam was ravaging much of the known world with what seemed like an unstoppable army.

Now, Rome was strong enough to maintain its monopoly on European thought, but it lacked the resources to counter Islamic aggression in the Middle East. Basically Rome was rich, but unwilling to spend the cash needed to find an army big enough to reclaim the lands won by Islam. The emperors/popes found they were quite content to be rich and comfy in a smaller empire rather than jeopardize their opulence for the sake of more land. It wasn't until Peter got things rolling with public sentiment (not to mention the fact that Islam was now sitting at the borders of the empire, greedily looking at Italy and France that the ruling Pope decided it was about time for a rebuttal to the Islamic campaign.

So, with Peter the Hermit riling the crowds, the people, demanded that the Roman Catholic Church take steps to reclaim the road to Jerusalem for all the pilgrims and make the Holy City accessible to Christians once again. This led to the first Christian Crusade, which secured a portion of the Holy Land for the Christians.

THE CRUSADES

> History is the register of the crimes,
> follies, and misfortunes of mankind.
> ~Edward Gibbon

Monty Python is now annoying me. If it weren't for the "Holy Grail" (and the start of Robin Hood) no one would give a damn about the Crusades, and I wouldn't have to write this subchapter. As it is, everyone knows that the Crusades happened and I'm condemned to cover them even though I don't see them as ultimately having any bearing on anything. But here's how they went anyway.

In 1096, the first Crusade freed a chunk of Palestine and set up "the Latin Kingdom of Jerusalem."[55] This did little to stave off the Muslim fervour. The second and third Crusades were basically limited clashes that only marginally affected anything in the region. The fourth Crusade, however, was a stunning success. The only real difficulty with this stunning success was that it occurred in the wrong city.

Apparently, after being sent by Rome to free the Holy Land from the Muslim hordes, the Christian army seemed to have gotten a little lost. They wound up in Constantinople-which was controlled by the Greek Orthodox Church at the time-and proceeded to sack and loot the whole damn city. A fifth Crusade was then sent out to fetch the fourth Crusaders, who had managed to take over Constantinople but refused to give any of the loot to Rome. The Muslims really had nothing to do with the fifth Crusade, as they were too damn entertained by the fact that the Christians were busily killing each other to bother getting involved.

The sixth and final Crusade was launched in 1270 and failed so miserably that the Christians went home and totally forgot about crusading. The Muslims secured their power in the Middle East and everything pretty much went back to being exactly the way it was before the Crusades started. All the stories you've heard about chivalry and piety and noble Christian warriors came from these scuffles we call the Crusades. (It was all just a useless bid to wrest control of the Holy Land from a superior army with a hometown advantage.

If this all sounds a little pathetic to you, try this: at the same time as the men were going off to this "holy" war, a bunch of children followed suit in what's referred to as the "Children's Crusade." The romantic propaganda the Church had been feeding folks inspired hundreds of children to march off to the Holy Land. The adults watched in awe as these kids made it across Europe, believing these children to be led by God.

Well, God led them to the shore of the Mediterranean, where a captain offered them free passage to Palestine. Once they set sail, God immediately led the children to the hold, where that same captain promptly shackled them. Those that didn't starve or die of disease were sold into slavery when the ship made port. So ended the Children's Crusade.

About the only good that came out of the whole Crusade thing was that the Crusaders managed to find and reintroduce a bunch of Greek texts that had been lost to Christendom since Nicaea-books by people like Plato and Aristotle.

You see, the Muslims had conquered vast territories and had managed to secure many of the antiquities of ancient Greece and Egypt. Instead of rejecting it all out-of hand as Christianity was wont to do, the Muslims proliferated the ideas of Greek thought for consideration. The Crusaders encountered these ideas and, when they returned in utter defeat, brought back copies of the books amid the booty they were able to escape with. As these texts weren't overtly religious in nature, they weren't declared heretical, so they were accepted as just weird "thinking-type" books that theologians didn't care about.

This allowed the discipline of philosophy to grow as an independent field of study, which has proved to be an unrelenting thorn in the side of Christianity from that time to this. As it was the Crusades that made this possible, I find it delightfully ironic every time I see a philosopher and a theologian screaming at one another. Aside from this, the Crusades didn't amount to much. Unless you're a Python fan.

THE INQUISITIONS

Nothing so needs reforming as another person's habits. ~Mark Twain

You'll learn everything you're ever going to need to know about the Inquisitions by watching Mel Brooks' the History of the World, Part One. In it, the Spanish Inquisition is portrayed as a cruel, sadistic, dark era, wherein the Church tortured innocent Jews and Heathens until they either died or "gave their lives to Christ" (i.e. died).

About the only real difference you'll see between this portrayal and the actual events is that Mel Brooks had a better soundtrack and more attractive nuns. The Inquisitions lasted from 1096 to 1545, and the thing that made them so incredibly bloodthirsty is the Zero Tolerance Factor. Loosely put, it meant that if you were under Roman rule, you were either Christian or dead… no middle ground. (Kind of a right-wing Christian's wet dream.) With the political power that Christianity achieved through Constantine, the Church kind of got lazy in the proselytizing department. They examined their literature and dogma, considered the best means by which to convey it, then thought, "Kill 'em if they don't agree."

With the Moors (the Muslims) on the march in Spain and Luther's Reformation taking off, Rome was really getting worried about the personal safety and purity of the Christian souls living in the outlying regions of their empire. They needed to find some way to cohesively maintain the beauty of the Christian word in an environment where evil influences threatened to lead the people away from the true salvation that is the Catholic Church.   Just kidding...

Rome was an empire. Like all good empires, she used her power and military to force herself on the world. Because Rome wanted both the land and the souls of the people living there, it made the fundamental mistake of declaring that it was not good enough for a conquered territory to just pay taxes to Rome. The citizens also had to be "true adherents" of Catholicism. (Oh..."Catholic." It translates as "universal ", meaning the one true universal Church. So Roman Catholic means Roman Universal-kind of an oxymoron, but hey...) Anyway, Rome secured its territories in Europe by gaining political control. Then, since taxes generated far less revenue than religious tithes, they sent in the Jesuits or the Donatists to "convert" the people who were not Christians. If the converts weren't easily persuaded, they opened their minds. Or their skulls. Whichever came first.

When the entire populace was either converted, dead, or too damn scared NOT to be Christian, the territory was then declared to be "Christianized" and Rome moved on to the next area. This went on for years. When the "New World" opened up, Rome did the exact same thing there—wholesale slaughter of those who wouldn't convert, and absolute obedience (and tithes) from those who kinda wanted to live. Is it any wonder Vatican City is still the smallest country in the world and yet one of the richest?

MARTIN LUTHER

> *Chance is perhaps a pseudonym of God when He did not want to sign.*
>
> *~Anatole France*

I can't slag on Luther too hard. The guy was pretty damned gutsy and did what he could under some pretty bad circumstances. His only real fault was that he thought for himself, a practice not condoned by the Church.

Martin Luther was born in 1483. He graduated from Erfurt University in 1505 with both a Bachelor's and a Master's degree. He had no major, and his education ran the gamut of courses: math, philosophy, languages, that sort of thing. He was raised, like the rest of Europe at the time, as a good Catholic. This meant he never saw the Bible. You see (not surprisingly), Catholicism had followed the ideas set down by Augustine about literature-you made up the explanations for what you wanted the people to believe, then you told them about it. They didn't need scriptural basis.

Why?

Because.

Because why?

Because they didn't that's why. And if you ask again we'll roast you alive as a heretic, okay? Now go whip yourself for being insolent.

(I bet you think I'm exaggerating this. Sadly, I'm not. That's exactly how they kept people in line.)

But Luther was a different kind of guy. He basically put up with having to take "no" for an answer long enough to figure it out on his own, then he told everyone all about it. How and what he figured out is kind of cheesy and weird, but you've got to understand that he was short-changed by the Nicaea crew. All he had to work with was the Bible, and even then he had to wait until he was in his twenties and in university to get a look at it.

Here's how his story goes…

LUTHER'S TALE

Great men are but life-sized. Most of them, indeed, are rather short.
~Beerbohm

In a really cool twist of fate, it was Luther's new job with the Church that was its undoing. You see, Luther went on to get a doctorate in theology and was ordained as a Roman Catholic priest in 1515. The irony is that he was put in charge of eleven monasteries belongings to his order of priests. The greater irony is that it was the Order of St. Augustine.

It was at this point that Luther began to diverge from Catholic teaching. Two things happened. First, he visited Rome. This was not a good thing for a thinking man. Everywhere he looked, he saw the Church fleecing money from the people for "indulgences." Indulgences were basically passports to heaven. For example, if your father had been a total asshole that beat your family regularly, stole from your neighbors, then laughed about it while sleeping with his mistress in his wife's bedroom, you'd normally say the guy was going to hell. UNLESS…

That's right! For a limited time only you can buy a brand-new, never-before-used "indulgence" from Rome's K-Tel Collection, Personally glanced at by the Pope on his way to the bank, for only $19.95. Visa and Master Card not invented. Please allow four to six weeks for deliverance.

Okay, suffice it to say Rome was not what the young Luther expected it to be.

As it turns out, it was seedy, grungy city full or greed and corruption. Rome was ranking in cash hand-over-fist from the pilgrims, and quite frankly, Luther was disgusted by it all. He'd expect something reverent and beautiful. Instead he got New York's Lower East Side.

The second event that turned Luther's life around was his famous Tower Experience. Even after the Rome incident, Luther kept his "faith" (a bad move, but at least he'd learned to have faith in the Divine instead of the Church). The problem was sin. The whole concept really messed the poor guy up. According to the Church, we are all born into sin because Adam and Eve (our progenitors) ate of the Tree of knowledge in the Garden of Eden. This "Original Sin" (that is, defiance of God's will) condemned all of us to being born with an inclination toward sin. This inclination is referred to as having a "sinful nature", and is used by Christians to explain things like this book. Having now read the scriptures, Luther couldn't reconcile the whole thing with a God who was, supposedly, good and just and loving. Mankind seemed trapped by it all. Sin was always more available than God was. Even the promise of Jesus being the Saviour didn't help, since the Saviour could only save you if you were able to go against every instinct you had and live in a pure and sinless life. I mean, let's face it, sinning is a hell of a lot more fun than purity.

This whole dilemma screwed Luther up totally. He gave up saying mass. He took a sabbatical from his teachings. Basically he sunk into a deep, theological funk that just wouldn't quit. The deeper he thought about it, the crueller it sounded. God came out looking like an evil psychotic that was playing head games with humanity— promising an eternal salvation that he knew no one could ever hope to achieve. We mere humans seemed to amount to nothing more than repugnant, insignificant playthings for a cruel and unjust God. We were all just ignorant fools looking around, saying, "Hey…where are we going and why are we in this hand basket?"

Then it hit him. Luther had a moment of *rahma* (it's pronounced ray-mah, and it means "divine inspiration") while reading chapter 3:21-24 of Paul's (yeah, had to be Paul's) letter to the Romans. In it are the famous lines, "All have sinned and fallen short of the glory of God, being justified freely by his grace through the redemption that is Jesus Christ."

"Wait a cotton pickin' minute here," thinks Luther. "This is a grace thing. We're saved by grace: the free, no-indulgences, no-money-owing grace of God. Sure, we're all slime, but God knows this. He set it up knowing this. All we have to do is accept this grace and we're saved. That's it. No work. No dues. Just accept it and go on with your life."

Now, on the off-chance that Christianity is now making sense to you because of these bright ideas, let us stop to consider one vital fact in this postulate. In order for any of this to work, Josh had to have been God Incarnate, come to Earth in human form, yada, yada, all the Nicene Stuff. If Josh was just a rabbi (as I contend), then this whole argument, and most of Christianity, falls apart at its sacred seams. Luther's philosophy, you'll recall, was what the nutbar Christians that Paul flipped on were all about-the guys that believed that since they were saved by grace, they didn't have to give a damn about anything they did for the rest of their lives. Luther merely reinvented this philosophy (minus the antisocial overtones) after Paul had stifled it. Anyway, Luther figured all this out while meditating on Paul's letter. This all happened in a tower, by the way, which pretty much explains why it's called The Tower Experience.

THE NINETY-FIVE THESES

> *I'll not listen to reason. Reason always means what someone else has to say.* ~Elizabeth Gaskell

A thesis is a point; an opinion or fact you put forward in a debate. It's normally followed by the opposite point of view, called the antithesis. The two points are then measured against each other to make a new point called the synthesis. This in turn may be used as a new thesis. The German philosopher Hegel defined this process and called it "the dialectic" and it's the way debates have fuelled for time immemorial. Except this one.

Luther came up with 95 theses, or points, that he thought the Church should consider and get back to him on with antitheses. They were written in Latin (as most scholastic things were), so the average Joe wouldn't have been able to read them. All the same, he took them down to the local church and nailed them to the door.

All Luther was looking for was some kind of intellectual response from the Church, some antitheses he could mull over and debate. That's not what he got. The theses, covering everything from indulgences to salvation to why the Pope needed cash to do what should be considered Christianity charity, were picked up by other scholars and copied. They were then sent whirling through Germany and were soon hot topics in every social circle, scholarly or otherwise.

The original Latin was quickly replaced with German so the average person could understand it, and in no time all hell was breaking loose. It wasn't long before Rome caught on and suddenly the sullen, quizzical Luther became the front man for a full-scale religious revolution. Luther was formally charged with heresy (a capital crime) and was summoned to Rome to stand trial. Not surprisingly, he didn't go.

Instead, he applied to Frederick III of Saxony (Luther's homeland) for protection. It was given conditionally, the condition being that Luther answer to the charges, if only *in absentia* (i.e. while absent from the actual court room). Luther did one better than this. He agreed to stand trial – *if* the trial were held outside of Rome itself, where he knew damn well that he'd be hung before the trial even began. Rome agreed to try Luther in the city of his choice, figuring it really didn't matter where they sentenced him to eternal damnation, since the result would be the same: the people wouldn't follow him anymore.

THE DIET OF WORMS

Don't wait for the Last Judgment. It happens every day. ~Albert Camus

No, Luther didn't eat worms. It's amazing how many times people ask me this.

A "diet" (pronounced "dee-it") is a mini-council of religious leaders. Worms was a city. Luther was finally and eternally excommunicated from Catholicism in April of 1521 at the Diet of Worms by the Holy Roman Emperor Charles. (He really needed a last name. The Holy Roman Emperor Charles just sounds like it needs "The Fifth" or "the Lion-hearted" or something after it.) Anyway, Luther was excommunicated and put under the ban of the Empire, which meant he couldn't live in any country under Roman rule. Saxony came to his aid yet again, ignored the ban and Luther moved in with Fred. Oh…sorry, Frederick III of Saxony.

Having basically gotten away with all this, Luther began to amass a huge following especially in Germany. Seeing chance for change, several monarchs renounced the papacy, using Luther's theses as reason. Monks and nuns were dropping out of the monasteries and convents in record numbers because of Luther's ideas of free grace without works. Why spend your life in a monastery if you don't have to? As a result of all this, the first new Christian Church since Constantine was quickly created. It rejected the papacy, the recitation of prayer, and the Latin mass. Instead it was more "user-friendly." Unlike the Catholics – who kept the Bible locked up on the altar – Luther, with the help of Gutenberg and other presses, distributed Bibles for the laity to interpret for themselves.

Since people were then able to read the Gospels in their own language, they could actually understand what was being preached at them in the services. An unprecedented emphasis was placed on the Bible (New and Old Testaments) as the authoritative text – not on the works of saints like Augustine. So it was that a messed-up priest from the capitalized Order of St. Augustine brought an end to the monopoly of Augustine and Constantine had held on Christian thought since the fourth century. My, that sounded dramatic.

THE PROTESTERS

In the years that followed (from 1540 to the present day), a wide variety of sects have arisen from Luther's teachings. These sects are collectively called, the "Protesters". Or, as your probably more used to hearing, the Protestants. They include the Lutherans, the Baptists, the Anglicans, the Seventh Day Adventists (an apocalyptic offshoot of Baptists started in America by William Miller) and the Methodists, to name just a few. All of the Pentecostal "Believe-in-Jesus-and-you-are-saved" evangelists like Jim Bakker owe their beginnings to Martin Luther's revelation about salvation without works. You'd never know to listen to them, but they do.

Of all of these sects, there are three that everyone asks me to cover. They are the Calvinists, the Mormons, and the Jehovah's Witnesses. I'll do the Calvinists and Jehovah's witnesses first. The Mormons are a bit more complex and fall a lot further away from Luther and Catholicism.

JOHN CALVIN

Okay, Calvin was "eccentric". It's my humble opinion, of course, but I genuinely think that the guy was a nutbar. I kinda liked Luther because the guy was just trying to figure things out. Calvin, on the other hand, was aiming to create a whole new dogma to replace the crap stripped away by Luther. And he succeeded. Were Luther was quizzical and kind of meandered his way into a new religion, Calvin grabbed the reins of Luther's reformation and turned it into hard-core "Church". Where Luther had concentrated on divine grace and forgiveness, Calvin's big thing was predestination and the sovereignty of God. He turned Luther's vision of loving, empathetic deity into the "Lord God Almighty" who *had already judged* humanity by His own whims.

Luther was known for being amiable and easy-going (once he was free from the Catholics), Calvin was a bastard to anyone who disagreed with him. Case in point: Michael Servetus, long-time friend and physician to Calvin. Servetus disagreed with Calvin on the issue of trinity. (Calvin agreed with the Catholics regarding the trinity, i.e. that the three elements of God—the father, son (Jesus), and the Holy Ghost—were all one entity that had manifested itself in three different ways. Servetus, and others at the time, believed that all three elements of god existed, but as three separate beings, not a three-in-one package deal).

Anyway, Servetus escaped Catholic persecution on this issue and found his way to Geneva— in Switzerland, the first Protestant state— where Calvin was hiding out from Roman persecution. Calvin welcomed his friend in and the two of them sat around and compared notes on Catholic persecution. Then Servetus explained why it was that the Church was after him. Calvin agreed with the Catholic stance on the trinity and had his friend burned at the stake the next day.

There's piety for you.

Calvin began the regime of hard-nosed, "listen-to-me-or-burn-in-hell" Christianity. There is a whole bunch of sects that have come out of this, including Calvinists (go figure), the Presbyterians, the Puritans, and basically anyone else who says that you're gonna roast eternally if you don't do exactly as we tell you…" (Except the Mormons, but even they own their ardency to Calvinist influence, socially if not doctrinally.

To Calvin, the way to tell if you're going to heaven or hell will show in the fruits of your labors. This means that those who have the grace of God will by the very nature of that grace want to work really hard and give lots of time and money to propagating Calvin's, er, God's word. Simply put, the idea was that *works*, meaning things done to say, "look at me, I'm doing this because God told me to", were bad because they were self-aggrandizing and lacked Christian humility. However, *work*, meaning labour of any kind that was designed to better your station in life, was good.[56]

This was because of the significance of prosperity. In the absence of the New York Lotto, social and economic prosperity could only be brought about by hard work. It was prosperity, rather than the actual *work* itself, that Calvin deemed was indicative of God's blessing. If you were successful, then God liked you. If God liked you, then you were going to heaven.

It seems a tad screwy, I know. But Calvin was biblically

sound in saying this. Throughout the Old Testament, from Able to Zechariah, God has shown His grace by blessing his favourite people with success. When Israel as a nation was in His favour, they won wars. When they screwed up, they lost. When a sacrifice was done properly, God favored the priests with success. If it was done poorly, no blessing could be expected and the priest had to start all over again with a new sacrifice. Miracles— in both the Old and New Testaments— were the ultimate examples of God's grace.

Success is what God's always been about, and this is what Calvin said was the best indicator of His blessing on an individual's life. If people could show that their lives were sound and good and prosperous, then it followed that they were in God's favour and would be going to heaven. If their lives were screwed up, then they obviously weren't in God's good graces.

CALVINISM AND CAPITALISM

> *God helps those who help themselves.* ~Benjamin Franklin

Capitalism pretty much explains the success of Calvinism. You see, there was another side to this whole predestination thing. While it was true that those that had grace would have an indication to do church stuff, it wasn't the only indication that you were heaven-bound.

Remember, predestination meant that God knew before you were even born whether you would roast in hell. (See you there, bring beer.) Since God knew this in advance, Calvin rationalized that God wouldn't waste success on those that were just going to hell anyway. This meant that if you were poor, blind, lame, orphaned, or in any way financially or socially lacking, then you must be a candidate for hell. If you weren't, then God would have taken better care of you. Along the same lines, if you're a rich, upstanding member of the Church and you suddenly go broke, then obviously your "grace" was false and God had decided to revoke your successful status to show everyone that you were going to hell.

What this meant, in practical application, is that only wealthy and successful people were considered holy. Wealthy and successful people really liked this idea. Wealthy and successful people became Calvinists because this meant they were going to heaven for sure. Forget about that whole "give everything you have to the poor and follow me" bit from the Bible. Instead, it's "Why waste all my possessions on poor people who are obviously going to hell? I'm rich because that's the way God wants me, and I wouldn't want to disagree with God, now would I?"

Moreover, the accumulation of wealth became something that was indirectly encouraged and sanctioned rather than despised, since the wealth itself was not the goal. Rather, it was the *by-product* of proper Christian behavior—you didn't strive for the wealth for its own sake, but for what it told you about your eternal faith. Of course, as an added bonus, the heaven-bound got to keep the money. The righteous industriousness that resulted from this theology is primarily responsible for the state of our economy and ecology, reinforcing the capitalist credo that "more is better".

More insidiously, Calvinism sets up a hierarchy of worth within society. This isn't an idle thought here. It's where the whole idea that artists, composers and poor maligned authors like myself are worthless comes from. To Calvinists, unless something generated concrete revenue it was seen as being valueless in society, and therefore indicative of God's disapproval. The twisted reality here is that this philosophy carried *way* beyond the doors of the Calvinist churches into society at large. We know Calvinists became wealthy. They also became the publishers, moralists, and civic leaders that have laid the foundations for Western thought, especially in America. It's their views that are taught to grade-school kids to make sure they grow up with a healthy respect for hard work and "proper values".

Okay, enough of a tangent. That is why Calvinism's all about. Let's move on. There are a few more Christian sects I have to piss off before I trash Islam. Guess which one is next...

A Typical Introduction

Unbidden guests are often welcomest when they are gone. ~ *Henry VI*

It's really late in the evening. Somehow you've managed to crawl your way home from whatever booze fest you were at and you find yourself lying in your own bed, wondering how you got there and why your underwear seems to be missing. You try to piece it all together (*"…it was something about a bet and a police car…"*), but the buzzing noise starts at the back of your brain and it won't let up. It keeps going, and going, and somewhere in your stupor you begin to understand that it's the doorbell. The realization hits full force that anyone who's going to be at your door at this time of night must be there for something really important. You summon up some hidden refuge of strength, drag yourself off the bed and stagger blindly for the front door. As you rush, you're trying to remember…

"a police car…Jake told me if I threw my underwear he'd…"

As you swing the front door open, you find yourself confronted by two horribly confusing images at the same time. The first is the sun. Somehow it seems to be up and looking an awful lot like 10 am out there, when in your reckoning it should only be about 4:30 or so.

"…I remember the cop was really pissed about something…"

The second confusing image comes in the form of two women in pink, flowery dresses who are smiling at you as if they really belonged on your front step at this oddly sunny hour of 4:30 am. Through the painful haze of daylight, you make out the **(e)** Watchtower Magazine in their hands and start hoping to whatever's up there that someone slipped something in your last drink and that this is just a painfully real hallucination. Before your mind can even to find hope in this idea, the older woman speaks.

"Good morning, sir. Have you considered the fate of mankind in the coming millennium?" she asks.

You scream, slam the door, and collapse on the Indian throw rug in the hallway, wondering why your girlfriend/boyfriend isn't talking to you, a vague memory of the encounter wafts through your mind. You absently rub the raw spot where the rug chafed your face and mutter something about guard dogs and Jehovah's Witnesses.

Yeah. We've all been there…

Jehovah's Witnesses

Those who speak of the Bible as a monument to modern prose are merely admiring it as a monument over the grave of Christianity. ~T.S. Eliot

Witnesses? Not really. But they're hoping.

Because of scenarios like the one above, good Heathens are forever asking one question over and over again: How can I piss these guys off so badly that they never come back? That part's simple. Just tell them you're intimately involved in (and enjoying) any numbers of the delicious sins that the Bible says deserve death. These include homosexuality, witchcraft (Wicca), and honoring false gods. (Lots to choose from there. And hey—can't decide? Spend a fun-filled weekend creating your own god, complete with personalized rituals. For best results, have the rituals include one or more of the other sins that deserve death.) Then, when they come to your door, lure them in and show them the fruits of your labour. A black altar with a pentagram. A shrine to Shiva. Or, for a low-key approach, invite them to browse your home library of videocassettes, including the illustrated Marquis de Sade and the complete Richard Simmons' *Sweatin' with the Heathens* workout tape. If they do come back, be worried. They're probably not there for Jehovah.

The question still remains: who the hell are these guys? Well, Jehovah's Witnesses are "officially" a Protestant Church. Barely. It was started by a guy from Pittsburgh named Charles Taze Russel at the turn of the century. The entire faith is founded on this guy's intricate interpretations of the Bible as given him by Yahweh, now called Jehovah because the King James guys. (Incidentally, Shakespeare was one of the King James guys. He helped translate the Greek and Hebrew for the KJ version, and was on the Bible team. So, in fact, the Bible is Shakespeare's most popular work, not *Hamlet.* He just never signed it.)

Anyway, the Jehovah's Witnesses are the original "millennium fever" guys. It's something that's just catching on now—the idea that the year 2000 will be the end of everything and it's all gonna change fundamentally for the betterment of mankind and stuff like that there. You've heard it before, I'm sure. Well, the Jehovah's Witnesses has a century's head start on everybody (except the Seventh Day Adventists). They're waiting for the new millennium, when they figure JC is supposed to judge the living and the dead and set up his—sorry, "His"—kingdom and a perfect Earth. They're called Witnesses because of a prophecy in Revelations that says that "The End" won't happen until "the Word has been preached in all the lands." This means that they're trying to bring about the end of the world by fulfilling the prophecy by telling you about "The Word". It doesn't matter to them whether you believe it or not. That's not their department. Their job is to tell you so that The Word has been witnessed to everyone on the planet so they can happily get on with the Apocalypse so they can set themselves up in perfect bodies on a perfect Earth afterwards wherein they can live without the evil earthly distractions that vex them nowadays. Like me.

In order to keep all His "Witnesses" safe during the "Great Tribulation" that's supposed to happen, JC has promised to get 144,000 of them the hell off the planet after all the witnessing is done and the evil anti-Christ is duking it out with JC. This getting off the planet is called the "rapture". It is basically like being beamed up to the enterprise, except you wind up in Heaven instead of the transporter room.

So the people that come to your door are witnesses that are hoping to end the world as we know it and then get out while the getting's good (rapture). In order to show God that they're righteous, holy people deserving of rapture, they donate their time doing missionary work for the church. As it's mandatory for them to be volunteering doing one might get to questioning the effectiveness of this in the sight of a god. Buy what the hell…that's what they're up to. They canvass the world looking for converts so they can basically say, "Hey, look how many people I brought in." It's works in exchange for grace, though they'd never put it that way. They believe the grace of God is freely given—it's just given more freely to those that canvass the world on Jesus' behalf.

About Charles Taze Russel. The guy was a con man. Even the most devout Witness has to admit that the vessel of this revelation was flawed. The guy spent a lot of his adult life dodging creditors and answering to charges of fraud, coercion, etc. He was basically from the Jim and Tammy Bakker school of religious leadership. The most prominent case in which the Church founder was implicated involved wheat—"miracle wheat," to be precise. He was selling these seeds that he claimed were a divine offshoot of manna, the bread that fell from heaven to feed the Israelites when they were hungry in the desert. These seeds were sold to devout farmers with the promise that they would yield a huge harvest from relatively small amount of seed.

The farmers bought it. The U.S. Food and Drug Administration didn't. A sample was tested in government labs and found to be nothing more than a low-grade bulk wheat germ. Russel was busted. He was charged with fraud and made a public disgrace. Of course, the church tends to ignore this aspect of its history, explaining that Chuck was just one man and the church is many people and you can't condemn the entire faith on one man's actions. This is logical—except, of course, for the fact that this guy was one of the founders of the faith (and worse yet… the creator of The Watchtower Magazine) and he's the one who created the interpretations and doctrines that are the crux of Jehovah's Witness.

Oh. One last thing. The Jehovah's Witnesses adamantly believe that all governments are currently under the direct power of the Anti-Christ. It's a big world conspiracy, wherein the forces of evil are slowly but surely taking over. They don't believe the Anti-Christ is coming—they believe he's already here and in power behind the scenes. Sometime very soon he's supposed to expose himself to the world as god-emperor of the planet and seize total control. To this end, I've done up my résumé in hopes of applying for the job, but I have not as yet found where to send it.

The flip side of this coin is also true. You see, they don't believe JC is coming back. They believe he's here. According to the faith, JC arrived on terra firma in 1914. You see, the Jehovah's Witnesses believe that Adam was created in 4026 B.C. and that human beings have been allotted 6000 years of existence until Armageddon. This figure is based on a "creative week" in which each of six days is equal to 1,000 years, with the Sabbath or seventh day being the beginning of the millennium. Simple arithmetic gives 1975 as the year Armageddon would arrive. But when 1975 came and went, the Witnesses had to "adjust" their chronology to cover up a failed prediction. They accomplished this by maintaining that no one knew exactly when Eve was created so the whole thing was out of whack.

Some of the older readers will remember the summer of 1975, when the Witnesses declared the world would end. This was because JC was supposed to make Himself known at that time— judge the living and the dead, that whole scene. The idea was that since he's been here since 1914, it was about time he actually did something.

Well, he didn't. The faith lost a LOT of adherents in '75. Those that remained created a new ideology that basically says, "Yes, Jesus is here. But only in spirit. Like a ghost. And only the holiest are actually able to see Him."

This inevitably leads me to asking any Witnesses I meet if they've ever actually seen Jesus. They always say no. (Though I'd love to meet one who says yes.) If they say no, I then explain to them that they're obviously not holy enough and that they should go somewhere and pray rather than trying to convert me to a faith they're obviously not holy enough to "witness". It pisses them off to no end. But hey, I figure if someone's going to show up at my door and preach to me, they should be holy enough to do so, right? I mean, we can't have half-assed missionaries out there corrupting the Word, now can we? (You don't have to say it. I know. I am an asshole. It's what makes life fun.)

So, the Witnesses are apocalyptics who maintain that we're living in the end times. They believe the Beast of Revelation and the Late-Great JC are here now and that we're all just a few years away from wrapping up the tale of the human race.

THE MORMONS

Both read the Bible by day and night.

But thou read'st black where I read white.

~William Blake

Joseph Smith II was born in Vermont in 1805. Until he was fifteen, he was basically a nobody like the rest of us. Then things got a little weird.

It seems that while wandering around the backwoods of Vermont, young Joseph came across two "personages whose brightness and glory defy all description." In a rare twist in this kind of tale, it wasn't JC and it wasn't angels. It was Moroni and his father, Mormon. Don't worry if you never heard of them from the Bible. They aren't in it. These two are an entirely new addition to the tale.

A few years later, Smith was visited by actual angels, who led him over the hills and through the woods to grandmother's hou... er, no. Try that again...through the woods to a secret hiding place, where they showed him a bunch of golden plated with inscriptions. The inscriptions were in what Smith called "Reformed Egyptian." The fact that Egyptologists then (or now, for that matter) had ever heard of this language didn't seem to hinder Smith's story. It was Reformed Egyptian. The main problem that Smith saw in all of this was is that he couldn't read Reformed Egyptian. "No problem," said the angel, and handed him a pair of magic eyeglasses. He put them on and suddenly he could read and decipher Reformed Egyptian.

He busily set to copying the whole thing out in English then it all took home where he published it as a book called *The Book of Mormon*. As a result of this interpretation (as well as other visions he had around the same time), Joseph Smith made a public declaration of the creation of new church, called The Church of Jesus Christ of Latter-Day Saints. The declaration was made in La Fayette in Seneca County, New York on April 6, 1830.

"So...what about these golden plates?" you ask.

Well, I'll tell you. The Book of Mormon was published and got an awful lot of attention. I'll go into detail about what was in it in a moment, but suffice to say it was enough to whet the whistle of every theologian, historian, and cryptographer this side of Mount Zion. In a flurry of activity, the whole world wanted to see the plates from which this book was translated. Scholars from around the world were suddenly descending on Vermont and Upper New York in droves, waiting to get a peek at these divine tablets. They never did. It seems these angels were shy or something. When the furor around the plates grew, the angels came back to Smith, told him to return the plates to their hiding place for safekeeping and made him forget where they were. No one outside of Smith and (presumably) his family ever saw the plates, and they were never authenticated by any of the scholars of the day.

The word "dubious" comes to mind here. Can't say why, but it does.

The Book of Mormon

Of making many books there is no end.

~ Ecclesiastics 12:12

Trust me; you can get one of these things for free. They practically force them on you if you show any interest whatsoever. The Book of Mormon is so named because the last book in it is called the Book of Mormon. Go figure. Like the Bible, it has other books in it that all add to the tale. The tale goes something like this...

You remember the story of the Babylonian exile from the Judaism section? This is where the first temple was destroyed and the Hebrew king got carried off to Babylon. Well, a funny thing happened on the way to captivity, as they say. You see, there were thirteen tribes of Israel that went into Babylon. Twelve came back and rebuilt the Temple when the Persians invaded. So what happened to the missing tribe? (Yet another deep, mystic secret.)

Me? I've always figured that they just assimilated into the Babylonian culture. I mean, it was amazing enough to figure that the people that stayed Jewish did so under such extreme pressure to give it all up and become good Babylonians. The idea that some of them did exactly that is no great surprise to me. But this isn't what Joseph Smith says.

Smith (oh, sorry—the angel that guided Smith) said that this tribe did, in fact remain the unified tribe. But somehow they just never made it back to Israel when everyone else did. According to *The Book of Mormon*, these guys hopped on a bunch of cigar shaped boats and sailed away. (Presumably on the Atlantic, but who knows?) Anyway, they sealed themselves inside these boats. There was no deck. No windows. Just a big, cigar-shaped tube floating along on the high sea. God, being the thoughtful guy he was in this story, packed a bunch of phosphorus rocks in with them so they could see inside the boat. Then the whole lost tribe floated on out to open sea and headed for the Americas.

They entered the New World, carrying their Jewish heritage with them, and continuing to record the divine influences in their lives—commandments, miracles, that sort of thing. The Book of Mormon also speaks of how JC came and visited them after he ascended in front of the apostles. (I get this image of JC flying through the air like Christopher Reeves in the Superman movies—taking off from Israel, flying across the Atlantic, then setting gently down in North America to chat with the lost tribe.)

The Book of Mormon (or BoM, as I like to call it) goes on to say that the people fell away from "the one true God" and became savages. (These would be the modern-day Native Americans.) The story goes that God saw the wickedness that was growing in the people and decided it was time that what was in your hearts should show up on your skin. To this end, He darkened or lightened people according to the love or hate in their soul. Black people were considered the most evil, whites the most pure.[57] (And hey…Smith was white. Coincidence or what?) The savage natives were reddish in color because they were at one time pure and therefore couldn't fall all the way down to being black-skinned. (Mormons truly believe this, by the way. Ask one of them sometime. Particularly if you're not white. It'll scare the hell out of them.)

Take note, though. These guys have a prophet all the time now. The old one is always replaced. Apparently, the new guy has recanted some of this facial stuff—something about the NAACP and huge riots gave them the divine inspiration to change it.

POLYGAMY

Marriage is popular because it combines the maximum of temptation with the maximum of opportunity. ~George Bernard Shaw

In 1843, Joseph Smith (now living among a thriving Mormon community in Illinois) declared that polygamy was okay. He was right, by the way. The Old Testament does back him up.[58] Remember, most of the laws of marriage and sex came from Augustine, not the Bible. In the bible, polygamy was legal. In Illinois, however, it wasn't. The Governor of Illinois ordered Joseph and his brother Hiram arrested for the crime of polygamy (and inciting people to polygamy) and both were summarily picked up and thrown in jail in Carthage, Illinois.

Folklore has it that a band of armed men broke in and shot both brothers. While this is essentially true, there's a few minor details that seem a little hazy, most notably the lack of a mob. You see the official story on this is that the local sheriff went out to get a bite to eat and when he got back the two brothers were dead.

Now, I've been to Illinois. I've also seen old-school American justice in action (most notably in Alabama). It doesn't change much, but I'm pretty sure that what happened was that the sheriff went out to dinner, accidentally leaving everyone else in the jail cells armed to the teeth except for Joseph and Hiram.

An hour later, he comes back and is astounded to find that somehow the brothers have been mysteriously pumped full of lead. He then asks around the jail to see if anyone saw anything and, amazingly enough, the other prisoners report that a whole mob of people had broken in and killed the brothers. "Oh dear," says the sheriff. "We'd better get an APB out on that mob. Unruly, you say? Okay. We'll get right on it. Right after dessert." So Joseph Smith becomes a martyr. There's nothing like a martyr to get things rolling in a religion.

Brigham Young

Wherever Law ends, Tyranny begins. ~John Locke

So now the Latter Day Saints are leaderless. For a bit anyway. It didn't take long before a man named Brigham Young took the reins and really got things going. This guy was fanatical to the infinite power. (There is a pun in there if you look closely enough.) Brigham was stern and intolerant of anything that even hinted at sin. He was a BIG FAN of both corporal and capital punishment, which he meted out freely.

He also wasn't stupid. By this time, he and the Saints had figured out that Illinois was not about to welcome their new religion with open arms. Since there was a lot of unsettled land out there, Brigham lead the whole bunch of them (about ten thousand or so) out of Illinois to a New Promised Land. In what amounted to a sort of new age Exodus, the whole religion hit the road in a wagon train bound for Utah—not because it was wonderful or promising or anything, but because it wasn't yet part of the Union. In 1847, Utah was Mexican territory. It was, however, only peripherally monitored by the Mexicans, who didn't give a damn if these Latter Day Saints had one or twenty wives. More importantly, Brigham Young could be the unchallenged Law for the Saints. His order would be carried out without question and without United States intervention. No piddling human rights stuff to worry about in Utah. This lasted, oh, about a year.

Unfortunately for Brigham's theocratic state, Utah was given up by the Mexicans about the same time his reign was just getting established. This time they weren't arrested, though. Instead, Washington recognized Brigham Young and the first governor of the state of Utah. Official statehood didn't actually happen until Wilford Woodruff, Brigham's successor, held power, but it was effectively a state during Brigham's regime. Woodruff was basically economically bullied into giving in on the idea of polygamy. He was given the promise that if he didn't give up polygamy the federal government would run the railway through Utah and make sure that Salt Lake City and Kansas City (Utah) became known as two of the greatest pornography, gambling and debauchery centers in America. Giving up polygamy definitely seemed the lesser evil.

The Mormons, as they are called, are seen as nowadays as a stoic bunch of stick-in-the-muds that don't do anything fun. No tobacco, alcohol, coffee, tea, etc.[59]... You begin to suspect that if belching weren't biological, they'd go to hell for that too. They're banned from having any hot liquids, including hot chocolate, coffee, soup, and Neo-Citron. From our point of view, a hundred years later Mormons seem archaic and "old-school". The thing is, it was the exact opposite idea that made them big. The LDS offered the people a religious novelty—a new chapter in a Christian tale that had grown stale. Here in the New World, the people wanted a "New Story", and that's what Joseph Smith gave them—a new book for the Bible after a thousand years of waiting.

In a way that's what they still give, having their prophet in Kansas City, ready at any time to tell you the latest news from heaven. There is a saying that you hear a lot in Mormon circles (I know... I traveled in Mormon circles for a long time). It goes like this:

"If god ever spoke to Abraham or Moses or any of the Prophets, then he's still speaking. It's us who stopped listening."

That sums up a lot of the appeal of the faith. It gives its people a sense that God is still with them and not hiding out in heaven, waiting to come down and judge us all at his leisure. People will do a lot if the figure God's right there with them, protecting and clearing the way for them. They'll take a lot more risks. Like showing up at your door at 10:30 am.

The Salamander Letter

> *The individual is not a killer, but the group is, and by identifying*
> *with it the individual is transformed into a killer. ~Arthur Koeslar*

These days most people know the Mormons from those sappy commercials that run late at night. I'm sure you've seen them... they usually depict some hard working father or mother who just hasn't got time to be a good parent. The parent usually has some epiphany wherein he or she suddenly sees their child's big blue eyes and realizes that family is more important than work. The commercials usually end with the words "Family... Isn't It About Time?" These ads are indicative of the warm, loving, family values that the LDS cherish so much. It's because of their deep respect for life and their love of all people that the Mormons church is most famous. Well, that and the murders.

I gotta admit that over the last couple years the LDS has done a spectacular job of ignoring these murders. I keep hoping that the government will force religions to have the same warnings in their ads as drug companies are forced to carry. I really want to hear that side-effect warning at the end: *"Warning: This religion may cause headache, nausea, dizziness, and, on rare occasions, homicidal rampages. This faith should not be administered with Buddhism, Hinduism, or while pregnant or nursing. Consult your physician for more details."*

For those that have not heard about the Mormon murders, here's the deal.

The Salt Lake City Bombings (a.k.a. Mormon Murders) took place in October 1985.[60] A guy named Mark Hoffman blew up two Mormons, Steven F. Christensen and Kathleen B. Sheets. Then, not entirely satisfied with his triumph, Hoffman went ahead and blew himself up. While I have to admit the body count was pretty low compared to other great religious idiocies, there's a lot to this story that makes up for the rather inept techniques used.

This whole fiasco started when a high raking Mormon leader bought the so-called "Salamander Letter" from Hoffman and damn near destroyed the church. It was, indeed, a letter about a salamander and it came awfully close to closing down this whole Mormon idea for good and all. It had supposedly been written by a guy named William McLellin, one of Joseph Smith's original Twelve Apostles that set up the church in 1835. The thing is, McLellin left the Mormon Church in 1838 and never went back. More importantly, he took a whole bunch of documentation with him when he left that supposedly told an independent version of Joseph Smith's angel tale. The Salamander Letter, bought by Christensen in 1985, was supposedly one of the documents that McLellin took with him when he left the church.

Now, lest there be any confusion, let me make this perfectly clear. I did say "salamander". As in the small, slug-like thing that crawls around in swampy areas. Understandably any salamander that could hope to destroy an entire faith would have to be somewhat unique as salamanders go. This one, for instance, was an albino.

This whole Salamander story of McLellin's supposedly dates back to October 23, 1830. Apparently this alleged salamander was wandering about the woods in upstate New York when who should he stumble across but a young Joseph Smith, out doing some black magic. The salamander, called by Smith's dark and evil powers, is summoned to serve Smith. As it turns out Smith was not looking for God or purpose or anything the Mormons say he was looking for. According to the Salamander letter, Smith was out hunting for cash by using evil magic spells to find hidden gold in the hills around his home. In this version of the tale it was the transfixed salamander that led Smith to the golden plates, not Mormon and Moroni. (Apparently salamanders are good for finding gold. Who knew?)

Anyway, the salamander leads Smith to the plates because they're made of gold and it had been told to find gold for Smith. As these tales tend to go, things didn't go smoothly for Smith. Instead of finding the bright, angelic Mormon and Moroni next to the plates, Smith was confronted by a nasty, spitting, evil wood spirit that was guarding the treasure. The story goes that Smith basically conned the plates away of the spirit through a series of ruses, lies, and manipulations. (This is not unlike Bilbo meeting Golem in JRR Tolkien's Lord of the Rings.)

In the end it all comes together and Smith gets the plates and starts the religion about the same way. But the essential difference in the role and character of Joseph Smith in the Salamander Letter might have undermined the foundations of the Mormon Church... if it actually existed. As it turned out, it didn't. The whole Salamander Letter tale was invented by Hofmann, who was using it to screw the church out of hundreds of thousands of dollars. Normally I wouldn't have a problem with this, however...

How to Get Bombed in Salt Lake

We are always making God our accomplice, that so we may legalize our own iniquities. ~Henri Frederic Amiel

It seemed impossible to the Mormon elite that sweet, innocent Mark Hoffman could be a forger, con-man, and a murder. He was a Mormon after all. It seemed far easier to believe he was another victim of some psycho- bomber (probably a Lutheran) who had snapped and was going about killing anyone associated with the "Salamander Letter" for some evil reason known only to Lutherans. (Ok... the Lutherans had absolutely nothing to do with this tale, but I figured I hadn't picked on them enough earlier on so I'm making up for it here.) Anyway, Hofmann claimed to have found this Salamander letter and borrowed tons o' cash, including a $185,000 signature loan that Hugh Pinnock, a Mormon Seventy (elder), had co-signed for.

Of course, as these things go, people got to wondering where all their cash had gone off to and why these letters hadn't shown up yet. To cover his ass on the loan, Pinnock arranged for a wealthy Mormon to buy the non-extant Salamander Letter from Hofmann and donate it to the church. The sale would've netted Hofmann enough of a kickback to cover the $185,000, and still make a pretty good profit. Unfortunately for Hofmann, he was a cheating, lying bastard who'd never had the Salamander letter to begin with, so this deal was never going to happen.

Christensen, who had dealt with Hofmann before, volunteered

to serve as a middle man for the movement of the letter from Hofmann to the church, so he had a front row street when Hofmann defaulted on the $185,000 loan and Pinnock wound up screwed. Since the Salamander letter never actually existed, Hofmann found himself increasingly unable to show it to people. Somewhere along the line Christensen figured out that the entire deal was a scam and, just like in the movies, he threatened to expose Hofmann. Hofmann then did what any normal psycho-thief would do: he blew the guy up.

The bombing of Christensen bought Hofmann some time, but not enough. So, to keep the ball rolling and buy some more time, he blew up another good Mormon, Katherine Sheets. As near as anyone can tell he picked her because she had some business dealings with Christensen and Hofmann figured people would think the bombings were business related. As this whole thing is referred to as "The Mormon Murders", you can pretty much see as how this little diversion failed miserably.

So it was that after two gruesome murders, Hofmann was rather annoyed to find that Mormons still wanted the Salamander Letter. Despite his bloody rampage, the deal was still on track and Christensen would be replaced by Donald Schmidt, the retired Mormon Archivist. This makes matters worse, as an archivist would be the one person Hofmann KNEW he could never pass a forgery off on. So Hoffman heads back to the hardware store, grumbling under his breath at the rising cost of pipe, nails, and sulphur.

This time he decides he'd decided to kill Ashworth, a Mormon lawyer. Unfortunately for all you lawyer fans out there, this is the guy Hofmann failed to get. On October 16th, Mark "Butterfingers" Hoffman tried to put a bomb in Ashworth's car, screwed it up and went boom.

Once Hofmann had blown himself up, it didn't take a whole lot of deep police work to piece it all together. Hoffman was charged with the murders and a bunch of lesser crimes in February 1986. At the beginning of the preliminary hearing, Judge Grant apparently thought that Hofmann was innocent. By the end, Grant was quoted as saying that Hofmann was "clearly guilty, a pathological liar with no conscience and no remorse."

A plea bargain resulted, with Hofmann pleading guilty to certain of the charges and promising to answer questions about his operations in return for a commitment not to seek the death penalty. Hofmann was given a full life sentence, which I think makes him eligible for parole after about a week and a half.

This whole ordeal should have impacted quite heavily on the Mormons faith, and I'm not just referring to the concussion from the bombs. When you stop to think of it, there were some pretty heavy theological challenges here. I mean, the General Authority and Gordon B. Hinckley, who were supposedly acting under divine guidance, were totally duped into this scam. One might figure that God, being their leader and talking regularly with old Hinckley, might have mentioned to his prophet that the guy he was dealing with was a psycho-killer bent on killing anyone who got in the way of his plans to rip off the church.

Yes, all these questions and more should have arisen from all this. But none did. The Mormons recovered from the $185,000.00 loss, took in a bunch more cash after that, then put it all into making those warm fuzzy commercials so the whole world can know how beautiful and pure the message of the Mormon Church really is. This has worked so incredibly well that if you question a Mormons about the dire events in Salt Lake City in 1985, virtually all of them will blink and ask "What Mormon murders?" If you get the chance, explain it to them.

The RLDS

About the time ol' Brigham was setting himself up as God-Emperor supreme in Utah, there were a bunch of Saints that decided Brigham shouldn't be in charge. Their idea was that the leadership should carry on down the paternal line of Joseph Smith, which would make Smith's son the effective God-Emperor supreme in Utah. Well, to make a long story short, Brigham said, "No, you absolutely cannot follow Smith's son, because I am the leader of this faith," at which time these Saints said, "Yeah, well, watch us."

Brigham then warned them that he was the Law in Salt Lake City and they couldn't disagree. These Saints then basically said "Oh. Okay. Well then, we'll just move on up the road to Kansas City (Utah) and set up shop there." Brigham flustered and pouted a bit but was little he could do, short of killing them all. Oddly enough, he didn't. So it was that these Saints moved off and founded the RLDS meaning the Reorganized Church of Jesus Christ of Latter

Day Saints. It's "reorganized" because they figure that Brigham Young had disorganized the whole thing by being the wrong leader of the faith. The RLDS is centered in Kansas City today. It's a lot more lenient than the LDS, mainly because the lacked Brigham's brand of leadership. Few people know about these guys since they don't have the sappy commercials of the LDS and they don't show up at your door. Legally (because the RLDS followed the lineage of Smith), the RLDS are considered the original Mormon Church. The LDS don't think so.

Both the RLDS and the LDS have prophets that say that they are the only Mormon Church. Both prophets still record new and exciting new from heaven called *The Doctrine and Covenants.* The LDS and RLDS version of this book is identical up to the split in the faith, form which time the two sects have followed their own prophets and therefore don't record the other sects' news from heaven. The sects don't get along, and are often found taking small but polite jabs at one another. The RLDS, for example, refer to the LDS as "Mormons" but put the emphasis on the second "o", thus making it sound like they are saying "Morons". It is not that exciting, which is why I omitted it to begin with. No bloodshed or holy war— just a bunch of classically "nice" Mormons disagreeing with each other. Abbot and Costello have better fights than these guys.

THE HOLY GRAIL

> *Millions long for immortality who don't know what to*
> *do with themselves on a rainy Sunday afternoon. ~Susan Ertz*

The Grail is a cup that was used at the Last Supper. Josh holds it up and says, "Take this all of you and drink from it. This is a cup. The cup of a new and everlasting covenant."[61] In some versions of the tale, JC also says, "He who drinks from this cup shall see eternal life." Uh huh.

Think "metaphor," folks. The "New Covenant"— eternal life through the promise of an awareness of the divine, a.k.a. *gnosis.* That sort of stuff. The one thing you can count on in history is that someone somewhere is going to be stupid enough to screw up the simplest statement. Like this one.

A lot of people have been after this cup throughout history because they actually believe that by drinking from it you can achieve eternal life. I don't even know where to begin to address that kind of logic. The thing is, the Grail was a cup—just a plain, ordinary cup that was supplied by the people from whom JC and friends had rented the room in which they met. It didn't even belong to them. It was just part of the service that came with the room. When the meal was over and the bunch of them took off for the Garden of Gethsemane where JC was arrested, someone would have gone into the upper room they'd rented and cleaned it up. The "Grail" would have been washed and put away like any other dish that was used at the meal. There was nothing special about it, and no gospel mentions it being around after they left the room.

People seem to want thing to be cooler or more mysterious than they are. This is the case with the Grail. Instead of just accepting the idea that JC used the cup during dinner to illustrate a concept, they took it literally and went off on Crusades and quests and things, looking for this holy cup that would bring eternal life.

The stupid part of it all is that people actually found it. Several times. In different places. Usually made of gold, with gems and fancy lettering. The real Grail would have been a simple clay cup with no adornments. The "Grails" that were found were obviously fakes. The whole myth is a mystery created from one line in scripture that was taken way out of context. Repeat after me: THERE...IS...NO... GRAIL. It was probably got broken serving mead to some Roman soldier a week later or something.

So much for the Grail.

CHRISTIANITY: SUM UP

I count religion but a childish toy,

And hold that there is no sin but ignorance.

~Christopher Marlow

Well, that's the section on Christianity. If you sitting there thinking, "Hey, wait a minute...he didn't mention MY sect of Christianity"— e.g. Pentecostal, Church of the Nazarene, Church of the Holy Foreskin, etc.—consider yourself lucky. (By the way about the foreskin thing... For a change, I'm not being blasphemous here. In the world today, there really are several Churches of the Holy Foreskin.[62] Indulgences weren't the only odd thing the Roman Catholic Church sold off in the Middle Ages. Holy foreskins[63], pieces of the Cross, nails from the Cross, Jesus' hair, His fingernails, you name it. And many of these artefacts are still meticulously preserved in various churches that bear their name.) Anyway, there are a hell of a lot of sects nowadays. What I've tried to outline for you is how Christianity as a whole evolved, not the subtle differences between the sects that keep them arguing.

What you've read here frames the foundations of the faith, the ins and outs of the political and social crap that led to modern-day Christianity. There's an old saying that goes, "Give a hundred men a hundred Bibles and you'll have a hundred religions." We've got a lot more than a hundred. The thing is, it doesn't matter whether you're the Pope, Billy Graham, or David Koresh. The religion you're dealing with has the same history, even if it doesn't share the same interpretation.

As a matter of fact, interpretation isn't even a big issue anymore. Currently, theologians and historians are busier with the implications of the Gnostic texts and the Dead Sea Scrolls than they are with the age-old debates about baptism or whether the Eucharist is God Incarnate. There is a new wave of inquiry taking place that deals with the grassroots questions that Constantine and the Nicene crew thought they'd quashed forever. I see this as good. There's a lot more out there in the Christian tale than the orthodoxy has ever let on over the years. As it comes out, it fundamentally changes what we know of the religion. There have always been rumors whispered in pubs, or in the privacy of a person's own home about things like Mary Magdalene being the first leader of the Church, or Josh not being divine. But with these texts appearing after so many centuries, there's a new chance for people to rethink the damage done to the so-called "one true faith" at its inception.

It may work out. A lot of pretty important people out there are starting to wonder about the orthodox version of Christian history. It's the kind of "wonder" a religion should inspire—the quizzical kind.

Chapter Three: Islam

After Mohammed died of natural causes, it became
increasingly unclear who would be the new head of the faith.

Religion: *Islam*

Established: 622A.D.

Main Prophet/Holy Guy: *Mohammed the Prophet*

Main Holy Book: *Torah, Bible, Qur'an, Hadith*

What to call the priest: *Imam*

What to Call an Adherent: *Muslim*

ISLAM

Fortune is always on the side of big battalions. ~Marie de Sevigne

Islam is a faith built on the heritage of the prophets,
priests, seers, and scribes that everything in this book has been
systematically trashing up to this point. As I seem to be in full
blasphemous swing here, I'm not about to slow up to be extra kind
to Islam in spite of its reputation as an extremely volatile faith. I

know what you're thinking. You're thinking there probably won't be a sequel to this book because I'm going to get myself killed for what I'm about to say about Islam. That's ok. The thought has occurred to me too.

I do have one thing in my favour, however, and that's a working knowledge of what Islam actually is, as opposed to the media hype that we see in the news every day. You see, Islam is not a religion made up of terrorists that are ready to sacrifice their lives to kill someone whom they feel has insulted "the one true faith." In fact most Muslims I know are thin, gaunt guys that wouldn't say shit if they had a mouthful. Of the hundreds of Muslims I've known I've only ever met one who I thought really could be nuts enough to be a suicide bomber. It's important to understand though that after I was introduced to the guy the other Muslim with us leaned over to me and whispered "This guy's fucked..."

Don't get me wrong... if you bad mouth Islam Muslims are gonna freak on you, but no more or less than a born-again Christian would if you insisted on reading this book aloud to them. Individual Muslims are usually ok. But there's a Borg collective thing that happens in Mosques that you should be aware of. The same guy that shrugs about your questioning his faith in a coffee shop will absolutely lose it on you if you say the exact same thing when other Muslims are around. I've known Muslims in a lot of different places around the world and I've always found this to be the case. It's not exactly empirical evidence, but as a rule of thumb I'm telling ya these guys can get pissed in front of their peers. How and why is what I want to talk about. First, though, were gonna have to cover the history of Allah and the foundations of the faith.

ALLAH

God is no respecter of persons. ~ Acts 10:34

Whenever you see Muslims in the news or 60 Minutes, they invariably have a clip of a bunch of guys bowed down low on small pieces of carpet chanting something in Arabic. About the only word you can catch that might mean anything to you is "Allah." Question: Who is Allah?

Anyone who said *"the God of Islam"* gets a zero and is sent to the back of the class. Allah is NOT the God of Islam. Islam is one of the religions that honour Allah, but He's not exclusively Islamic. It's the language thing that's getting you here. "Allah" is an Arabic name. Translate it into Hebrew and you have Yahweh.

That's right… Allah is Yahweh, a.k.a. El-Shaddai, a.k.a. God. The "one true God" of Christianity and Judaism-the same God that Adam, Moses, Abraham, JC and the rest of the bunch supposedly talked with, the God of the Covenant. Same God, different language. You wouldn't believe how many people are amazed to find this out.

"So," I hear you ask, "What's the story? If it's the same God, how come it's not the same religion? Why all the fighting?"

In a less-than-amazing twist of fate, the answer is far more political than religious. It all dates back to the fifth century, about the time that the Roman Empire was collapsing in on itself and Christianity was on the rise. The Codex was set down by then and, after a few more ecumenical councils, it was turned loose on the world as the Holy Bible. The Jews were dispersed around the globe, trying to find safe haven from Christian persecution, and the Middle Age of Mankind was just beginning.

About the only place in the known world where any safe and amicable trading was going on (without bands of thieves or the Roman military stealing everything) was in Saudi Arabia. There's a trade route through the desert there that exists to this day. On this route there were three major cities/oases. They were Mecca, Medina, and Taif. Of these, Mecca was the biggest and most important. It was here, in Mecca, that Mohammed, the prophet of Islam, was born.

MECCAN RELIGION BEFORE MOHAMMED

A god that let us prove his existence would be an idol. ~Dietrich Bonhoeffer,

This is not only the same tale as Abraham's several millennia before, it also occurs in exactly the same area. Mecca is actually only about 50 miles from the Red Sea that Moses supposedly parted. There are a few differences from the Jewish tale and this one, mainly because a lot of time had passed and the polytheistic guys had had time to refine the names and ideas of the *elohim*.

However, it's essentially the same story all over again—the dawning of monotheistic thought in a polytheistic culture.

You see, what we're looking at here is a bunch of these same old Bedouins. It's amazing how much comes from these guys. (And I bet you only thought they were good for postcards.) In the fifth century, they were going strong. A bunch of them had settled into Mecca at the time (which kind of makes them less nomadic, I suppose), and they brought their idea of gods with them. Unlike Abraham's time, these guys had a thing about rocks. In their theology, rocks somehow carried the power of the god whose spot they were taken from, so the whole area is full of people carrying pet rocks.

These Bedouins had their version of the pantheon or the elohim. It was all very complex and convoluted (since there were so many areas that were considered holy or powerful). Of these, only three gods become really important here. The first is the moon goddess Allat.[64] She's still worshipped in various cultures today (including Wicca, but I'll cover that in the third book of this series). The second important deity was Al-Uzza believed to have something to do with luck.[65] Since the worship of Al-Uzza involved human sacrifice, you pretty much have to stop and ask who it was lucky for.

These gods (and almost all the others) were worshipped at a place called the Kabah. The main feature of the Kabah was a cube with a whole bunch of icons and the sacred stones (pet rocks) associated with the gods; a shrine, essentially. It was built over and around the sacred Black Stone which, along with the cube, still sits in Mecca today. Personally, I think the Black Stone is a meteorite that someone saw come down and kept, but no one really knows. As the Black Stone is still considered very holy to the Muslims, calling it a meteorite is likely a major step toward offending the faith. (I'm now wondering if I'll make enough off this book to split security costs with Rushdie. Probably not.)

Anyway, there was this big black rock in a cube with lots of other smaller rocks and trinkets from every god. Once a year all the tribes-who spent a whole lot of their time in bloodthirsty wars-called a truce for a month and went on a pilgrimage to Mecca to honour their chosen deity. Mohammed and his folks didn't have to travel far, as they lived in Mecca.

Okay, you know Allat, the moon goddess. And you know Al-Uzza, goddess of luck. So where does Allah come in? Well, Allat was one of the top gods in pre-Islamic Mecca. Al-Uzza was right up there too, but Allat was basically #2 in Kabah popularity. In fact, she was so well known that very few people ever bothered with the most powerful god in this region, whose name (you guessed it) was Allah.

Allah was mysterious to the polytheists. He was rarely heard from and seldom (if ever) worshipped. Even though he was the # 1 god in the region, he was so elusive and distant from the people that no one had ever bothered to carve him a place in the Kabah. He just "was." People figured he was above everything and everyone, so they never bothered with him. Allah (to the polytheists) was a "god's God"— something humans could never really figure out.

Until Mohammed.

Mohammed

Rather than getting people pissed at me by describing what Mohammed looked like, I'm going to let the Hadith explain it. Here's what it says about his appearance:

"Muhammad was of a height a little above the average.

He was of sturdy build with long muscular limbs and tapering fingers.

The hair of his head was long and thick with some waves in them.

His forehead was large and prominent, his eyelashes were long and thick, his nose was sloping, his mouth was somewhat large and his teeth were well set.

His cheeks were spare and he had a pleasant smile.

His eyes were large and black with a touch of brown.

His beard was thick and at the time of his death, he had seventeen gray hairs in it. He had a thin line of fine hair over his neck and chest.

His gait was firm and he walked so fast that others found it difficult to keep pace with him.

His face was genial but at times, when he was deep in thought, there were long periods of silence, yet he always kept himself busy with something.

He did not speak unnecessarily and what he said was always to the point and without any padding. At times he would make his meaning clear by slowly repeating what he had said. His laugh was mostly a smile. He kept his feelings under firm control - when annoyed, he would turn aside or keep silent, when pleased he would lower his eyes."
~Shamail Tirmizi.

This description is given by Tirmizi, one of the Muslim Caliphs in the fourth century. It's said that this guy had a photographic memory, and as such his accounts of Mohammed are considered flawless. People believe a lot when they need to. Regardless, sooner or later I am going to get shot but-- the meantime-- let's take a look at the 'historical' account of Mohammed's life...

It should come as no surprise that Mohammed made his living tending camels. Mecca was an oasis, after all. He was employed by a rich widow named Khadija. (Don't ask me how to pronounce that.) She was fifteen years older than Mohammed, but all the same, they must have gotten along fairly well. So well, in fact, that when Mohammed was 25 and she was 40 he married her. The couple had six children and did a pretty good business in the camel trade. This was Mohammed's life in the years before prophet hood. Kinda dull, but he and family managed to eke out a comfortable enough living to be content.

The only portent of Mohammed's destiny seems to have been a guy named Zayd.[66] No one really knows who this guy was or where he came from, but we do know that he had an influence on Mohammed. You see, Zayd was a monotheist-a rare thing in Meccan society. We don't know all the details, but we do know that Zayd chastised Mohammed for idolatry and polytheism long before the religion of Islam came about. Muslims see this as foreshadowing the divine intervention that was to come. I tend to look at it more as laying the foundations for the religion Mohammed would invent a decade later. Of course, they're Muslims and I'm a Heathen, so these small differences of opinion are apt to arise.

MOHAMMED'S CALL

Man proposes, but God disposes. ~Thomas A. Kempis

Mohammed had become something of a religious oddity before his call to prophethood. He had taken to practicing an ascetic lifestyle. Not wholeheartedly, mind you. I mean, he still had the kids and the camels and the wife and everything. But it seems the whole Al-Uzza thing just wasn't doing it for him. Instead of sacrificing at the Kabah as he was supposed to do, he'd go off and meditate alone in some quite place, trying to find some ultimate Answers. He wasn't having a lot of luck. This is how it was that Mohammed happened to be sitting in a cave on a mountain one day when his whole world did a one-eighty and he suddenly found himself up to his eyeballs in ultimate answers.

Okay, so there's Mohammed sitting on a mountain, thinking things over: He'd probably done this a few hundred times before with no real result. He's probably a little bored or depressed. Like a lot of people today, he's feeling like he's not getting anywhere with this whole spiritual search thing. The sun goes down and he's alone up there, pitch-dark except for the stars and the moon. He's deep in thought when he gets to feeling like something's wrong. He's not sure what, but something just suddenly doesn't seem to feel right. He casually looks up, trying to figure out what it is. Not having sunglasses back then, he puts his open palm above his eyes to block the sun so he can look out over the plain and maybe figure out what's wrong. Right about then it hits him: it's night time. There shouldn't be sun.

He drops his hand and looks up. Good news and bad. The good news was that the sun was in fact set and had not mysteriously risen in the middle of the night. The bad news was that the "sun" was actually a giant being of light hovering over him with a silk scroll in its hand. (For Muslims this is good news, I know. But I highly suspect that Mohammed did not see it as such at the time. Personally, I'd have been scared shitless.)

To make matters worse, the being (whom you find out later was the archangel Gabriel) holds out the scroll and says:

"Read"

There's nothing scarier than being half-asleep on a mountain and having an archangel show up out of nowhere with a silk scroll commanding you to read. Unless, of course, it's being half asleep on a mountain and having an archangel show up out of nowhere commanding you to read when you're illiterate-which, as luck would have it, was what Mohammed was.

"I can't read," says Mohammed.

"READ!!" the angel says again, getting agitated. (Note: According to most biblical scholars, it's generally considered a bad idea to piss of an archangel. I'm quite sure Mohammed was no biblical scholar, but I am also sure that at this point he had a firm grasp of this theological postulate.)

"I cannot," Mohammed says, probably wondering what his chances were of getting out of this alive.

"Read," Gabriel says again.

"What can I read?" Mohammed said.

"Read in the name of the Lord who created," Gabriel says, "Created Man from a clot of blood. Read: and the Lord the most beautiful/ who teaches by pen will teach man that which he knew not!"

Mohammed read the scroll.[67]

AFTERMATH

Our deeds determine us, as much as we determine our deeds. ~George Eliot

Personally, I think Mohammed really believed that something happened on that mountain. Not because of the Islamic argument that Mohammed "suddenly" became literate. This point doesn't hold for me because he lived in a major trading city-he could have learned to read anytime and just not told folks. No. The only reason I think something actually happened on that mountain was because of what Mohammed DIDN'T do. He didn't run down the mountain like Moses and say, "Hey, I've got a message from God here. Listen up." Mohammed did exactly what any decent healthy human being who thinks he'd spent the night on a mountain with the archangel Gabriel would have done. He flipped.[68]

Whether or not anything really happened is irrelevant. Personally, I think Mohammed believed something happened and that's the important part of all this. Unlike a lot of other prophets, Mohammed was acting out of a real belief in something, not just your average politics, greed, and avarice you usually get from divine messengers. His religious fervour was genuine. And that, as history shows, is always a dangerous thing.

When Mohammed finally got back home it took a long while for his wife to settle him down. Sure, he had wanted a few answers, but this whole messenger idea was way too much for him to handle. (This whole story is found in The Hadith-a collection of stories about the life of Mohammed. It's an important part of all branches of Islam, as it's where the stories of Mohammed's campaigns or his reactions to things like Gabriel showing up are found. So, basically, the Quran is supposedly the words of God, and the Hadith are supposedly the words of Mohammed.)

Anyway, the Hadiths tells how Mohammed's wife "tested the Spirit" that was in him. Basically what happened is that Mohammed became what you'd call a "trans-channeler." He'd have some form of "change" or trance wherein he'd speak the words of Allah. While in trance state, Mohammed could recite the words of the silk scroll (something he could not do out of trance state).

The contents off this scroll (as relayed through the entranced Mohammed) are what we call the Koran, or "The Reading" (meaning the reading of the silk scroll). When he wasn't in trance, Mohammed made no claim to godhood or divine knowledge. He was just an ordinary guy who (he said) was picked for no real or apparent reason to be the vessel of Allah's message. If the scriptures can be believed then Mohammed hadn't chosen and didn't want the job of prophet. This is why I think Mohammed actually believed what he was saying— because he supposedly didn't want it to happen.

The Faith

A hopeful disposition is not the sole qualification to be a prophet.

~Winston Churchill

Mohammed gets over the initial shock of his encounter and gathers his wits. Then thinking it all over he began to wonder if he's just gone mad. (Write your own joke for that line. I'm trying not to get killed here.) For a brief time, things around home go back to normal. Camel sales, kids, home life. That sort of thing. Mohammed is just getting to feeling like it was all a bad dream when (you guessed it) Gabriel shows up again. And again. And again. (That's the thing about disobeying a divine edict. Angels don't give up.)

Like Jonah from the Old Testament, Mohammed was basically stalked night and day. But, compared to Jonah, who was eventually swallowed by a fish and puked up three days later, Mohammed got off easy. Gabriel merely harassed him. He kicked him, prodded him, and goaded him. It took a while, but finally the persistence of Gabriel overshadowed any fears Mohammed had of the people to whom he was supposed to preach. Mohammed gave in, and started telling people what had been happening to him. Coincidentally, his capitulation occurred during Ramadan, when Mohammed's audience would be the largest of the year.

Since the Kabah was the center of religious worship, he decided to start there. He wandered downtown to where all the tribes were assembled to honour their gods and started explaining all that Gabriel had told him. The crowds listened carefully as Mohammed recounted his tale from start to finish. When he concluded, a brief silence fell over the crowd-followed almost immediately by laughter. They all pointed and laughed and carried on. His own tribe disowned him, embarrassed that he would make such a fool out of himself in public.

This was no Sermon on the Mount. More like Mount St. Helen's. With the exception of a very few who was converted (law of averages given any large crowd), the whole city turned on him.

It was kind of like what happened to the Christians in Rome. These guys were polytheistic. What Mohammed taught was monotheistic. As the people of Mecca (like Rome three hundred years earlier) were not about to abandon the gods they'd worshipped all their lives, it seemed a whole lot easier to "abandon" Mohammed. They did so in the traditional, time-honoured Bedouin ritual of abandonment: sharp knives and clubs.

MECCA TO TAIF

Ever let your fancy roam; pleasure never is at home.

~John Keats

Mohammed persisted in his efforts, but ultimately failed to convert Mecca. The polytheists accused Mohammed of being allied with the Christians or the Jews. They also accused him of being possessed by demons. He'd been at this for four years before Mecca finally got to him. His wife had died. His tribe basically hated him. It was getting seriously dangerous for him to walk through back alleys alone. He had managed to convert about three dozen people, but this was hardly enough to make it worth his while. Things were just too dangerous and unyielding in Mecca. Mohammed packed up his life there and left for Taif, where he found some welcome apathy from the people (as opposed to open animosity), but little in the way of converts. It all settled into a routine of teaching a small group of faithful listeners amid a city that didn't really care one way or the other.

In order to understand what happened next, you have to understand a bit more about Mohammed's character and theology. You've probably gathered that what he taught was monotheism. But there was a bit more to it than that. Mohammed maintained through the inspired words of "The Reading" that Allah was the only true God. All the other "gods" were basically seen as either nonexistent fantasies or (as in the Christian view at that time) lesser beings that should not be worshipped. The only being that was deserving of worship was Allah.

Although Mohammed utterly rejected the idea that there were any other gods, he paradoxically maintained a unique version of inclusiveness in his theology where the Jews thought they were the "Chosen People," and the Christians maintained that you were only saved through the Holy Roman Catholic Church. Mohammed didn't feel he had exclusive knowledge of Allah/Yahweh/El-Shaddai. Rather, Mohammed taught that God had been trying to get through to people all over the world in many different ways and, more often than not, he was being ignored or misinterpreted. God was working for a united people, not sects of different adherents who all heard him but believed his grace to be unique to their culture. For Mohammed there was only one the God, who wanted to get rid of all the dissension so that everyone could live peacefully under His law. Therefore, if you worshipped another god and could somehow prove (using a Holy Book) that your god was actually God by a different name, and then you were fine. To Mohammed, his visions were just the next step in the evolution of the interaction between humanity and God.

As a good Heathen, I should point out here that this whole thing seems a lot more like devolution than evolution. This "interaction" between God and humanity came at a huge price: absolute obedience. The happy polytheists were being asked to surrender their gods of fertility, sex, debauchery and just plain fun for a single God whose idea of a happy human life was to spend most of it honoring and worshipping Him. This precept is what gave rise to the name of the faith: the word Islam means "submission," specifically submission to the Law of God as outlined in holy books around the world-not just within Islam, but in all the religions that had been founded by the interactions of "the one true God" with humans. The other thing you have to understand is Mohammed himself. From all accounts, he started out as an average type of guy. But when he went public, he did so with fervour. People talked about the "fire" that was in his eyes when he spoke.

Whatever you think of his message, you have to acknowledge that he was one hell of an orator. The guy was described in The Hadith as having an unearthly charisma when he spoke. Whether they agreed with him or not, people seemed to recognize that he had a very real personal power and authority that made people listen. This may be why He was such a threat to the polytheists in Mecca. Of course, this may also just be folklore, written long after Mohammed died. After all, the Meccans that saw him as a threat did manage to run him out of town. Granted, the guy got his revenge, but that's still a couple sub-chapters away. At this point they had managed to get rid of him, which I figure kind of brings the whole charisma thing under some scrutiny.

Anyway, Medina...

MEDINA, 622 AD

Muslims date the beginning of the Islamic era from this date---622 AD. It's called the Hijrah. As with the Hebrew tradition, it's just a word in another language that sounds intimidating because it's not translated. It simply means "The Migration" and refers to Mohammed's relocation from Taif to Medina-from relative obscurity to full-scale prophet and leader of the people. If you're ever idly wondering when this whole Islam thing got started, this is the date to keep in mind. You'll sound really informed and intellectual if can spout it out offhand at parties. "622? Why, that was the year Mohammed took over Medina, wasn't it?" It works. Trust me on this one.

Mohammed didn't just casually wander into Medina and take over, by the way. He was invited. It seems the city was pretty corrupt and falling apart at the time. The local government was ineffectual at best; lining their own pockets and letting everything go to hell. By 622, even the politicians had given up on the idea of order, since no one was listening to them anyway Medina needed a leader, someone to galvanize the city and make it strong again. It had all the people and resources you could need. What it didn't have was someone they could respect to lead them. Rumors of Mohammed had reached Medina. The people there had heard how powerful a speaker he was, and a group of them recognized that he had just the kind of charisma they needed in a leader. What literally happened was that a bunch of these guys from Medina showed up in Taif where Mohammed was teaching, and said, "Hi! Want a city?" Of course, this is a rough translation from the ancient Arabic, but you get the idea. Mohammed accepted and moved to Medina.

THEOCRACY

Thus far, most of what Mohammed had been credited with had been through divine inspiration and trance. Here, in Medina, he showed what he was made of. He walked into a city that was falling apart and in less than a year had entirely restructured it and made it a force to be reckoned with. The polytheists and Jews that lived in Medina took offence to what Mohammed was doing, but most of these groups just didn't exist after a while. Funnily enough, they either converted to Islam or "left" within a year. A combination of charisma and an iron fist brought the entire city into line for Mohammed and by 623 AD Medina was the first Islamic theocracy, entirely run by the laws Allah had outlined in the Koran ("the Reading of the Silk Scroll'). In the West, Islam is known as a faith you don't want to mess with. There is historical fact to back this up, and it begins here. Islamic theocracy is stringent in its adherence to the Law— not out of cruelty, but because it's what they believe God has ordered. Muslims live by the same code of ethics set down in Leviticus, but, unlike many Christian and Jewish sects, they really live by it. Read Leviticus sometime and you'll see how many things there are that call for the death penalty. The God of Islam was no more or less demanding than the God of Abraham or Josh. The difference was that the Muslims abided by (and still abide by) these principles very closely. They haven't softened the message of the scriptures with interpretive doctrines that allow humanity to exercise forgiveness on God's behalf. Where the Bible or the Koran says a person should die, they kill them. The thing is, if you're living a good Christian or Jewish life, you should have no fear of Islam. Heathens, on the other hand, are just supposed to be killed. I don't travel much in the Middle East.

PEOPLE OF THE BOOK

> *"The Jews, in spite of their hostility to the Prophet, were so impressed by his impartiality and sense of justice that they used to bring their cases to him, and he decided them according to Jewish law."* ~ Abu Dawud, Sunan Dawud

Islam does not demand that every Jew and Christian agree with them and become Islamic. Muslims usually do, but Islam does not. That's a misconception of the West. The whole problem between the Jews and the Muslims in the news today is political, not theological (at least from the 'Islamic standpoint). As mentioned above, Islam recognizes what they call "people of the book."

What this basically means is that Yahweh/Allah has been busy worldwide and they aren't about to kill people just because they have abided by a prophet that came before Mohammed. Christians and Jews are seen as people who have listened to and followed Allah's teachings, but just haven't gotten the whole story. These aren't people who deserve death. They should be taught, not punished. If they don't listen and they reject the Prophet, then they're considered kind of dense, but not evil. As long as they worship *"the one true God,"* they're basically considered to be on the right path, if a little astray. They are still protected by Allah, since they are worshipping him under a different name.

The devotees of Judaism and Christianity (and any other religion that has a "book" that reveals a monotheistic theme) are considered to be like children-lesser informed groups that are to be taught and led by Islam to the fullness of the scriptures as contained in the Qur'an. I know. It just doesn't fit with every conception you have of Islam, does it? We'll get to that. For now, understand that this is the doctrine of the faith. Like all other doctrines of Islam, the adherents abide by it. In a theocratic Muslim state, there is a legal and ethical tolerance, even an acceptance of, Judaism and Christianity. Anti-Semitism is not only Islamic, it's illegal. Okay... back to Medina...

THE TAKING OF MECCA

All great civilizations are based on success in war. ~Kenneth Clark

Okay, Mohammed is the head of Medina. He rallies the city to produce a crack military, and is set at the helm of a new faith called Islam. So what does he do? Well, he was raised in Mecca. From the time he had received his vision, he had always wanted to see the false gods of the Kabah rejected and "the one true God," Allah worshipped there. To this end, he went to war with Mecca. That in and of itself was radical, but like every other military activity Mohammed undertook, this move had the mark of the military genius he would show throughout his career. He started off by attacking caravans travelling past Medina on their way to Mecca. For the most part, these were relatively small incidents-a bit of looting, a few guards killed, nothing monstrous. The notable thing here was the timing: he attacked during the annual truce, when all the good polytheistic tribes set aside their differences and went to Mecca to honour their gods. Mohammed, being a monotheist, figured that this was apt, since these guys were calling a peace on behalf of false gods. The thing about it was that the tribes couldn't fight back and Mohammed knew it. This REALLY pissed off the Meccans, who set to planning a counterattack as soon as the month was over. There were three major battles between Mecca and Medina.

According to the text, in each battle Mohammed was well outnumbered and should have lost. However, each time he had a new and exciting surprise waiting for the Meccans. In one battle, he had his men dig a huge trench at the base of a sand dune. In the bottom of the trench he put sharpened stakes about eight feet long. The Medians backed up twenty paces from the ditch and waited. When the Meccans mounted their attack, the Medians just of stood there, watching the superior army barrel down on them. When it got close enough, Mohammed told his men to taunt the Meccans and get them really pissed off, so they'd ride all the faster into a battle they were sure they'd win. The Meccans didn't see the abrupt drop of the ditch until it was too late. They flew right over the edge, impaling themselves on the stakes beneath. Mohammed's men merely edged up to the side of the ditch and finished off those that had survived the fall and the stakes. In another incident (the battle of Uhad), Mohammed was again well outnumbered.

This time, the Muslims lost and Mohammed was injured in the mouth. The Meccans, knowing they'd won the battle and seriously injured the prophet, headed home feeling victorious. Mohammed was not about to let this happen. In spite of his injuries and the obvious fact that he'd lost the battle, Mohammed himself mounted a horse and followed the Meccan army all the way back home, chastising them for their idolatrous ways. There was no further fighting that day, but Mohammed managed to take the wind out of their sails anyway. I mean, picture this. You've just defeated these guys in battle. You're covered in blood and tired at the end of a long, hard day, and you look behind you and see the head of your enemy's army riding up on horseback, screaming and yelling at you about your religion. Nobody bothered to draw a sword or go after him. They all just kind of rode on, thinking; "This guy's either really holy or really wacko. Either way, he's got guts."

Just before the final battle for Mecca, a group of Median Jews, figuring Mohammed was going to lose anyway, had secretly made plans to turn against Mohammed and side with his enemies. If it had worked, it would have divided Mohammed's army at the height of battle, opening his ranks to Meccan offence. It never happened.

Mohammed caught wind of the plan and instead of letting on that he knew about it, he spread rumors through Medina that the Meccans were going to betray the Jews. Inversely, he had spies spread rumors through Mecca that the Jews were going to betray the Meccans.

By the time the battle happened, Mohammed had everybody so damn confused they didn't know what to do. Mohammed won the battle. As a special thank-you to the Jews for their disloyalty, he had the men beheaded and the women and children sold into slavery. Thus began the perpetual mistrust between Jew and Muslim.

The Death of Mohammed

> *A man's dying is more the survivor's affair than his own.*
>
> *~Thomas Mann,*

Okay we jump ahead a few years here. Islam has secured the area that is now Saudi Arabia and has begun conquering the Middle East and much of the Mediterranean with about the same success rate they had against Mecca. Mohammed personally led the Muslims in a total of 27 campaigns and countless battles, so that by the tenth year of the Hijrah (the calendar of Islam), Mohammed became the effective emperor of much of the lands that were the Roman Empire a century earlier. His turf eventually became known as the Ottoman Empire, and lasted from 1299

to 29 October 1923 under Islamic rule. It was a pretty good run, as empires go.

It was in the year 642 AD that Mohammed went on his final pilgrimage, called his "Farewell Pilgrimage." Go figure. While on Mount Arafat near Mecca, he preached to thousands of the devout. He ended the sermon by turning to the crowd and saying, "Have I not conveyed the message?" (Meaning "*The Reading*.") The whole assembly answered, "Oh, Allah! Yes!" Then Mohammed said, "Oh, Allah...be Witness!"[69] (This last comment was actually supposed to be directed at Allah, basically saying, "See, I did what you wanted. I told them.") Mohammed went on to reveal to the crowds that he was dying, and that this was his last pilgrimage. He returned to Mecca after that, where he grew progressively worse. Tensions among the devout grew high, worried as they were about the faith and the messenger of it. [70]

On the day he died, Mohammed came out of his house for morning prayers. Since he was still too weak to lead the prayer, Abu-Bakr (a long-time ally and devout Muslim) had been leading. People saw Mohammed and thought he was getting better. The truth was that he was basically just saying goodbye. Later that same day, the rumour went around that the Prophet had died, and people were getting panicky. Umar, Mohammed's right hand man, threatened to kill anyone who repeated the rumour, saying that the Prophet could not die. He was screaming at the people to stop the rumour when Abu-Bakr came into the mosque (temple) and heard him. Bakr immediately left and went to the Prophet's home where Mohammed's wife, Ayeshah, had placed Mohammed in her own bed. There Abu saw that Mohammed was indeed dead. He kissed Mohammed's forehead and went back to the mosque, where Umar was still ranting about how the Prophet of Islam could not die. Abu tried to be subtle and alert Umar with a whisper, but it didn't work. Umar kept shouting. Finally Abu-Bakr out-shouted Umar and the whole building went silent. Abu then said simply:

People! For those who used to worship Mohammed, Mohammed is dead. But as for he who worships Allah, Allah is alive and does not die!

Before anyone could react, Abu raised his hands for continued silence, then read the following passage from the Quran:

Mohammed is but a messenger; a messenger the like of which have passed away before him. Will it be that, when he dies or is slain, you will turn back on your heels? He that turns back does no harm to Allah, and Allah will reward the thankful. [71]

So ended the life of Mohammed.

Politics is the art of preventing people from
taking part in affairs which properly concern them.

~Paul Valery

When Mohammed died, the people needed a new leader. It's amazing how many sects have been invented from exactly this scenario. The thing is, Islam was getting rich fast. Now, when I say rich, I mean filthy rich. These guys had managed to take over huge metropolitan cities like Constantinople, Cairo, and Damascus- places where art and literature had been at their apex. With these cities, Islam inherited some of the most valuable items in existence. Grecian artefacts. Roman friezes. All the gold and silver and gems that had been the wealth of Rome were now quickly acquired by these desert Bedouins on their campaigns through the Mediterranean. Confronted with the majesty of these cities, these rural folks did the only thing they could think to do. They looted it all.

What you wind up with in the years immediately after Mohammed is an army wherein even the lowliest foot soldier is dragging along sacks of treasure that would make his family financially independent for generations. We're talking about an amazing amount of cash and jewels here, all of it falling into the hands of these marauding Islamic warriors. The thing was, what do you do with it all? With Mohammed dead and his followers becoming the wealthiest men alive, there was a real possibility that it would all go to their heads. After all, Islam was supposed to be a faith built on the ideas of humble servitude to Yahweh/Allah. There had to be a cohesive factor in all this or it was bound to fall apart quick.

The "cohesive factor" came in the form of the caliphs. Think of them as Islamic popes-the unquestioned leaders of the faith. The caliphs were not appointed by God or elected by an elite like their Roman counterparts. They were elected by plebiscite. Every Muslim was called upon to cast a vote for who they thought should lead them. The first to win this election process was a guy named Omar. He reigned with no real trouble until he was killed in his own palace by a Christian slave who escaped and knifed him. Uthman, the son-in-law of Mohammed, replaced Omar. Uthman began to structure Islamic society, creating a hierarchy of lieutenants that would be overseers in the regions where he couldn't maintain control personally. The problem was that he appointed these posts to relatives and friends, not to the people in the areas they were supposed to govern. This caused a lot of resentment in Mecca in particular, where a lot of the people who were with Mohammed from the beginning were passed over for appointments. This eventually led to Uthman's assassination by his own people.

I don't need to go through the whole list of the caliphs. What I do need to do is jump ahead to the last caliph. Who that may be depends entirely on who you're talking to, which I suppose gives you a clue as to how the line of caliphs came to an end.

POLITICS AS USUAL

I figure I could give you a whole lot of Arabic names here or I could just give you the *Reader's Digest* version. Take a wild guess which way I'm gonna go with this.

Okay, here's the story. The caliphs did okay until the Umayyad Dynasty, circa[72] 720 AD. Then the problems start. Naturally, the big dividing question had to do with who got to be the leader of the faith. Since Islam had grown really big over the years, a true plebiscite had become impossible. There were too many people that lived in too many places. No phones, no Internet, and no way for the full body of Islam (the Umma) to cast their vote. Still, they needed a leader, so something had to be done. It all came down to two ideals.

The first was the approach was the orthodoxies. They believed that a caliph can only be elected by the whole of the community and if that couldn't happen, then they'd have to get by without a caliph until they found ways to have everybody vote.

The second approach came from the guys in power (go figure). Their idea was that the leadership should pass through the lineage of Mohammed. Coincidentally the last elected caliph was a descendant of Mohammed. Amazingly enough, this side was supported mainly by a guy named Hussein who just happened to be the younger son of the last caliph. Hussein (no...not Saddam) was a descendent of Mohammed and claimed the leadership of Islam, declaring himself caliph. For about a week.

You see, the vast majority of Muslims didn't take to the idea of anyone arbitrarily setting themselves up as caliph. In a predictable move, the orthodoxy got together and removed Hussein from his position as head of the faith. They left the rest of him, mind you. They just took the head. It was mounted on a stick and taken back to Damascus, where it was paraded around the street as a warning to anyone else who'd try to do the same thing. This led to the first split in the faith of Islam. The traditional Muslims carried on pretty much the same way they had since the last caliph died. These guys became known as Sunni Muslims. About 70 per cent of the Muslims worldwide are Sunni. These guys are basically cool and don't believe in blowing things up or attacking large trade centers with big planes.

There's very little difference between Sunni eschatology (i.e. end-of-the-world stories) and Christian eschatology, except that it includes the character of Mohammed and the ideas of obedience outlined in "the Reading of the Silk Scroll" (otherwise known as the Quran). While they believe that Islam carries a superior message to that of Judaism and Christianity, they also abide by the laws regarding the *People of the Book* and basically look on the Jews and Christians as undereducated followers of "the one true God" Allah/Yahweh. They coexistence with the secular world and, since they are unable to elect a caliph and establish a rightful leader, they believe they should listen to their local assembly, follow the five pillars of Islam, and live under the law of the land until a rightful leader can be elected. If they're living under a regime led by a total asshole they are permitted to oust/kill him, but that's just common sense, not religious fervour. For the real religious fervour you gotta look to guys like Bin Laden, but we'll get to that in a bit.

Shi'I

God is not dead. He just smells funny. ~Frank Zappa

The name Shi'I means *"Party of Ali"* (named after Ali, Hussein's father and the last guy that both the Sunni and Shi'I agreed was supposed to lead them.). Unfortunately for the rest of this chapter, the "Party of Ali" isn't the drunken keg-type party we'd all have liked it to be. It was a religious party. The term itself is an oxymoron.

To the Shi'I, Hussein (the guy that lost his head) was a martyr. They have a day of mourning to commemorate his murder every year. It's nowhere near as interesting as commemorating some guy's head on a stick could be with a little creative planning, but they do it anyway.

After Hussein was killed, the Shi'I immediately replaced him and the movement grew. There were a total of 11 of these descendants of Mohammed to officially reign over Shi'I, ending with a guy named Mohammed al-Mahdi whom they refer to as the last "divinely guided" caliph. According to the folklore, Mohammed al-Mahdi was taken bodily away to heaven, where he is supposed to stay until he decides to return to Earth and bring about an age of bounty and prosperity. This isn't officially the "end of the world," just an era of plenty. Anyway, the Shi'I are kind of waiting for Mohammed al-Mahdi to return, being as how he is a direct descendant of Mohammed the Prophet and he's supposed to bring about a new age for Shi'I. They're also waiting for the End like all other religions, but as al-Mahdi is supposed to show up first they're waiting on him.

The Shi'I maintain that Abu-Bakr was a jerk and that everyone who had anything to do with leading the faith when it wasn't in the hands of the descendants of Mohammed were corrupt idiots to whom Muslims should never have listened. They also believe that the true interpretation of the Quran was never given to these guys, but was instead passed down through Mohammed's family. As a result, the Shi'I believe they are in possession of knowledge that the Sunni lack and are therefore the true faith of Islam. Sunnis of course differ, but really don't care what the Shi'I believe. There's dissension between the sects, but not outright war. With the notable exception of Iran (Shi'I) and Iraq (Sunni), the two sects coexist (the fact that Sunni outnumber Shi'I ten-to-one might have something to do with this).

All Muslims believe in the Creed of Islam; the "No god but God" bit that we talked about earlier. That's what makes them Muslims. They also all agree that Mohammed was the true leader of the faith as ordained by Allah and one shit-kicking angel named Gabe. The problem was that they all also agreed that Mohammed was dead and, as this seemed to detract from his ability to lead the people, arguments soon erupted.

Now, we have the basic idea of the Sunni... the guys that

were in the majority. They believed that Mohammed had nominated a political successor who could lead things (the Caliphs). Most importantly, these guys figured that the Quran and the Hadith were all they needed to guide them. They just abided by what the books said and left it to the judges and courts to fulfill the will of Allah. As for leadership, they do what they can to live under Islamic law, but it's not essential for them to have a "divine" leader. The spiritual-moral authority was to be exercised by the *ulama*, a group of specialists in matters of religious law, collectively called the *shariah*. It was their job was to make up all the laws and rules of conduct based on what the Quran or the Hadith said about life.

The Shi'l took issue with this whole idea. Their beef was that the guys doing the interpretation didn't have the whole story. They believed that the depth and meaning and all that there religious stuff Mohammed talked about was somehow too precious for mere mortals to glean themselves. Since there weren't supposed to be any more prophets coming before the end of the world, the Shi'l looked to the next best thing: a relative of a prophet. Since the Shi'l believed that the leadership of the faith should never have gone to anybody except a blood relative of the prophet it should come as no surprise that this idea was strongly supported by Mohammed's relatives.

The guy the Shi'ls thought should be in charge back then was Ali, Mohammed's cousin and husband of Mohammed's daughter, Fatima.[73] The Shi'l maintain that after Mohammed gave his farewell speech outside of Mecca he appointed Ali to lead the people. The Sunni say this never happened, but didn't care a hell of a lot. The Sunni like this Ali guy and believe he was the last of the four "rightly-guided" caliphs, but don't buy into the whole family tree concept of leadership. Ali, they figure, was leading the people because he was an ok guy, not because he was a relative of Mohammed.

All Shi'l leaders are all supposedly descendants of Fatima and Ali, who are in turn descendants of Mohammed. As there are a hell of a lot of people in the world who claim to be descendants of Mohammed the prophet there tend to be a lot of candidates for leadership around these days, which makes the whole issue of leadership about as clear as a butterfly ballot in Florida.

IMAM

"Teachers teach more by what they are than by what they say."

— Anonymous.

Ok, here we get to the topic of Imams. It's one of those words that's guaranteed to get confusing, and you're gonna need a basic gist of it if you don't want to wind up staring blankly at Muslims when they talk to you. The word *Imam* means 'leader' or 'pattern'[74]. Making lots of sense already, huh?

Usually when you hear the word today it refers to anyone who's leading a prayer in a mosque. That kind of imam (usually spelled with a small 'i') is a layman that doesn't need to have any formal training or special lineage or anything. He's just the guy the community picked to lead the prayers. Probably the guy with the clearest voice. Then there's the Sunni idea of an Imam with a capital I. They use to the term to refer to the line of Caliphs we were just talking about. The word Caliph and Imam are interchangeable to Sun

nis. They also use the term in the same way military guys use the term "Sir". It's a sign of respect. When Sunnis refer to lawmakers, teachers, and theologians they use the word imam.

Now, there's also the Shi'I definition of the word. The Shi'I use Imam to refer to the original Caliphs that the Sunnis liked, the Caliphs they added but the Sunni don't agree with, and the missing Caliph that got dragged off to heaven. All these Caliphs are called Imams.

If you can't keep all this straight, just do what I do. Every time someone says the word *imam*, assume they're talking about the guy that calls out the prayers. You'll be right about 75% of the time. When you're not, the Muslim you're talking to will say something like "NO… I mean Imam So-And-So!!!". If this happens you'll know they're talking about some important Muslim holy guy, and you should just run screaming.

THE GOLDEN AGE OF ISLAM

About a hundred and fifty years after Mohammed died, the Islamic movement became known as the Islamic Empire, mainly because they got really, really big. At the time they controlled land from Syria to southern China, well into India, south through to what had been the Persian Empire and Saudi Arabia, through Egypt and across North Africa, and up into Spain to the Pyrenees. For the geographically challenged out there, this is what cartographers refer to in technical terms as "a really big chunk of land."

This is the era where they invented Baghdad. Having all this money and power and stuff, the ruling Caliph basically just looked at an empty stretch of land and said "What the hell... let's build a huge city there. We've got nothing better to do and I want a big gold city, dammit." So, they built him one. Baghdad became one of the most prosperous cities in the world. For 400 years, from the mid-9th century until 1256, Baghdad was the center of art, literature, science, and all things intellectual. No more war, no more bullshit about killing anyone who wasn't Islamic. During this era Islam flourished and grew as both a nation and a religion, reaching levels of technology and social change that many places are still catching up to. The telescope, microscope, paper, our number system (1,2,3,4,5...) and a thousand other things were all invented and refined in Baghdad in this era. For those who think the Islam never did anything truly great, it should be noted that it was in Baghdad in this era that alcohol was first distilled and the process for making hard liquor was created. This was a time when Islam was truly at its peak; a time when it was a faith of love and prosperity and kindness. So, of course, they were all slaughtered mercilessly.

In 1256 the Mongols wandered by, noticed all this wealth and prosperity, and sacked the place. The entire culture went down the tubes, and all the art, literature, and prosperity was replaced by a lot of really pissed off Muslims.

The faith that stand on authority is not faith ~Ralph Waldo Emerson

It was during this 'Golden Era' that a lot of the intellectual arguments happened in Islam. It was also at this time that a lot of the small sects of the faith started up. Coincidence? I think not.

As seems to happen every time you have more than one divinely led leader with secret knowledge from God they eventually got to disagreeing with each other. You'd figure that God, being the omniscient kinda guy he is, might make some allowances for human stupidity. No such luck.

Shi'I, like all other stoic, unified faiths quickly degenerated into a bunch of sects. Unlike the Protestants, though, these guys never really call themselves a new "religion" like the Baptists or the Pentecostals. They just consider themselves new "schools" within the Shi'I sect. This is why the religion tends to be seen as far more unified them Christianity. These "schools" are a lot like the Protestant side of Christianity with a whole bunch of different groups that all fall under the same name. (i.e.: Baptists, Lutherans, Anglicans, and Calvinists are all Protestant churches even though they're quite different. The same is true within Shi'I.) Here's how this whole spilt thing went down…

Ali, the main guy when Mohammed died, was supposedly vested with the power of *ta'wil* (inner teaching, or wisdom derived from closeness with Allah[75]) and is recognized by all the Shi'I as being the first *Imam*. All subsequent Imams have to be of the progeny of Ali and are appointed by the dying Imam before he shuffles off the mortal coil. This, of course, is a recipe for disaster.

In all of history this process only really worked five times. After that it all seems to go to hell in a hand basket starting with the Sixth Imam (or the fifth, depending on who you're talking to, which kind of explains how far afield all this goes). Anyway, Jaffer-as-Saddiq is the Imam in charge when it all gets screwed up. It seems that there was some confusion as to which son he had named to be the next Imam (yeah, like you wouldn't see that one coming). You see, the son who had the most favour in the eyes of the Muslims was Isma'il, the eldest. Many maintained that Isma'il was the guy named to be the new leader. This assertion was seen by some as rather hurtful by Isma'il's younger siblings who honestly felt that they had better qualifications for the job as leader of the faith. They, for instance, were still alive. You see, Isma'il had somehow managed to take that great dirt nap sometime before his father did, which some folks saw as a detriment to his ability to lead.

As these tales tend to go, it seems that not everybody thought that rigamortis was an impediment to true leadership. Surprisingly enough, there was actually a fairly large contingent of devotees who decided that this whole death thing was overrated and that Isma'il was, indeed, the true leader of the faith. As Isma'il himself never really offered an opinion on the subject (being dead and all) these folks went right ahead and made him leader.

As it turns out Isma'il was a tad lax in his duties, so his brother Musa assumed the responsibilities of being Imam. Thus began the first major division in Shi'I, as Musa's line became known as 'the Twelvers' (ending in a 12th Imam who died with no kids to pass the title to). These guys went on to become the most orthodox branch of Shi'I who believe that Isma'il was supposed to lead them way back when.

THE KHARIJITES

Fanaticism consists of redoubling your efforts when
you have forgotten your aim. ~George Santayna

I know I know... any time I start doing the "*Kh*" thing at the beginning of a name I might as well put the word BORING in big bold letters. If it's any comfort to you, this is the beginning of all the nutbar Taliban crap so you probably want to read this...

Ok, follow me here... While old Ali was still alive, there was a bunch of guys who decided he was an idiot. These guys weren't Shi'I or Sunni... they were before all that. They were called the *Khawarij* or *Kharijites*, meaning "*those who come out from impropriety*"[76]. These guys were the fanatical bible-thumping (sorry, Quran-thumping) ones who decided no one else in the world was as holy as they were and everyone needed to go back to the word of God in the book and ignore all this silly human bickering. In the West we call these guys Biblical literalists and elect them to school boards in the Southern States. Wisely, the peaceful and decent majority of Muslims, led by Ali, decided it was better to slaughter these guys then to let them write school policies. There is much we can learn from Islam.

The Kharijites believed that the Quran was the sole authority, that they could revolt against any form of secular Muslim rule, and indiscriminately killed all unbelievers, including Muslims who didn't join them. They also claimed all property belonging to non-adherents as booty. It was all rather akin to the American War on Drugs. They claimed that anyone guilty of a sin was an evil infidel with no rights who should be tossed from Paradise and made to suffer in hell for all eternity for their transgressions against the established dogma.

Ali spent much of his time fighting against the Kharijites while he was in charge of Islam. Fortunately, Ali was pretty damned good at this whole kill, slaughter, maim thing, so the movement kind of stopped moving eventually. It just kind of laid there bleeding and screaming until it died a sick horrible death at the hands of Ali's troops. If only we'd done this with the Pilgrims…

MU'TAZILAH, THE "FREE-THINKERS"

The attempt to make either the Bible or tradition infallible
is an attempt to shore up ecclesiastical power and control.
It is never an attempt to preserve truth. ~John Shelby Spong

Not long after the Kharijites, there was a rationalist movement in Islam that was loosely based on some Greek and Christian philosophies. Called *Mu'tazilah* (or *"Free thinkers[77]"*) their big thing was opposition to the Islamic concept of pre-determination. They taught that man had free will, as opposed to the main Islamic idea that humanity was just a pawn to Allah's great plan. They also questioned the Quran as holy text, using some rather deep and annoyingly long-winded reasons that aren't worth going into. (It had a lot to do with whether or not God's words were still His words if they were written down. As He has no form, neither should His words, so how could anything be written and still be His words? And so on *ad nauseam*. Get bored now.)

As these guys were sort of the opposite extreme from the Kharijites, they too were slaughtered, maimed, killed, and otherwise discouraged. This was a lot like the predestination debates in Calvinism and the Catholic Church in the 1600s which, I might add, are equally worth mentioning, glossing over, and moving past before anyone falls asleep.

The main thing this school of thought contributed to Islam was to create a reaction. They were trying to get the people to open up and think outside the box. Instead, the Sunnis in particular had to defend their beliefs, and did so by making sure nothing changed. This was where the institutionalizing of Islamic beliefs really started... where everything was set in stone so you couldn't change or edit anything. It was in reacting to these guys trying to soften the dogma a bit and make Islam more interpretive that the dogma became entrenched and unalterable. I hate it when that happens.

THE WAHHABIS

The Wahhabi Tenets:

Only God can be worshipped.
Holy men or women must not be used to win favours from God.
No other name other than the names of Allah may enter a prayer.
No shaving of beard. No abusive language.
People must be dressed simply. Women may not drive.
Mosques must be built without minarets or ornaments.

These guys piss me off. I mean, they really, really piss me off. Just to be fair I am attaching an endnote *here*[78] that is a link to a defence of the Wahhabi movement, but I'm not going to have a hell of a lot of good to say about them. My account is one-hundred percent biased, openly admitted.

You'd think that if some joker in the 1750s was going to go digging up old Islamic philosophy he'd go for the free-thinking stuff, right? Wrong. Just when Islam was settling in to being a successful, peaceful, and overall decent religion of Sunnis and Shi'Is that weren't out there killing anyone or being fanatical, a guy named Muhammad ibn Abdul Wahhab goes and digs up that whole fundamental Kharijite crap that Ali had managed to get rid of. This is the root of a lot of Islamic fundamentalism in the world today. Without Wahhabi, Islam would probably be like the Catholic Church today... not a great thing, but not going out and killing thousands of people in Allah's name to show how holy they are. Here's what happened...

During the mid-1700s the Wahhabi movement spread like wildfire in Arabia.[79] Following in the stupidity of the Kharijites a thousand years earlier, the Wahhabis destroyed shrines, tombs, and anything else they saw as contrary to their version of Islam. In 1806 the Wahhabis conquered Mecca and the damage Ali had kept in check was allowed to run rampant. They replaced the silk shroud on the Black Rock with a simple black curtain (a major thing if you're Islamic), burned and stripped the tomb of Muhammad, and declared that it should be a simple tomb of a dead person, not a shrine. (To this day there's a screen around his tomb to prevent people from praying there because these guys figured honoring Mohammed was a sin. Granted, Mohammed probably would have agreed with them but still, I hate the fascism involve here.) This is one of the few times in history that Muslims actually stopped going to Mecca for pilgrimages because it got to be too expensive and too fanatical for the average Muslim to go.

The mainstays of the Wahhabi movement were eventually wiped out by the Turks, (yay Turks!) but Wahhabi has remained in various forms to this day, notably in Saudi-Arabia. The ruling house of Saud is descended from the Ibn Saud, a Wahhabi. These are the ultra-fanatical, *"destroy everything that isn't exclusively Islamic"* types we all know and love from CNN. Like *the Taliban* in Afghanistan, the guys who destroyed the 2000-year-old Buddhist statues because they weren't Islamic.

OSAMA BIN LADEN AM TALIBAN

Fundamentalism isn't about religion. It's about power.

~Salman Rushdie

The actual Wahhabi movement as it existed in the 1750s is utterly rejected by most Muslims nowadays, but the theology and sentiment is still very much alive in groups like the Taliban. More importantly, it was this movement (and the oath the Saud family took to this movement) that is the root of the Saud family control over the region. The radical right-wing Wahhabi sentiments are what give the crown power in Saudi Arabia, indirectly if not directly. In 1964, when members of the royal family deposed King Saud, they had to get a *fatwa* (a religious declaration) justifying their actions before the new king could be put in place. This is where Bin Laden fits in to this whole thing.

You see, Bin Laden grew up in Saudi Arabia amid a culture of hard core supporters of the Wahhabi Islamic *tradition*. Note the emphasis on the word *tradition*. Bin Laden is not Wahhabi; he just sort of likes the fundamentalist ideals of the movement. During the Gulf War, when the monarch allowed American planes and bases into Saudi Arabia, the old school guys totally flipped. They thought the use of Saudi land by non-Islamic forces was the epitome of evil, and there was a call for the religious guys to oust the king as had been done in 1964. The problem was, the States supported the king and, well, they had lots of guns. Because the U.S. was allowed into Saudi Arabia and still maintains bases there, Osama bin Laden and his ilk declared the king to be an "apostate" (your basic evil bad guy deserving of a good killing under Islamic law. See "*About the Author*" at the back of this book for more details.)

If you watched TV after the Sept. 11 bombing of the Trade Towers you'd have seen that a whole bunch of Imams stood up and declared that Bin Laden did not represent their faith. They were basically right. The average Muslim can get really pissed about religious or political crap, but their mullahs doesn't tell them to go out and kill people or destroy everything that's not Islamic. If you start hearing that kind of rhetoric, you're probably dealing with a Wahhabi of some descript. Unless of course you are dealing with a Qutbite, which is Bin Laden supposedly is. A *Qutbite*. Honest... I am not making these names up.

Qutbites are named after Sayyid Qutb (1906-66) He was a good secular writer in the 1920's in Egypt. After WWII, Qutb went massively extreme and started writing about Islamic lore, Islamic tradition, and the Islamic take on politics and the world. He published his first book while in the United States in 1949 which he ironically titled "Social Justice".

When he got back to Egypt in 1950, Qutb joined the al-Ikhwan al-Muslimun (the Muslim Brotherhood) in openly opposing the government of Jamal Abdul Nasser, which (for those who don't know) was never a healthy thing to do. Qutb spent most of the rest of his life in prison after that.

Thing is, Qutb was no scholar. Most of what he came up with in jail was his own musings about Islam under oppression. Say, like, being in jail or something. As his life got harsher, his writings became harsher and more radical. Not surprising for a guy in prison, Qubt created a theology that opposed authority and called for all Muslims to punish the sin and corruption they saw around them. Sinners HAD to be punished in this life. Like, say, the big guys in the prison shower with him. There HAD to be a comeuppance. Qutb believed that the Muslim nations needed to rise up and slay the evil shower guys.., er, dictators who had profaned the world he saw around him. Sin had to be punished. Islamic law had to mete out death and execution in the name of a holy and vengeful god, so as to right the wrongs of the oppressed and through the blood of the wicked cleanse the world of wickedness..

Egypt executed Qubt in 1966.

The movement that's come out of this, Qubtites, is pretty much the same as the man. It's based on a reaction to authority, notably the U.S.. Where Qubt had seen Nasser as being evil and corrupt, his movement now sees the West (and the U.S. in particular) as being evil incarnate deserving of a good killing. This whole idea of the West being godless, hellbound scum is a common enough theme in modern Islam, but the Qubtites have a mandate from their leader that tells them to actually go out and fight against the evil shower room oppressors.

Anyway, the modern Wahhabi in Saudi Arabia maintains that this is the movement that Bin Laden belongs to. They may be just trying to cover their asses after 9/11, but who knows? Adherents of both groups will go on and on about how different they are and how Wahhabis s based on tradition and lore while Qubt is based on reactionary musings and no history or depth. However, both groups are vehemently Islamic and would happily kill you for being gay, drunk, debauched, an educated woman, or me. When they're about to lop your head off with a sword it's kinda hard to care which sect they're from; Qubt or Wahhabi.

SUFISM

The longest journey is the journey inwards of he

who has chosen his destiny. ~Dag Hammarskjold

Sufism is the loving, warm, mystic side of Islam. What I refer to as *'spiritual masturbation'*.

You'd be hard-pressed to find a real Sufi. They're rare. Less than five percent of all Muslims ascribe to the sect. Anyone who's gone into a new age book store recently has probably seen some book on Sufism and thought, "Ooh...sounds deep and mystic. Better look at this." Like a lot of stuff, it only sounds mystic because it's not in English. The name of the sect, Sufi, is not some profound and important term designed to instil respect and reverence. It's an Arabic word for a person who wears cheap, coarse cloth made of inferior-quality wool— the Arabic equivalent of burlap[80]. It just doesn't sound so mystic when you call the sect "People Who Wear Burlap," does it?

People Who Wear Burlap is the esoteric sect of Islam. It first appeared somewhere around (oh, sorry...circa) 1700 AD, so it's a fairly new thing. It's called People Who Wear Burlap (or Sufi, for the Arabic people out there) because the adherents of this sect are often seen wearing burlap or other forms of cheap, undyed cloth. This isn't done as some forum of statement. They wear it because they don't give a damn about what they look like and, since most Islamic countries would kill them for going naked in public, they have to wear something. So they wear burlap. It's cheap, it's simple, and they don't have to worry about it. The Sufi believe that the teachings of Mohammed are deep and enigmatic and full of levels of interpretation that only a purified soul could ever hope to understand. To this end, they lead an ascetic life, often as beggars or menial laborers. They spend their time in deep thought, trying to fathom the depths of the Koran and the life of Mohammed. Anyway, the Sufi believes in an "inner search," much like the Buddhists and the Cabalists and a bunch of other "ists" from other religions. To achieve this, they engage in self-denial and meditation (both of which had their place in the Pillars of Islam, but these guys took it way further).

Like the Cabalists, Sufis believe that all is one, and that we need to align ourselves with the one pure Divine Light. The Divine Light is Allah, and Mohammed was the messenger of that Divine Light. So were Jesus, Moses, and all the others. You can see why Sufism isn't really considered a split in the Islamic faith. It's just too damn passive and accommodating to start any trouble. Sufis advocate a "knowledge of the Divine" that is reached through meditation. It's not an actual conversation with God, or with an angel as Mohammed had (as hearing God would make you a prophet, and being a prophet after Mohammed was considered heresy, since Mohammed said he was the last one). Their revelation was more concerned with witnessing the Infinite through meditation, not interacting with it. It's all very much like the Buddhists' concept of Satori, or momentary enlightenment. Sufis call it Marifa.

The issue of leadership (Shi'l or Sunni) doesn't affect Sufism at all since they're on an "inner search" that doesn't involve the material world. As a result, both major sects of Islam have just kind of looked at the Sufi and shrugged. Most Muslims regard them as an oddity-something you pass on the street on your way to get groceries. They just "are" which is about how Sufis like it. They can attend daily prayers with either major sect with no hassles, or they can just kind of sit on their own and pray on some side-street somewhere. Either way, they abide by all the laws of the Qur'an and the officials generally don't worry about them. Unlike the other sects of Islam, Sufism has an inordinate emphasis on love.

I learned a lot at the Baha'I feasts I attended.

BAHA'I

Religions die when they are proved to be true.
Science is the record of dead religions. ~Oscar Wilde

Here's a word of advice: Don't refer to Baha'I as "a sect of Islam." Muslims get really ticked and Baha'Is take it as an opportunity to explain the faith to you. Either way, you're trapped in a deep conversation about religion with someone who actually believes it. This is fine if you're bored, but don't try it as a matter of course. The Baha'I faith came out of the Shi'I sect of Islam in about 1850. I pick 1850 as a date because this is the year the Bab (pronounced "Bob") was executed. "What," I hear you ponder, "is a Bab?" Well, it's a gate. Bab is the Farsi word for gate (*Farsi* being one of the main languages spoken in Iran). "So," you ask, "how does one go about executing a gate?" Let me try this again.

There was this guy named Ali Mohammed, who called himself the Bab, or gate. He was a teacher who believed there was a way to communicate with Muhammad al-Mahdi (who, I'm sure you remember from the previous section, was the last imam, who was carried off to heaven and would come to begin a new age of peace). Ali Muhammad believed that Allah had set up a series of gateways to the divine sphere to allow this contact. He wasn't exactly referring to prophet hood. It was more like a mystic window to heaven, reminiscent of the Sufi ideas. It was this kind of gate that Ali pronounced himself to be. Not a prophet. A gate. The differences were subtle, but there. Unfortunately, the Shi'Is missed the subtlety. Ali Muhammad was executed for heresy in Baghdad in 1850. The "gate" closed.

MIRZA HUSSEIN ALI

Imitation is the best form of flattery. ~Charles Caleb Colton

Mirza Hussein Ali was a student of Ali Muhammad. He was the son of a prominent government minister so he had some political ties, but they were tenuous. His father never really supported him. With the "gate" dead, there was a large vacuum to be filled by someone who could carry on Ali's teachings about the coming age of peace and the return of Muhammad Al-Mahdi. Being a good student of Ali, Mirza thought, "Well, this needs fixing." To this end, in 1863, Mirza Hussein Ali declared that he was the prophet that Ali Muhammad the Bab had foretold. He changed his name to Baha Ullah (The Glory of God) and began teaching about peace and love and prosperity, so naturally he was immediately arrested. Much of Baha Ullah's life was spent in one prison or another.

He wasn't executed, mainly because the Ottoman Empire (which was Islamic) wasn't in the habit of arbitrarily killing folks. This was in the era before the annoying Wahhabis screwed everything up, so you were allowed to think a bit. The problem with Baha Ullah was that he thought a tad too much. You see, before you could be executed for heresy at the time, you were given an opportunity to reconcile your ideas with the Quran. This gave Baha Ullah the chance to prove he wasn't an outright heretic. As he was considerably better at defending his teachings than Ali Muhammad, he lived quite a long time and did much in the way of confusing the religious authorities of the day. No one ever nailed him with a point he couldn't somehow justify, so they kept him alive but in prison.

His most ardent opponents would be seen wandering out of his prison cell with a perplexed, ponderous expression on their face as they went off to consider Baha Ullah's latest "interpretations" of the Qur'an. It got to be a running joke, and in time Baha Ullah's answers to his charges became the stuff of legend. Whether they were heretical became irrelevant. They were provocative, and that's what saved his life.

He got himself quite a following during his time in prison. Teaching during the Victorian era, Baha Ullah set down some principles that are still being perfected by the politically correct today. He rejected polygamy and slavery. Because he saw the true unity of all faiths worldwide, he rejected the idea of Jihad or holy war. Basically, he restated the Islamic idea of "the one true God," but went far beyond Islamic teachings in his quest to show how all the faiths are destined to be one, including those that were not seen as being "of the book" (i.e. Hinduism, Taoism, Buddhism). He also advocated that a single, universal language be instituted so that all people everywhere could understand each other. This, he felt would reveal just how similar the religions were and how God had been active in them all.

It was naive as hell, but people liked it. They still do. Perhaps the most radical thing Baha Ullah did was to institute provisions for the total equality of the genders. Within Baha'l, women were (and are) regarded as total equals to their male counterparts. In fact, Baha Ullah prophesied that in time politics would become exclusively the domain of women-not because of any takeover bid, but because the age that was coming would no longer demand the warlike skills that males had brought to politics. He felt that women would be better at planning and diplomacy, while the men would be more comfortable in things like architecture and construction.

Okay, it was still sexist, but hey, we're talking about the 1800s here. These ideas were pretty radical.

I seek only to understand the mind of God. All else is detail.

~ *Einstein*

Baha Ullah instituted a faith that was a lot easier to live by than Islam, so people liked it. Prayer became a personal issue rather than a formal, state-run event five times a day. Personal meditation became the focal point of the faith rather than organized meetings. More importantly, Baha Ullah reinterpreted the holy texts of Islam, Christianity, and Judaism and rejected the idea of evil incarnate. Demons and angels were interpreted as allegorical rather than physical beings. This was a major change for a people who had been fed the doctrine of a celestial battle between good and evil. All of a sudden, evil was beaten. It didn't exist. There was only a personal relationship with the Divine, unhindered by Satan and his minions. With this concept went the concept of sin-or, rather, the judgment for sins. If you did something "wrong," Baha Ullah saw it as a transgression between you and the Divine. No one was about to walk up and punish you for it. Of course, this didn't defeat the rule of law. If you were a criminal, you could still be charged and imprisoned, but this was seen as a measure to give you time to work things out with the Divine while protecting people's lives and belongings from your criminal activities. It wasn't meant to be punitive.

One of the other big revelations of Baha Ullah was the reconciliation of religion and science— a singular effort in the realm of prophet theologies. He basically said that if science proves a religious belief wrong, then science wins. This puts faith where it should be-in reality. Baha Ullah believed that there would be no dissension between the two ideals (science and religion) as the new age grew.

He said that science would become more advanced and precise, allowing for a fuller revelation of the nature of God. The rationale was that God created a physical universe and that (at least while He's in it) there was no need for Him to break the rules of nature. Miracles were then interpreted as aspects of nature that we as humans hadn't figured out yet. Pretty decent thinker, this Baha Ullah. The downside of this (for Muslims) was that it degraded the importance of the Koran as the only authoritative text. Baha'Is were encouraged to decide on the scriptures based on an empirical and scientific inquiry. While nothing that came out of such inquiry was overtly anti-Islamic, both of the major sects of Islam rejected the idea that the Koran could be proved wrong according to Baha Ullah's teachings.

When Baha Ullah died in prison, the leadership of the faith was taken up by Abbas Effendi, who unfortunately lacked Baha Ullah's knack for stalling judgment from the political leaders of the day. The relative tolerance for the faith that Baha Ullah had managed to maintain was lost. Baha'I became illegal in all Islamic countries-a heretical faith punishable by death. The persecution of Baha'Is still goes on today in Shi'I-controlled states like Iran. It was Abbas Effendi who introduced the faith to the world. Since the Baha'Is were being slaughtered in the Middle East, the adherents fled to Europe, the United States and Canada, thus proving, as the Jews had before them, that persecution generally leads to expansion. The faith would have stayed a sect of Islam had it remained in Iran. By persecuting it, the Islamic states transformed it into an entirely independent religion and spread it around the world.

Wherever Baha'I has gone, it has employed the teaching technique that Baha Ullah insisted on: "Win the world one heart at a time." This means proselytizing. No pamphlets. No street missionaries. A person who is Baha'I is supposed to just live their life normally and be the best person they can be. This makes Baha'I the only faith that you never have to hear about, which I genuinely like. If you inquire about the faith, a Baha'I will usually give you one of Baha Ullah's books to read. If you've lucked out and asked at the right time of year (Ramadan, the month of fasting), they may invite you out to one of the feast nights. If you ever get the chance to attend, I highly recommend you feign genuine interest and go. The food is genuinely damned good.

Baha'I Politics

Each community sets up a Local Spiritual Assembly. These are people who volunteer to take care of whatever administrative stuff comes along. They also have the legal right to marry people, seeing as how they fulfill the role usually assigned to priests. A person can serve for a year or twenty years on a LSA, but usually the positions are bounced around to those who have the time to do the stuff needed. Above them is the National Spiritual Assembly, same idea, larger landmass. At this level, you're also afforded an income (sometimes), since you don't have time to do anything but NSA work. Above this is the World Assembly in Haifa. These people are also elected from the local assemblies. They do things like petition at the UN to help get Baha'ls out of Iran and end the persecutions. They're also involved in humanitarian groups like Amnesty International. All levels of the faith have an "open book" policy on finances. All monies donated by the faithful are accounted for and even your average Joe off the street can wander in and say, "Hey. how did you guys spend all the money you were given last year?" They're supposed to give out a detailed list-no omissions, no "secret allotments." I haven't tried this yet but if they came through I'd be impressed.

Were I were to pick on anything here, it would have to be the origin of the faith. Most modern Baha'ls have fallen so far from the original premise set out by the Bab that they don't recognize Baha Ullah's claim to being the last imam, Muhammad al-Mahdi, as being an element of Shi'l Islam. This disparity is further complicated by the fact that the Bab never declared Baha Ullah to be Muhammad al-Mahdi. That's who was supposed to show up and enter in this whole new age of prosperity and peace- Muhammad Al-Mahdi, not a regular mortal from Baghdad named Baha Ullah. You'd figure that the Bab-who had had regular visions of Muhammad Al-Mahdi in heaven-would have recognized Baha Ullah as the last imam returning from beyond when he saw the guy in his classroom. He didn't. But they provide great feasts and strive for world peace and all that, so I cut them some slack. They have my indifference if not approval. (By the way, I'm still technically Baha'l, if your look it up on their computer lists. But then again, I also still belong to Catholicism, Mormonism, and some faith in Mexico involving giant lizards and hallucinogens. At least, I think it was a faith.)

Anyway, if you're just your average Heathen, Baha'l is basically one of the easier faiths to endure. They don't bother anyone. They keep quiet. They not supposed to proselytize or annoy you, and they don't tell you you're going to hell. They just kind of drift around, having their get-togethers and meditating quietly on their own, all the while trying to free hostages and create peace on Earth.

Lately they've been advertising in magazines etc., so I think they're probably getting a tad commercial. It'll probably get worse.

'BLACK' ISLAM

I have a dream… ~Martin Luther King Jr.

I hate religions, but if I had to throw money at some religion it would probably be this one. They strive at every opportunity to piss off the white-bred Christian groups in the States, and I just can't help but want to support such a noble goal. Besides, I figure I better cover these guys in the book as they call themselves the Nation of Islam these days, so everyone's going to figure I should have put them in. The truth is I see then as a political movement disguised as a religious movement, which is probably why I don't feel so bad liking them a bit.

The first real "Black Muslim" was a guy named Timothy Drew. In 1913 he left his home in North Carolina to move to New Jersey. There he adopted a new name, Noble Drew Ali, and proceeded to become an enduring thorn in the side of right-wing Christians world-wide. Truly a man after my own heart. The down side of all this is that he did it by founding a new church called the *Moorish Science Temple of America.* I figure he knew that the religious side of this would sell faster than a political movement would, but who knows? Either way he decided that the blacks had God on their side and they were gonna win out over the bigots in the States. His idea for saving the black Americans from all the bullshit and bigotry was for them to *"discover their national origins."*[81]

Basically, what this boiled down to is that he'd figured out that the politics of North America was run by bigoted idiots that were never going to regard his race as truly American. Understanding this, he decided they should all go back to what they were before they got dragged across the ocean and dropped into this mess over here. This meant that all the blacks were to refer to themselves as Asiatic, Moors, or Moorish Americans. More importantly (for some odd reason) this also meant that they should all be Muslims (as the Moors were also Muslim.)

Now all of that's ok in and of itself. The WASP population of the U.S. basically shrugged at this whole *black Muslim* idea. But Drew then started teaching that Jesus was a black man killed by whites. As every good Christian in America was positive that Jesus was a white man with blonde hair and blue eyes, this didn't go over very well. Drew Ali was forced out of New Jersey and a half dozen other places before settling into Chicago. There he allied with a guy named Claude Green. Green "mysteriously" winds up dead, and Ali was charged with the crime. Then, while out on bail, Ali himself "mysteriously" winds up dead. Funny how that happens sometimes.

After Drew Ali died, the Moorish Science Temple became the Temple of Islam, headed up by a rather light-skinned black guy named Wallace Fard. Some say he was black, some say black-oriental, others say he was "whitish". Regardless, Fard claimed to be Ali's reincarnation born in Mecca. Fard's mission to America was to set the "captives" (Black Americans) free from "Caucasian devils" and the "White man's religion" (Christianity). He never explained how reincarnation seems to have lightened his skin. Must have been all the white light... who knows? Anyway, Fard led things until the 1930's.

Elijah Poole and Malcolm Little

> *The Negro revolution is controlled by foxy*
>
> *white liberals, by the Government itself.*
>
> *But the Black Revolution is controlled only by God.*
> ~Malcolm X

Elijah Poole was a disciple of Fard, and later a leader in the Temple of Islam. When Fard left in 1935, Elijah Poole (now Elijah Muhammad) assumed leadership and changed the name of the sect to the Nation of Islam. One of the Poole's best and brightest was a young kid named Malcolm Little. The name fit him... he was a scrawny kid with big glasses who looked like he couldn't fight his way out of a wet paper bag. Little was arrested several times for petty theft until, in 1952, he took off to Detroit, joined the Nation of Islam, and became the unparalleled mother-of-all-pains-in-the-ass to White Supremacists and right-wing Christians everywhere.

When he became a Muslim, Malcolm Little dropped his

Christian last name and replaced it with a simple X to show his disdain for "Christian" names. Now called Malcolm X, this scrawny kid became the scourge of Christians everywhere; the scary bedtime story white Christian parents told their kids to make sure they were good. Malcolm X and the Nation of Islam did more to shake up the established Christian power base than a thousand years of Christian apologists had been able to do. Suddenly Christians weren't the top dogs anymore. By educating Black Muslims and making they knew their rights, Malcolm X orchestrated some of the most effective social protests in American history. That, combined with a rhetoric that rivaled Christianity for sheer bigotry and violence, kept good little white-bred Christians locked away in their homes quaking in terror until Malcolm X was assassinated on February 22, 1965. I like that. For an all-too-brief time in the 1960s the Pentecostal and Evangelical Christian groups all but shut up for fear of incurring the wrath of the Nation of Islam.

Kudos, Mr. X.

Louis Gene Walcott Farrakhan

> *"Do you have blacks too?"* George W. Bush

Today the movement is led by another rather exuberant leader named Louis Farrakhan. Farrakhan's carried on well in the tradition of pissing off pretty much everyone. In the summer of 2002, amid growing tensions between George Bush and Saddam Hussein, Farrakhan wandered over to Iraq for a major publicity binge, publicly supporting Iraq against "American aggression". Some called for him to be charged with treason for this, others wanted his citizenship revoked. In his own defense Farrakhan pointed out that all the black men that the United States honors are dead and can't change anything.

The religious aspects of this movement are definitely less important than the social reforms it calls for. The Nation of Islam is, first and foremost, a political body. It isn't officially or unofficially connected to any standard Ismaili, Sunni, or Shi'l community. Its theology is assumed to be Islamic and they abide by the "Five Pillars". But the practical goals of the Nation of Islam are pretty far removed from any other Muslim group. They center almost exclusively on the struggle of disenfranchised blacks in the United States. Under Farrakhan there's been quite a bit of anti-Israeli sentiment, but again this is political, not religious.

Looking For Martin Luther: Summing Up Islam

There shall be no compulsion in religion. Quran 2:263

Okay, that covers Mohammed's life, Sunni, Shi'I and the other schools or sects.. That's the bare bones of Islam. It's all about the Silk Scroll and what it revealed to Mohammed about how to live. It's about abiding by the Pillars of Islam and believing in the monotheistic creed, *There is no god but God, and Mohammed His messenger.* That's it. Aside from that, you work, you get married, have kids and live your life.

Like Christianity, Islam has sects and splinter groups the character and theology of which differ as dramatically as Carmelite nuns do from Southern Evangelicals. Where Christianity is divided into Catholic and Protestant, Islam is divided into Sunni and Shi'I. Where there are hundreds if not thousands of Protestant churches, there are an equal number of Islamic "schools" that, like their Christian counter-parts, are as independent of the whole as David Koresh was from the Pope.

I see Islam as a faith that's looking for its Martin Luther... a reformer who can tie the moderates together into something cohesive while putting the nutbars out to pasture. So far most of the reformers who have come along in Islamic nations have been executed. There are some in the West though, and it lends a bit of hope that it'll all calm down eventually. But who knows?

Anyway that's enough Islam stuff. We have a whole other continent to piss off, and I'm running out of book...

Religion: *Vedism (What became Hinduism and Buddhism)*
Established: Pre-history
Main Prophet/Holy Guy: *Vedic Monks*
Main Holy Book: *Vedas*
What to call the priest: *master/ teacher*
What to Call an Adherent: *Vedic*

Vedism

> *In every country and every age, the priest has been hostile to liberty.*
>
> *~Thomas Jefferson*

As this is the opening paragraph, I am supposed to write something that grabs your attention and makes you want to keep reading. Unfortunately, the stuff I have to cover in the first couple of sub-chapters is anything but fascinating, so I worry that by the time I get to the cool stuff you'll have gotten bored and gone off to read something by Stephen King. As I need the money more than he does, I figure I've got my work cut out for me here.

To this end, I seriously considered starting this chapter off with my famous 'Pig with a wooden leg' joke, but the mere mention of this idea has brought hordes of opposition from everyone that's ever heard me tell it. Alas, the pig must wait. Instead, I figure we'll just dive right in and cover the monotonous stuff as quick as possible so we can get back to the bloody, gory, fun stuff we all love.

So ok... the East. Big place. Lots of people, lots of religions. It's said that Hinduism alone has 330 million gods. The idea of trying to fully explain each of these gods should logically seem daunting. To try to explain them all in a few small chapters should logically seem impossible. It should come as no surprise, then, that I failed the Logic course I took at university.

It's not actually that difficult though. You see, there's a common thread to all these faiths that ties them together in a way that most folks aren't aware of. A common ancestry if you will. Once you get to understanding this basic foundation for all the Eastern faiths, the differences between Hinduism and Buddhism fades and you can see where it all actually came from. Unfortunately, to do this, we have to wade through a whole heap of archeological data and historical crap that's about as exciting as Ross Perot. Fortunately though, I think I can get through it all without having to use a pie chart.

So There's This Pig With a Wooden Leg...[82]

The first clergyman was the first rascal who met the first fool. ~Voltaire

It all started in India a very long time ago. (Not the pig... the Vedics.) We're talking somewhere around 5,000 BC, a time when the true natives of India lived and worked in the Indus valley. They had houses, public baths, that sort of thing. All in all, they were way ahead of the rest of the world at the time. Rome wasn't even thought of back then. Mohenjo~daro in the Indus Valley was one of the few (if not the only) center of human civilization on the planet. The rest of the world at the time was a cruel and uncompromising place, full of ravenous hordes of bloodthirsty marauders that would kill you in an instant just for the plain old fun of it. Not unlike the L.A. Freeway.

Now, as near as we can figure, these original Indus Valley folks were an easy going lot that farmed, tended to their families, and generally loved and honored all things. They weren't war-like, and had no ideas of conquest or domination. Instead, they lived quiet lives that genuinely reflected a willingness to get along and care for the people and land around them. Naturally then, they were slaughtered mercilessly and wiped off the face of the Earth.

The guys that killed them were called Aryans. (not the ARIANS, as in Hitler youth. These guys came way earlier and were way more successful.)[83] These are the white folks. Originally from the Ural plains of Russia, these guys moved out over the globe, killing pretty much anything that happened across their path. As near as we can figure, this all happened somewhere around 4,000 BC. As the indigenous culture had clubs and the Aryans had horses and blades, the indigenous folk were pretty much decimated, though enough of them remained alive to form a low-life class of servants called the Shudras. (Yay. More mystic words. *Shudras* means servant. We're gonna get a lot more of this mixed language stuff in all the Eastern faiths, so bear with me on it.)

The Shudras are the servant class. They're basically your average conquered people, considered low-life and generally abused. You see the same thing in every culture, but there's a bit more to it in this case. You see, before the Aryans ever got to India, they'd already set up a class system of their own. The Shudras, the servant class, was just tacked on at the bottom of a totem pole. On their own, the Aryans had three classes already established and going strong. Here's the reader's Digest version of them...

Kshatriya: The Warrior class. These are the guys directly responsible for offing the Indus Valley Civilization, and pretty much every other civilization they came across. They're a bunch of bloodthirsty, cruel marauders bent on conquering and subjugating the entire world. They also made bad house guests. Not surprisingly, these guys held the political control of India, as anyone who disagreed with them tended to wind up flayed and gutted.

Brahmin: The English translation for that won't make a lot of sense yet. It's a variation of Brahman (with an 'a'). As I haven't gotten into the Brahman stuff yet, just nod as if I'm actually making sense and keep reading. I'll get to it in a bit. Anyway, these guys are the priestly class of a religion called Vedism, a pre-Hindu religion. They considered themselves to be the first class of people, second only to the gods. As the Kshatriya didn't care a hell of a lot about what the Brahmin said, the priests got away with this. I'll go into way more detail about these guys than you ever cared to know in a little bit.

Vaisya: The folks that actually did the work in the society. Merchants, farmers, that sort of thing.

Ok, those are the four classes, if you count the Shudras, a.k.a. servants. This class system is still alive and well in India today, thousands of years later. They don't call it a class' system though. They refer to them as castes' (*jati* in Sanskrit.) In practical application the caste system is basically a racist thing. Because the Aryan conquerors were white, being white became a good thing. Inversely, the natives were black skinned. (A cool theory on all this: the reason the Hindu gods are all blue skinned is because the Vedics were black skinned. The early Vedics couldn't paint in a black because it all wound up looking smudged with no shading or depth. Instead they used blue, the closest color to black. So the images you see of Shiva being blue are actually supposed to represent black skin.)

The color of your skin became a signature of caste, though

officially your caste was by lineage. If your family is Brahmin, you're Brahmin. Seldom was anyone not of the caste they were born into, though the acceptance into the caste had to be made official in a coming of age ceremony called the second birth.' (hmmm... Born Again Vedics...) Anyway, that's the basic political structure of India in about the forth millennia BC, which is where I want to jump into things. It was in this political structure, that Vedism, the Mother Of All Religious Carp, was created.

THE VEDAS

Not Darth.

The Vedas are books. ("Veda" is actually the Sanskrit word for "knowledge", but when you refer to the Vedas you're talking about the books.) They're considered really holy and sacred, and are the foundation of almost all Eastern religious thought. Think of them as the Torah of the East. Collectively they form the back bone of both Hindu and Buddhist thought, so I figure this is as good a place as any to start chopping.

It should come as no surprise that the Vedas, like all other good, holy, and all-encompassing theological books, have an uncertain origin. Some folks say they're leftovers from the original Indus Valley folks. Others say they were written by different masters (more on that in a bit). But basically no one really knows. Like the Bible or the Torah, they're just "holy". Period. End of discussion. Should you be so bold as to inquire who wrote them you're told it was someone really holy who knew what they were talking about. Unlike the Jews who actually claim there were specific authors (IE: Moses, et al) the Vedics don't even bother pretending. To them, the Vedas are just really old and really sacred books. I agree with half of that. To get the gist of these Vedas and what they're all about, I gotta cover the philosophy of the Aryans and how it became Vedism. This all gets interesting really soon. Honest.

THE PHILOSOPHY

I don't know if God exists, but it would be better for
His reputation if He didn't. ~Jules Renard

Ok, there were all these gods and goddesses and demons and all the standard religious fare. These guys had pretty much deified everything that flew, crawled, or just happened to pass by. It all added to a growing pantheon of barometric-pressure deities. But there were a few thinkers in the lot, and it was what the thinkin' folks were doing that really added to the plot. There came up with this theory on existence... the first real explanation for reality that didn't involve some giant turtle carrying the planet on its back or some such thing. Their idea went something like this:

We know we are alive. Generally speaking, this doesn't tend to be such a good thing since it all gets miserable and painful pretty quick and sooner or later you die. Usually painfully, with lots of boils and nasty festering wounds seeping greenish-white fluids. (Ok... a bit much on the graphic description there. But hey, you didn't want lunch anyway.) The thing was, it all seemed pretty useless.

The thinkers of the day then looked at the nature of life and decided that there was a finite amount of it around. Living things seems to have a quality of animation that they called the *Prana*. It was kind of what we might call a soul, but it wasn't really a personal being... just a force that inhabited and drove living stuff. This Prana, they decided, was from a central font of all Prana, that they called *Nirvana*.

The thing was, Prana was removed from Nirvana, which to the Vedics was a problem. They figured that as long as the Prana remained separated from Nirvana, it was destined to keep floating around miserably, going from lifetime to lifetime and generally hating it all. Only by getting all Prana back to Nirvana could the suffering of life be stopped. The problem was that the Prana had this tendency to WANT to come back, even though it was miserable to do so. The wheel of life, which they called Samsara, kept drawing Prana in because the Prana kept wanting stuff. The desire for stuff, be it a cheese sandwich, walking along the beach or torturing small furry animals, is what they called Karma, or the action of the Prana.

While the Prana was intent on doing things here in Time and Space, it would never get back to the Oneness of Nirvana. Therefore, it became the goal of Vedics to get rid of all karma, thus allowing for all Prana to reach Nirvana. The problem was that even if we could divest our own lives of all karma, this still didn't stop dogs and cats from doing, well, dog and cat things. The Prana of animals seemed problematic.

This is where the Vedics invented the idea of the *atman*. The atman is basically exactly like the Xian soul. It's uniquely human, and its karma is entirely dependent on the actions of the human who possess it. This, thought the Vedics, was where we have to start. Dogs and cats (and all other lower life) would be destined to come back once they died no matter what they did, so we had best just work on getting humans to Nirvana and just hope the lower creatures re-incarnate as humans later on and thereby reach Nirvana. So, that's the philosophy. We're all headed for this absence of Self or atman, wherein we give up all our *karma* (or personal actions) and cease to be individuals. We become One with all things, and finally find an eternal peace that isn't dependent on the physical world.

This philosophy is pretty much standard in all Eastern faiths, mainly because the vast majority of them owe their heritage to Vedism. The objective— getting rid of the self or atman to achieve eternal bliss— is standard fare in all eastern beliefs. It's the way you get to that stage that differ, which is how you wind up getting all kinds of religions out of the same premise. Vedism acts like early Judaism does as the launch pad for other belief systems. In the same way that the Mormons, Catholics, Muslims and Jehovah's Witnesses all started from Abraham's deal with El-Shaddai, Hinduism and all the Buddhist sects derive from Vedism.

Ok... that's enough Vedism. There's more to it, but frankly it just gets more and more boring from this point on. You can read the Vedas if you want more on it all. Right now though, let me show you how all this becomes the Hinduism you recognize from the Beatles albums.

It may be that our role on this planet is not to worship God,

but to create him. ~Arthur C. Clarke

Moksa is an ancient Sanskrit word. I can't help it. Hindus never really bothered using English words for this stuff, so I'll have to keep using Sanskrit words. I suspect this has something to do with the fact that English wasn't invented for about three millennia after they started writing all this down.

Anyway... *Moksa* (or *Moksha*) is Sanskrit for 'liberation' or 'freedom'. It's the Hindu equivalent of Nirvana. So Moksha is Nirvana. *Nirvana* is a place full of depressing and narcissistic songs so puerile that you'll be tempted to slit your own wrists at the very thought of having to listen to another morose line of—

—*oh,* wait.

Sorry.

Wrong Nirvana.

Let's try that again...

It's the place you go if you're free off all attachments when you die and are able to prevent your self, your *atman*, from being tied up in the physical world again. Both Buddhism and Hinduism adopted this idea of the perfect Nothingness from Vedic thought; the idea that the only way to escape the suffering of life was to escape life itself. Both Buddhists and Hindus believe in this Ultimate End to life. Teleologically then, the two are the same. It was only in their ideas of how to get to this end that the two religions differed.

So, having found a proper excuse to sound intelligent using the word *teleologically*, let's get started...

THE UPANISHADS

*An apology for the devil: it must be remembered that we
have heard one side of the case. God has written all the books.*

~Samuel Butler

The Upanishads is the book that killed Vedism. Sure, Vedism was an old and strong religion and everyone loved it, but the Upanishads changed all that. You see, the gods of Vedism were gods of things like water, wind, air, and magic mushrooms; all the stuff that the people could see and marvel at. The thing is, by the second century BC people had stopped marveling. Frankly, fire was just not that amazing anymore. Neither was wind or water. Air, if it had ever really been something to be amazed at, had lost its divinity. Theologians tend to ponder the deep significance of this transition, wondering at the complex meaning in the people's dissatisfaction with the archaic gods. Me? I see the Upanishads as a pretty simple story.

I figure it happened like this: A couple guys were sitting around the fire, gabbing about the day's work and shooting the shit. Then one guy looked up from the flames and said *"Wait a minute... this is just a fire. There's nothing divine about a fire. I mean, it's nice and all, but it's not exactly a living thing now is it? Why are we calling this a god when we can create it or destroy it at will?"*

The other guys around the fire would be slightly intrigued by this statement, and would mull it over deeply while they beat the first guy to a bloody, fleshy pulp for being a heretic. Still, those that remained to watch the heretics' carcass burn in Agni's flames would sit and think to themselves "Yeah, you know... the guy had a point. Why DO we call this fire thing a god?"

Well, the Brahmin were quick to catch on to this whole scenario. They knew damn well that the "fire is a god, wind is a god" story wasn't going to hold much longer. They needed an out. With communities regularly harnessing wind, fire, and air to their own ends, it didn't take long for them to see that if these things were gods, they were pretty weak gods. By the third century BC India had become a society with a viscous outbreak of sanity, with people asking some very basic questions about these religious rights they were attending. They were starting to wake up. Something had to be done.

The Brahman, being smart guys, basically looked at the poor lost sane people, and said: "Y'know, you're right. Agni? He's nothin'. Soma? Atharva? Forget it. These guys are petty. Hardly worth worrying about."

The people, seeing the obvious evidence of this, agreed and were happy.

And the teachers said "BUT..."

The people then groaned and checked their assets, knowing where this was headed.

"But," continued the Brahmin, "There's more to this story. All these little gods? They're just itty bitty representations of other big gods that you can't see." And the people marveled at this story, wondering how much of their annual income these bigger gods would want. Happily they were to find that it was roughly the same graft as the minor gods wanted, so everyone shrugged and basically said "Okay, there are these bigger gods that we can't see but have to keep happy with worship and tithes and crap. Got it. Now leave us alone."

And so Hinduism was born. Not that they called it Hinduism. That term was hung on them by the Europeans centuries later. The Vedics just saw this new revelation about bigger gods as being a bigger truth, which explains their name for this new approach; *Sanatana Dharma*. It's Sanskrit again. Sorry about that. It means *"Eternal Truth*[84]*'*. Not that I ever intend to call it that, but I figure I should explain that the name Hinduism is a European invention. To the Indians, this whole thing was just an extension of Vedism that was designed to create (sorry, "reveal') a higher god that you couldn't see or feel but had to worship. This is a standard approach in all religions when the people get smart enough to start asking for proofs of divine influences. Create a god so big and unknowable that you never have to show him to anybody. It worked for the Jews and Christians, and it worked here for the Vedics. Suddenly the Brahman was too big, too vast to be understood. When the people asked where this Brahman was, the priests developed a neat catch phrase *'Neti neti'*, or *'Not this, not that'* to explain that the Brahman was beyond human conception and had no human attributes. It merely *'Is'*. Yet again the people shrugged, decided they were never going to figure it out, and left the details to the Brahmin. The tide of sanity was quashed.

The Upanishads were written as the first book to reflect this passing of old gods into new; the tale of the higher ups taking over and leaving behind poor old Agni and Athurva, who all but died with the passing of Vedism. Soma, on the other hand, did rather well for himself touring with the Grateful Dead until Jerry Garcia died, whereupon he retired to a counter-culture commune in California where he is still tended to by aging hippies and flower children.

THE PANTHEON

In the beginning Man created God;

and in the image of Man created he him. ~Jethro Tull

The Brahmin came up with this hierarchy in the second century BC that went something like this: there are 330 million gods, of which Agni and Soma were just two smaller versions. But the 330 million are actually only avatars. An *avatar*[65] (Sanskrit, literally "down-coming") is a manifestation of a god... sort of a mask the god wears to come down and deal with pesky humans. This whole concept is important, as it forms the base of all Hindu thought from that time to this. It works like this: above all the small piddly incarnations or avatars of the gods, there are three prime manifestation of godliness.

These are Brahma (without the "n", so he's a small god, not the Brahman, the godhead. What can I say? It's confusing.) Shiva, and Vishnu. Brahma, Shiva, and Vishnu are, in turn, avatars of the one true god or Godhead, known as the Brahman. The three in one are called the Trimutri... the Hindu Trinity. If you've ever browsed any Hindu art you'll probably have seen an image of a guy with one body but three faces, one looking forward, one left, and one right. That's the Trimutri. The faces are Vishnu, Shiva, and Brahma. It's always reminded me of an ex-girlfriend of mine. Don't ask why.

What we wind up with at the end of the Vedic era when Hinduism gets started is this idea of these three gods that are actually one God, but really aren't one God because all three keep being seen separately, even though there's only one body in the Godhead. But they really are only One God. Except that there's three of them. In one. Sort of. It's all very mystic and deep and they'll explain it to you someday if you work hard enough. In the meantime, just accept the mystery of it and support the priestly caste.

And the Catholics think they're unique.

This doctrine turned out to be pure genius. What it meant was that every two-bit little god from every small town in India could be recognized as part of Hinduism because they were all "Avatars.' You see, if your family happened to not have been Vedic but instead worshipped a giant wombat god with large teeth and glowing red eyes, they would have been seen as outside the truth under Vedic thought. Now, however, the giant wombat god would be interpreted as an avatar of one of the big gods, and you were free to honor him and pay tithes to Shiva/Vishnu/Brahma at the same time. A Brahmin might be called in to determine which of the three gods it actually was, but generally it didn't matter. The Wombat God was Brahma, Shiva, or Vishnu in disguise, and the Brahmin collected the tithes from everyone for using their gods.

THE GOAL OF HINDUISM

Karma Karma Chameleon... You come and go...~Boy George

There is no religious belief that has been so screwed up and turned around by the West as the tenet of Karma. Pretty much everyone has heard the word, and no one can give you a real meaning for it. People figure it's just some deep mystic word that has something to do with getting what you deserve.

The word Karma literally translates from Sanskrit as "doing"', as in "What are you doing with that gun?". In the Vedic tradition it referred to what people were *doing* with their lives. (i.e.: a Brahmin priest's Karma was sacrificing, a soldiers Karma was fighting... you get the idea.) The idea of Karma had nothing to do with fate or doom or pay back. More importantly, there is no real concept of "Good" or "Bad" karma. There was only karma, the doing of things. This whole karma thing is pretty much the most important aspect of this Eastern stuff, so I gotta get it clear. Here's how it works, at least as far as Hindus are concerned...

Since the days of Vedism, all karma has been known as a

bad thing. You see, there's this whole Wheel of Life that they call Samara. You're tied to the Wheel of Life by your desires, actions, and intentions. Both good intentions and bad intentions keep you coming back. Since both Hinduism and Buddhism see this as a bad thing, the idea of both religions is to free yourself from Samara by freeing yourself from all karma. However, this would generally mean doing and wanting absolutely nothing, which tends to leave one dazed and starving to death. This is fine if you're trying to get a job as a super model, but as a theological concept it didn't hold for the Hindus.

Here we get around to the Bhagavad-Gita. It's a really long, drawn out poetic epic that I highly recommend you never read. The plot sucks and frankly so do the characters, Krishna included. In the poem, there's this big battle that's about to happen and Arjuna, the hero of the story, is freaked out. Not because he's afraid of the battle, but because he's afraid of all the karma he's about to create by leading the battle. He figures he should just die and get it over with rather than worsen existence by making more karma for the souls (atmans) that he's about to dispatch to the great beyond. These souls, he is sure, are just going to come back. Worse yet, he feels the whole thing is just gonna make his next incarnation that much worse, since he had the chance to stop the battle but didn't.

Enter: Vishnu, disguised as Krishna, disguised as Arjuna's chariot driver. (Hindu lore is full of these multi-leveled disguises.) Krishna proceeds to explain to Arjuna that he's getting all worked up about nothing. He explains that the absence of karma does not mean the absence of action. Instead (says Krishna) it's the absence of attachment to the action. That is, it's ok for you to go out and slaughter tons and tons of people, lopping heads and raping cattle, provided you don't actually take any pleasure in it. You're just supposed to Ado' it. No thought. No glee. Just do what you are meant to do and carry on doing it until you die. Then, if you haven't attached yourself to your actions, you're free of the karmic attachment of the world and are free of Samara, the Wheel of Life.

Arjuna basically says "Yeah, hey, cool. That works for me." and goes off to kill while Krishna a.k.a. Vishnu wanders away happy to have aided the warrior on his deep mystical trek.

The implication of this story is pretty fundamental to the religion however. You see, what all this meant was that people need not and should not remove themselves from society in order to rid themselves of karma. Instead, they were to stay as good soldiers, wives, farmers, whatever, and work in the knowledge that they were fulfilling the role rather than creating karma. Sounds pretty lame for a major concept, but you have to figure that this idea allowed people to keep doing stuff instead of just starving under a tree as one might otherwise think necessary under the rules of karma. Indian culture was allowed to carry on raping and pillaging and conquering without the guilt of having created karma. I suspect the faith would never have gone as far as it has if they'd all just given up and starved in obedience to their beliefs.

One other major thing in all this is the role of the god. You see, according to the idea of the Brahman, the Ultimate Expression, all things are destined to go to Moksha, or Nirvana, sooner or later. This included the gods. They were seen as being on the same road to Ultimate Expression, but were just a tad further along it than we. In essence, we and the gods were the same stuff... creations of the One... but the gods were just closer to the One. They were seen as kind of older siblings rather than parental figures, helping us to get where they are and, eventually, into Moksha. This sibling role is entirely different from the Western ideas of God the Father. God the Father knew all. The gods of Hinduism, though almost all knowing, were kinda fallible and could make wrong judgments.

Shiva

The Universe is full of magical things, patiently waiting

for our wits to grow sharper. ~Eden Philpotts

What we in the god-biz call the proto-Shiva was a Vedic beast master. It was this image of a strong and powerful god who had dominion over all the animals. In Vedism they called this god Rudra. In Hinduism he was given the new name Shiva, which roughly translated as Auspicious', or so says Ninian Smart. Page 137, The Religious Experience of Mankind. There. A real reference note. And I bet you thought I couldn't do it, didn't you?

Anyway, Shiva is the sustainer of all life, the source of all yogic power, the great and eternal meditative force in the universe, yada yada, you get the idea. Major guy in the Hindu pantheon. His devotees (yogis) smear themselves in ashes and sit around contemplating the temporary nature of the universe. (I had a weekend like that back in '97. The charges were dropped.) The ashes are supposed to remind them of how fleeting the world is, and how they're going to end up dead. (Catholics stole this practice for Ash Wednesday by the way. Their *'Remember Man that thou art dust and unto dust thou shalt return'* line directly mimics Shiva worship.)

Shiva is the god of the ascetic. The one you'd go to get in touch with your inner self and understand your place in the universe. All the hippies that traveled to India to 'find themselves' during the sixties would have wound up in some form of Shiva worship. Oddly enough, he's also the god of creativity and creation. His symbol (a phallus, or penis shaped pillar) represents his power as creator and maker of the universe. It is said that it is the dance of Shiva that keeps creation happening, and that if he ever stopped dancing then chaos would rule. Like all Hindu gods, Shiva goes by a ton of different names, as does his wife, Kali. You may have seen Kali... usually represented as a black woman with a skull around her throat, possibly with large fangs and evil eyes. (Like most of my dates.) She's also a creator god, but is more famous for her role as destroyer. The two were made for each other.

Ok, just before I finish off, I am curious about something. Let's have a show of hands: How many of you out there are astonished that I didn't crack a joke about the huge penis shaped pillars of Shiva?

Yeah. Thought so.

VISHNU

"If I were two-faced, would I be wearing this one?" ~Abraham Lincoln

Vishnu covers all the basic stuff that Shiva misses. Where Shiva does the ascetic trip, Vishnu is more about the external world of worship and ceremony. It was Vishnu that went down and disguised himself as Krishna, a.k.a. the chariot driver for Arjuna in the Bhagavad-Gita. (I know I know... it's a whole lot of Indian names in a row and it's all gonna get confusing. I'm trying. But it's kinda like trying to order a peanut butter sandwich in a gourmet restaurant.)

Anyway, Vishnu is all about ceremony and the physical world, like the war Arjuna was in. Shiva, being the deep mystic guy, would never have bothered with it.

Basically Vishnu is the god for Hindus who would have grown up to be Born-again Christians had they been raised in America. The mythology even has a bit set aside to appeal to the apocalyptic nutbars of India. Instead of the Jesus figure, it is Vishnu who comes back in the end to judge the living and the dead. He does so in his guise as a Kalki, the dark god o' judgment.

And that's Shiva and Vishnu in a nutshell. You don't really have to worry about Brahma, the third guy in the trilogy. He kind of faded away after being invented. Basically he was just a basic representation of the Brahman, used to link Shiva and Vishnu into one character. A middle man for a theology that wanted all the gods connected into three gods, then those three linked into one god called Brahman. Without the third character, the image would only have two faces and it wouldn't seem to be looking all ways. Shiva and Vishnu would also seem separate, which contradicts the ideas of a unified godhead that the Brahmin were trying for.

YOGIS

Ecstasy is a glimpse of the infinite; horror is full disclosure.
~Kirk Schneider

Yoga studios are pretty much everywhere nowadays. Yet another left over from those intrepid hippies that went off to India and came back with deep meaningful insights and social diseases their family doctors had never even read about. Start off by forgetting everything you ever knew about yoga studios and yoga classes. It's 90% crap, and has very little to do with the religious basis for yogic meditation. These days it's mainly just a feel-good health thing that improves breathing and posture. These benefits of yoga are actually supposed to be side effects, not the goal. As strange as it may sound, yoga was not invented to be used in shopping malls or home videos.

A yogi, or one who practices yoga, is a worshiper of Shiva, the mystic god. Before all the yoga meditation got started the yogi was supposed to renounce normal human life. He was supposed to withdraw from society, have no goods or clothes, and be entirely ascetic in nature. Now, I've been to a few yoga classes in my time. (Not that many granted, but is it my fault that they don't provide ashtrays? You'd think they'd never seen a guy smoke a cigarette before.) Anyway, these days it's all about breathing, flexing, and exercise, so I don't tend to find my way into these places much. Funny that.

The thing is, yoga is not a fitness program. I find it really bizarre that it's been accepted as such. Sure, you can go on and on about the health benefits of yoga, but there are health benefits from a lot rituals, say like doing the Stations of the Cross, or climbing the steps of a Mayan pyramid to perform a blood sacrifice to Huitzilopochtli, but you don't see people emulating these rights for health reasons. It sounds absurd when you put it that way, but the comparison is a sound one. Yogic practices are designed to get the adherent closer to Shiva, not fitness.

Now, try to pronounce Huitzilopochtli. I dare ya.

The yogic mystic is usually an outcast kinda guy that's relinquished all things material to follow his path to Shiva through constant meditation. We call them Yogi's over here. Yogi' and Yoga' are both words meaning 'yoke', as in the thing you use to control oxen. It's a Control' or means' to achieve mystic stuff. The guys that practice the Hindu mystic stuff are not actually called yogis. They're *syad*,[86] a term that just means "holy man.' The word Yogi' does come up in a lot of names, but it's not used as a title. Just a name. It would be like having the middle name Pope.

The real yogis are guys that leave the society and wander around either stark naked or wearing the traditional saffron robes. They carry canes to lean on and just kind of wander around praying to Shiva and meditating. They're supposed to be regarded as outside of the caste system (which, I figure, probably gets a lot of lower caste folks into it.) In reality they're usually looked upon as pariahs... accepted, but not generally like. Unless of course you get bit by a snake, in which case they love them. One of the big ways these guys eat is by getting rid of snake venom demons.

Anyway, it's not all that exciting a life. The people that made yoga a popular past time definitely took only the best parts of it, omitting things like caking yourself in shit and ashes. Which, now that I think of it, is kind of too bad. I can think of a lot of people I know who practice yoga that I would love to see caked in shit and ashes.

Anyway, all this exercise is just a phase of the yogi stuff. They call it Hatha-Yoga, Hatha meaning 'Force'. So Yogis use the Force. It all about a path that leads further and further away from the physical, Samsara, to a freedom through Moksha or liberation into Nirvana. As they get better at this they supposedly are able to be so far removed from the physical that pain and suffering and the ills of the world no longer affect them, which is where the whole sleeping on a bed of nails thing comes from. They strive to put their bodies through stuff that you shouldn't be able to endure so they can master the karma of pain and suffering and be free of it. We have a similar sort of ritual in North America. We call it Jack Daniels
.

SECTS

Whenever you find that you are on the side of the majority,

it is time to reform. ~Mark Twain

Ok, yet again, this religion technically doesn't have sects. They are a unified faith that has different 'Schools of thought'. It's a standard line religions use to explain why they disagree but are still one religion. The Hindus manage to keep this solidarity because the definition of 'Hindu' is so broad that virtually anyone can fit in and call themselves an adherent. (IE: They believe Jesus was an avatar of Vishnu.) All the yogic stuff we've been looking at generally comes from the Samkhya school. There's also Mimamsa, Vedanta, and others. These different schools basically allowed whatever was popular with the people at the time to be represented in the faith.

Take Mimamsu for instance. It's big thing was piety and good will. They believe that the reward for a good and pious life was an eternal residency in heaven where you get to hang out with the gods. This so fundamentally disagrees with the premises of Hinduism, but is still accepted if not agreed with by the whole. But you're welcome to believe this if you want.

Another good one is Vedanta. The word actually means "Veda's End" meaning the end of the era where the little gods ruled and Shiva and Vishnu took over. Technically it's a really old idea, but there's this modern day Vedanta that has nothing to do with the ancient stuff but is being accepted worldwide as Hinduism. It's actually just New Age stuff in a Hindu package. It talks about the unity of all religions and finding peace and contentment though all the scriptures in all the religions, all that crap. It's the same stuff Baha Ullah passed off as Baha'I and it came into being about the same time. It was started by a guy named Dr. Radhakrishnan, who was president of India in the early part of this century. The theologies were picked up by guys like Aldous Huxley and Christopher Isherwood. Anyway, a lot of what the west knows as Hinduism is actually this Vedanta stuff. The thing is, it's not the traditional Shiva/Vishnu cult stuff that you see in India. It's more like Shirley Maclean; all unity and wonder and personal power. But hey, it sells.

That's the crux of Hinduism. It's just Vedism, your typical barometric pressure deity religion, now evolved into a convoluted hierarchy of big, unknowable gods that are all avatars (masks)of the one big god Brahman. It works because no matter what you sit down and make up as a religion, some priest will be able to come in, take a look at your notes, and tell you which of the three main gods, Shiva Vishnu or Brahman, it is that's pretending to be your god.

If you wander into a Hindu temple you're gonna see tons of idols and her dozens of stories about different gods. Ignore it. They're really only working on the three main ones, and even those three main ones are actually just one big god that's all things, the neti neti (not this not that) idea mentioned earlier. All the names and myths are just leftovers from Vedism, though they'll get ticked with you if you tell them that. Your average adherent doesn't usually know much about the whole avatar concept. They're raised with the stories of the many gods, and later on (if they care to learn it) they're told about the one big one. For this reason, someone who worships a Wombat god in India may not know that it's actually Vishnu, Brahma, or Shiva they're praying to, though their priest should be able to tell you about it.

BUDDHISM

Real knowledge is to know the extent of one's ignorance.
~Confucius

Chop Suey was not invented in China. It was invented by a chef at the Waldorf Astoria in New York City when some big wig asked for "something Chinese" and the cook had to throw a bunch of stuff together and make it look Chinese. An interesting parallel to this is that spaghetti, the most famous of Italian dishes, actually was invented in China and was imported to Italy by traders.

Aside from the increasingly obvious fact that I'm hungry as I'm writing this, one could get to wondering what, if anything, it all has to do with the history of Buddhism. The answer, you'll be less than surprised to find out, is absolutely nothing. But for a change I do actually have a point.

You see, like the spaghetti thing, a lot of people just assume that Buddhism was invented in China or Japan, mainly because that's where we always see the temples and stuff. Some folks might hazard to guess it came from Tibet, mainly because that's where the Dalai Lama and Co. are from. You'd be getting closer, but still off a bit. The truth is, Buddhism comes from the exact same guys that brought you Soma, yogis, Shiva, and the whole Brahman Bunch. Buddhism is Indian in origin, so we're gonna have to go back to the early Vedic crap yet again so I can show you how all this Buddhism stuff came about.

Ok, remember the era where fire and water and pretty much anything else just might be divine? Well, before the Brahman came up with the idea of avatars and really got this whole Hinduism thing happening, there were a lot of people asking questions that the Vedics just couldn't answer. One such person was Siddhartha Gautama, son of the Kshatriyan warlord, prince of India, and spiritual godhead of Buddhism. We'll can him Sid.

Sid was born in 563 BC just outside of Kapilavastu, on the India/Nepal border. This is still about 1000 years before the Muslim invasion, so everyone there at the time was either pre-Hindu or Vedic, with a bit of Jainism thrown in for the hell of it. (Oh... Jainism. It's a really old religion in India that's full of deep wisdom about how to get to Nirvana and be One with all your ancestors and stuff like that there. Jains are followers of the Jinas... ancestral worship basically. Extremely holy and important. Really important. Almost deserves its own paragraph.)

Anyway, we're talking about a civilization that had this mesh of Jain monks, Vedics, and early yogis all wandering around the countryside trying to get to Nirvana, while in the cities the Brahmin are getting the whole Hinduism thing going, trying to sew all the Vedic beliefs into one big religion. Okay, so this is what Sid was born into.

There's a lot of stories about Sid's young life that I will summarily toss out the window here. Most of it is probably crap, and even if it isn't it has no bearing on what he did or said to start Buddhism. They're just folk tales about how precocious he was and how everyone around him knew he was to become a powerful and enlightened master. As all these tales were written after he grew up to be a powerful and enlightened master, I think the veracity of these tales is somewhat suspect. (IE: Crap) Here's what we know of the guy...

Sid was born the son of a Kshatriyan raja, or clan leader. This means he was born into the caste that was supposed to kill, rape, maim, and order people around. As a good Kshatriyan, he was supposed to take over the family business (killing) when he got old enough to do so, and was destined to be the new leader of the Kshatriyans.

He grew up fairly normal as near as I can tell. There are stories of him being hidden away from the world lest he never see suffering, but I'll get to that. The evidence is, he did grow up and he did get married. He had a couple kids, and until he was 29 he lived a perfectly normal life for a Kshatriyan prince in 500 BC. Then, like many a great religious figure before him, he snapped.

SID'S REVELATION

When Sid got to 29, he was basically fed up with trying to figure out this whole existence thing. The myth has it that it was at this time that he saw an ascetic monk wander by, and this inspired him to give up everything he knew and become an ascetic. Personally, I think it had more to do with being fed up with the whole wife, kids, family, and responsibility thing. Either way, he slipped out the window in the middle of the night and took off from his family, leaving the whole wife and kid thing behind him. Near as I can tell he'd basically gotten to the point where scratching out a living, working like hell, then dying just seemed like a pretty useless concept, so he takes off with this monk who, supposedly, knew what was what and why things happened.

I should explain that this spousal abandonment (sorry... mystic calling) fulfilled a prophesy supposedly given about Sid when he was a baby. You see, there were these three "sights" --- things Sid saw--- that became really important. The first was a sick guy, the second a dead guy, and the monk with the ascetic lifestyle was the third. The prophesy mysteriously predicted exactly what happened to Sid; when he saw a sick guy and a dead guy, it introduced him to the suffering of the world. Then the monk wandered in and showed him the ascetic lifestyle. Inspired by the monk's life, Sid took off with the monk to try to find an answer to life's suffering by starving and whipping himself. It was a special kind of logic that.

The monk taught him that he should whip himself, starve himself, and hope that some deity or ghost would drop by and explain what the hell was happening and why life sucks. Buying into all this, Sid settles into a new life of abusing himself in hopes of gaining some insight. Amazingly, it took a couple years of this before Sid realizes he's getting nowhere. No gods. No ghosts. Just misery, starvation, and a few cool scars to brag about to his monk buddies. In the end though, all the hope he'd put into ritually abusing himself kinda fell flat, and Sid was left feeling like an idiot.

The day finally comes when he looks up from his daily whipping and says "Screw this." Having done the whole monk trip and gotten all he could from it, he decided it was all useless. The monks didn't have any more of a clue as to what was happening than he did, and all the starvation and whipping in the world wasn't about to give him the answers. He packed up his gear, walked away from the monks, and headed into the forest to figure it out on his own.

ENLIGHTENMENT

Discovery consists of seeing what everybody has seen and thinking what nobody has thought. ~Albert Szent-Gyorgyi

Pretty much everybody has taken this whole "Enlightenment" incident and made a lot out of it. The Buddhists love to tell you about the Bodhi tree Sid sat under for days on end, and there's a lot of bizarre stories about how gods and goddesses appeared to him while he sat there, but it's all crap designed to make it all look holier than it was.

What actually happened here is that Sid lost it. I mean, completely lost it. He's been frying his brain for years trying to figure out why people go through so much agony just to end up dead, and no matter where Sid looked no one seemed to know the reason for it all. (This was obviously before coffee was invented.) Frustrated and fed up of looking, Sid found himself a nice secluded tree, sat down, and snapped.

"That's it." he said to the Universe "I've had it. I keep trying and trying, and what do I get? Nothing. Zilch. Nada. No gods, no goddesses, no reason for being. Just a whole bunch of idiotic religious tripe that never actually explains anything."

The universe barely noticed his rant.

"Ok, we do it this way," Sid said, explaining his game plan to the Universe. "I'm going to sit right here. If there's an answer to all this, it can find me. I'm done chasing after it. I'm gonna stay right where I am, and I'm not moving until someone or something explains this whole existence thing to me. I don't care if I starve to death or die of thirst or get eaten by the next Bengal tiger that wanders by. I am not moving until this universe explains itself to me."

The Universe, totally unaware that it was being challenged, just ignored him.

"I'll be right here." Sid said to the rather silent Universe. "Under this tree..."

Well, the universe, being as insensitive then as it is today, said and did nothing. So, true to his word, Sid said and did nothing. He just sat there, staring down all of existence and hoping it blinked before he did. And so he sat.

And sat. And sat.

Being genuinely pissed off and having absolutely no intent to lose this celestial standoff, Sid stayed where he was. He ate bugs that crawled over his hands when he could, and sipped dew or rainwater when he was thirsty. Other than that, he didn't move. Didn't flinch. He just kept staring day after day, hoping sooner or later the Universe would cave and let him in on the joke. The tension was thick, and something had to give. In the end, the Buddhists will tell you it was the universe that caved. Me? I am fairly certain it was Sid.

What happened, according to Sid's own story anyway, was that the Universe kind of opened up to him. He ceased to be just "Sid" and he came to understand that his being, his atman, was only a small part of the whole universe. When what he called Ultimate Reality opened up, he as an individual person kinda disappeared. He experienced what it was like to not have an individual self anymore, but be part of the whole of the universe. When what was Sid ceased to matter, suddenly it was all beautiful and eternal and full of bliss and joy. It was only his self, his atman or soul that kept him thinking it was all horrible and painful here on old Earth. He realized that he, the tree, the rock, and an ion field in Alpha Centauri were all the same thing. The idea of a self, thought Sid, was what kept us away from this eternal sense of bliss.

This is what the Enlightenment was; the realization that an individual self is an illusion and that we (and all existence) are more properly one big energy mass. When we give up on the idea of being an individual, we achieve Enlightenment. This, by the way, is how Sid gained the name Buddha. It means "the enlightened one." All the same though, I think I'll just keep calling him Sid. It just sounds better.

So Sid had his answer. Understanding that he no longer existed, he got up, brushed himself off, and wandered back to town totally unaware of the inherent contradiction in this action.

When we remember we are all mad, the mysteries disappear
and life stands explained. ~Mark Twain

When he got back the first thing Sid did was set to making a theology out of all this. The theology was based on his Four Noble Truths, paraphrased here for your entertainment:[87]

1: Life is shit. Get used to it. You're gonna suffer all your life and die a horrible painful death with no idea why. No matter what you do, it will all eventually fail and everything you love will rot away, and there's not a damn thing you can do about it.

2: Life is shit because people keep wanting things that are just going to disappoint them. Take lasagna for instance. If you really love the stuff, you spend time working up an appetite and dreaming and hoping for the lasagna. Then, when it's served, you reach the apex of the lasagna pleasure. You eat it, and suddenly the lasagna desire is fulfilled. You then have to start from the very beginning again, working up an appetite, looking for lasagna, finding lasagna, then eating it again. Like the lasagna, no pleasure you could ever find on Earth can be permanent. You will always be on a roller coaster of cravings; searching, finding, enjoying, then searching again.

3: Life would not be shit if you as an individual didn't have these cravings. If you didn't want or need anything, you wouldn't be caught on the roller coaster of desires, fulfillment, and desires. You could, as Sid had, give up on the idea of a "self" that wants "things" and just be part of the universe at large, never wanting or needing for all eternity. That way, when you die, there would be no desires that would draw you back into the world and your energy would reach Nirvana, the one place where you can be eternally happy and content. No roller coaster, no failed desires. Just eternal Nothing where you don't exist because all you are has reverted back to being One with the universe.

4: The only way to be free of your cravings and release yourself from Samara (the Wheel of life) is to follow the eight-fold path.

Now, I hear you ask, what is an eight-fold path? Well, it's a lot like a 12 step program, but with monks instead of sponsors and you don't get a six-week badge for sobriety. It's really just a "How to be a nice, passive monk that doesn't want anything" list. It demands things like "Right thinking" and "Right breathing" and all that. Pretty basic to Buddhism, but not relevant unless you want to buy into all this and forsake your "self" in favor of eternal nothingness. I love the roller coaster myself.

POST-ENLIGHTENMENT

> *Happy is he who can give himself up.*
>
> *~Naguib Mahfouz*

Things begin to get weird as soon as Sid returns. You see, he first wanders back to the monks he was hanging around with before he snapped, and tells them that he's figured it all out. They, of course, were rather curious and implored him to tell them what he has learned. The conversation went something like this:

"Tell us what you figured out Sid." a monk asks.

"Why am I talking to myself?" Sid responds.

"Huh?" the monk says..

"I'm talking to myself. Why am I talking to myself?" Sid says.

"Huh?" the monk says again, figuring he'd missed something.

"I'm talking to myself." Sid reiterates.

"Yeah... I got that part." The monk responds..

"It's a unity thing."

"Uh huh."

"You see, as we're all just one thing, then my telling you anything is really just me talking to my self." .

"One what?" The monk asks.

"Huh?" says Sid.

"You said we were all one. One what?"

"Well... one. You know... One. Capital O."

"Oh."

"Yes... O. Capital."

"So, we're all a capital O?" the monk asks.

"Yes. Er, no. Sort of. I mean... we're all one One."

"Let me get this straight. Are we one "O" or one One?"

"One One."

"Oh."

"And the two of us are both these Ones, have I got it?" the monk asks.

"No! There is no two of us. Just the One. The Ultimate, Undivided, Total Unity of the Great-and-All-Encompassing One."

"And we're both this, er, One thingy then?"

"YES!!" Shouts Sid.

"With a capital O?"

"Yes."

"Oh." the monk says, and wanders off to spend the rest of his life meditating on the true joy and bliss of the One Great and True Capital O.

Sid kept teaching though, and did manage to get a lot of people to understand and aspire to his idea of a permanent bliss by getting rid of yourself a.k.a. atman. He taught about how to go off and meditate so you can get rid of all your karma so when you die your energies are free to go off never come back.

While Sid did seem to believe in the existence of gods, he decided that the gods themselves were in the same boat we were: condemned to existence until they can be free of all karma. As the only way he thought they could do this is through Enlightenment, he basically said that they too needed to listen to him or suffer for all eternity. This put Sid above the gods, since only through his teaching would they ever find happiness.

You gotta admit... the guy had balls.

SID'S DEATH

There is a time for departure even when there's no certain place to go.

~Tennessee Williams

For someone who said he didn't exist, Sid lived for a long while. He died of food poisoning after eating a roast pig in Sri Lanka when he was somewhere in his 80's. That's it. Nothing special. No angels or trumpets. He just keeled over from eating a bad piece of pig. Kinda lacks the bloody, gruesome death scene religions tend to lend to their founders, but what the hell. If Mohammed died of old age, why can't the Buddha die of poison pig?

Like all other faiths, it didn't take long after the founder's death before the original message started to be re-interpreted and everyone started yelling and screaming and calling each other heretics and liars. It's kinda what I like about religions actually. As happened in Christianity, the infighting started and kept growing, with two very opposing ideas pushing to the forefront. In Christianity this whole scenario happened because of Martin Luther and his problems with the pope. In Buddhism, it all started because of the rain.

THE SANGHA

"Rain, rain go way, come again another day."

One of the cornerstone ideals in Buddhism is *ahimsa,* which literally translates as "not killing." The idea here was that you shouldn't kill anything, even for food, because all life is on a path to Enlightenment and killing would only create more karma for both you and your lunch. Besides, the chicken would have to start a whole new life just to get back to where it was when you battered and deep fried it. So... no killing. Period. (Note: You could eat meat, say like Sid's pig, if someone GAVE it to you. You just couldn't kill it yourself.)

The problem was the rain. You see, even while Sid was still alive there got to be this problem of the rainy season when all the bugs would come out in force. You couldn't take a step without killing a half dozen of them. The monks, not about to let themselves kill, would have to be totally immobile during this season.

Sid's answer to this was the Sangha or assembly; a place that would be screened in before the rainy season and very carefully swept and cleaned so that no bugs would be there. Then, when the rains came, the monks could gather there where they could move about without killing anything. When the rains stopped, the monks could go back to their trees and continue meditating alone in the forest. This place, the Sangha, was the first place that Buddhist monks ever gathered under one roof instead of living alone in the wilds. (Incidentally, Sid stole the idea from the Vedics, as did the Hindus. All three religions have Sanghas for basically the same reason; ahimsa, or not-killing.)

It should come as no surprise that it was here, in the Sangha, that a bunch of crowded, wet, and half-starved monks first found dissension in their ranks.

ARHAT, BODHISATTVA, AND BUDDHA

Lots of folks confuse bad management with destiny. ~Kin Hubbard

As these things go, a hierarchy was immediately established. Since God wasn't a problem here, the Buddhists didn't have to deal with who was blessed by a god to lead them. Instead, it all had to do with how enlightened you were. The monks after Sid set up was a hierarchy that went like this:

At the bottom was the poor slob who wasn't a monk, didn't meditate, and would never reach Nirvana in this lifetime. One step up was the monk, a guy trying to find satori, or temporary enlightenment.

Above him was the Arhat, kind of a living saint that had reached satori but was still in his body so that he could teach before he leaves to Nirvana when he dies.

Then comes the Bodhisattva. The Dalai Lama's one of these guys. He's a Buddhist monk who reached full enlightenment and died, but made a noble promise never to go into Nirvana (even though he could) until every soul precedes him. He reincarnates and comes back over and over again to help people achieve Nirvana. He's on an eternal quest to enlighten all existence. According to his oath, he will only enter Nirvana when the last soul precedes him.

What this inevitably means is that at the end, when all the normal souls are in Nirvana, there's gonna be a bunch of these Bodhisattvas at the entrance doing a Three Stooges Routine... "You first", "No... You first.", "No, after you.. I insist."

Above the Bodhisattvas was the Buddha. That would be Sid, and a few guys like him; people who had achieved all there was to achieve and had shuffled off this mortal coil, never to return. The followers deified Sid after he was gone, making him into a godhead; the One True Buddha, or Enlightened One.

Now, if you've got this whole Buddha, Bodhisattva, Arhat concept down you have a pretty good handle on Buddhism in general. A lot of what Buddhists do today has more to do with venerating these guys than achieving personal enlightenment as Sid said you should do. Instead, over the years, there grew a whole pantheon of Buddhas and Bodhisattvas that could be worshipped and prayed to for help and guidance in getting to Nirvana. Or, if you didn't think you're gonna make it to Nirvana, they could help your crops grow or some such small favor. Of course, in order for them to help you you'd have to go to a temple and sacrifice accordingly to them, so the monks finally found a way to make a living.

THERAVADA, HINAYANA, AND MAHAYANA.

I am prepared to die, but there is no cause
for which I am prepared to kill. ~Mahatma Gandhi

This stark difference in attitudes toward Sid's philosophy changed things a lot. So much so that the original guys, the ones that still thought Sid's teaching was about sitting under a tree and reaching enlightenment, became considered a little lost and out of it.

It worked like this; the belief system Sid set up was called Theravada. It means "Way of the elders". The newer idea of the Bodhisattvas and sacrifices and all that stuff became known as

Mahayana, or "Wide vehicle". They picked that name because they felt that their idea of help from the Bodhisattvas allowed more people to reach Nirvana, or at least a better reincarnation. Theravada, they thought, was only good for those that wanted to sit under a tree and meditate. With the help of the gods, er, Bodhisattvas, you could get an express trip to a better place.

Needless to say the Theravadas didn't like this whole idea, and the fights soon started. As there were more Mahayanist than Theravadas, the old school ideals started to die out. The Mahayanist movement grew quickly as Theravada declined, and pretty soon the vast majority of Buddhists were Mahayanist. After a bit, the old guys were just considered oddballs, and are still referred to today as Hinayana, or "smaller vehicles". Ok, the language thing doesn't quite capture it, but that's a pretty big insult to the Theravadas in their own language.

By the eleventh century when the Muslim invasions of India were in full swing, the older Buddhism, Theravada/Hinayana, was already pretty much dead in India. People just hadn't bought into it anymore. Even Mahayana, the Bodhisattva worshipping side of it, had begun to die out. In true Hindu form, the Brahmin priests had managed to convince a lot of the Buddhists that Sid was actually an avatar of Krishna/Shiva, so the whole movement kind of just fizzles out and meshed into Hinduism.

Theravada remains in Sri Lanka to some degree, but by the 12th century it had given up on India entirely. Instead, it moved across Asia and settled in to places like China and Japan, which is where we need to go to follow the history of Buddhism through to present day Jujitsu classes. Here's where I start getting into trouble with the Buddhists. You see, in India, there were only Theravada and Mahayana. When Buddhism got to China in the first century AD, it was like light hitting a prism. Suddenly there were tons of sects of Buddhism arising, and everyone seemed to have their own idea of what Sid and company were all about. Although a lot of places in Asia accepted Buddhism, I've decided to start China, mainly because I just spilled coffee on the Thai notes and it's gonna be an hour or so before they dry.

Religion is a candle inside a multicoloured lantern. Everyone looks through a particular color, but the candle is always there. ~Mohammed Neguib

Buddhism basically just wandered into China. No wars or big theological debates. It just kind of wandered in without anyone really noticing. This happened somewhere around the first century AD, when India was trading spices for silks along what's known as "the Silk Road". Traders would go back and forth between the two countries all the time, and somewhere along the line some Buddhist monk whose name history forgot wound up in China.

When he got there, he met up with the existing religions; Taoism and Confucianism. It was the interaction between Buddhism and these faiths that caused all the sects. So, rather than running through about a thousand sects I'll just give you the Reader's Digest version of how all this went down.

The Taoists that listened to the ideas of the Nirvana and the unity of all things basically already agreed. Taoism has this whole concept of "balance", the Yin and Yang of things. To them, the Buddhist philosophy was just an added insight into the nature of existence. The idea of being One with all existence fit perfectly with the Taoists idea of being One with the Tao.

Basically all you really need to know about Taoism is that they believe in one all-encompassing thing called the Tao (pronounced "Dow" as in Dow Jones Industrial). If you surrender yourself to the Tao and work within it your life is easy. If you work against the natural flow of energies by thinking and planning stuff out you're gonna have a hard time of it. It's where George Lucas stole the idea of The Force from. Think of everything Yoda ever told you and you'll have it down pretty well. If you have any other problems, pick up a copy of the Tao Te Ching or, better yet, The Tao of Pooh. (Also the sequel: The Te of Piglet).

Confucianism on the other hand has no real theology or explanation for why life is. It's actually just a system that teaches you how to behave. It was started by a guy named K'ung Fu Tzu, which is where the name's from. We in the West couldn't say it properly so we slurred the name K'ung Fu Tzu into one word: Confucius.

In about 500 BC, K'ung came up with a system of how to

get along in society that everyone's been raving about ever since. It's basically a patriarchal and imperial system that lets you know who you serve and who should serve you. (The man serves the Emperor, the woman serves the man, the child serves the parent, etc., etc.) It's all very stoic and rigid, but it kinda had to be. It was invented to keep a bunch of bloodthirsty marauders together in one society without killing each other. As China still exists, it seems to have worked.

Anyway, Mahayana Buddhism wandered into China and encountered these two faiths, Taoism and Confucianism. When you look at the gist of the two religions, you can kind of understand how Buddhism worked in nicely. The Taoists accepted it as part of their own belief system with the idea of the unity of all things (which they called the Tao).

Confucianism, for its part, really didn't care about the religion unless it interfered with the social structure and the only place that happened was with the Sangha, or Buddhist temples. (The Sanghas became temples in time; while they were originally there as refuge from the rainy season, it didn't take long before monks moved in and stayed there all year long. Besides, the Mahayanists needed a place for the people to give alms, in exchange for which they'd pray for the poor bastards who would never be enlightened.)

Anyway, about the only place that Buddhism offended Confucianism was with the idea of a temple. Confucianism has this whole idea of family obligations, and abandoning your family and moving into a celibate monastery just wasn't their idea of good family behavior. But even this faux pas didn't really cause a stir. Eventually the Confucians just sort of shrugged and let them go.

Because Buddhism was so readily accepted it became a real "religion" in China. Governments started to back it, and huge temples were built and maintained by various warlords and emperors. The Bodhisattvas became powerful images, and wars were won and lost because of the backing of the monks and their godhead, Siddhartha Gautama.   The fact that he was dead from a pig overdose several hundred years earlier didn't affect anything. He was now divine, and as such could back armies and bless emperors.

Every path serves a purpose. ~Gene Oliver

There are hundreds of sects of Buddhism that have arisen in China and Japan. As all of them are Mahayanist and I've given the basics of Mahayana, I see running through each sect as being redundant. All you really have to understand is that the indigenous religions had their effect on Buddhism, and there was a lot of cross pollination of religious beliefs. Confucianism and Taoism bled into Buddhism, which is where you get the new sects from for the most part.

There are only a couple I want to look at, the first of which is Ch'an, also known as Zen.

Both "Zen" and "Ch'an" mean "meditation", so what we're talking about here is a Buddhism that focuses on meditation. The name difference is only because Ch'an is popular in China and Zen is Japanese, but it's really the same thing. Of course, they'd hate you for saying so.

Zen is nothing more than the Mahayanist Buddhism that's crossed with Taoism. They took the ideas of Nirvana and tantric meditation and crossed them with the Taoist idea of working "within the Tao." You'll remember that the Taoists believe that everything is easier when you give up on planning things and just "be", allowing the Tao to guide you. By adding in the element that living this way also rids you of karma (you just "are" and therefore don't create or experience karma) you create a system wherein the adherent strives to rid himself of his atman/self, while still working within the world.

The reason this became so big is because of the military implications of it all. You see, the biggest problem any army has is the natural cowardice of its soldiers. Put anyone in a situation where they're gonna die no matter what and you can pretty much guarantee that a certain percentage of them are going to lose it and flip out rather than killing the enemy. Zen/Ch'an solved that problem.

If you are a Zen soldier, they teach you that you as an individual (as an atman) cease to exist. You simply exist as one small part of the universe, in what Sid called Satori or temporary enlightenment.

In this frame of mind, you don't care about being hacked to bits by an enemy. You focus only on the act of fighting, and are "One" with the world around you while fulfilling the role of warrior.

It's all mystic and deep, but the thing is it worked. In the fifth century when Buddhism was getting settled into China, the emperors were quick to figure out the military benefits of this mind set. One of the best examples was under Emperor Ming (No... nothing to do with Flash Gordon).

Ming had an elite troop of warriors he kept aside specifically for battles he figured he'd lose. When the armies assembled on the battlefield, he would draw his main force back and send a hundred of these guys to the front. The enemy would be watching, expecting this force to attack at any second.

Instead, at the command of the emperor, all 100 men would draw a specially designed sword and have it hovering above and behind them. Then, on another command from the emperor, all 100 men would bring the sword forward and down, slicing off their own heads. As the bodies fell, another hundred men would step up and stand over the bodies, drawing the same kind of swords.

The effect was incredible. The enemy, seeing what these men would do on behalf of their emperor, would be scared stiff. Many battles were totally avoided with this maneuver. The enemy, in my opinion wisely, typically opted to high-tail it outta there rather than face these psychos. Can you blame them? This story is more than just a genuinely chilling image. It's the reason Buddhism so many monarchies and Emperors financially backed Buddhism in the East: it worked for warfare.

Thailand

Folklore has it that when Sid got older he explained to his disciples that the path to Enlightenment was one of self-reflection and personal meditation. The Buddha, he said, was merely a sign post that points the way along the path. The path was to be walked alone. That's the cover story anyway. Here's how I figure this all went down...

Sid, being eighty years old or so at the time we're talking

about here, started to care less and less about the fervor of youth. As tends to happen, the quest for the deeper meaning to life was replaced over the years with an even deeper yearning to be left the hell alone. Like most older guys, Sid just wanted to spend his last years kinda relaxing and being free of all the idiots he had to deal with his whole life. As he was still the resident godhead in the area, it got rather difficult for him to find a moment to himself. There was always another lost soul coming up to him out of the blue looking to him get them into Nirvana. (Lost souls, it seems, can be rather tedious and annoying when you're trying to nap.) In the end, Sid figured that as he couldn't get out of being the spiritual godhead, he could at least get out of the responsibility. So, when the next lost soul came up looking for guidance, Sid was ready.

"Master, how shall I find Enlightenment?" his devotee would ask.

"You must find Independence." Sid says.

"Missouri?" the devotee replies.

"No... the other Independence. Independent revelation." Sid says.

"Oh" the devotee says.

"Independent revelation... as in, you don't need me." Sid explains.

"I don't?" the devotee says.

"Nope. You never did really. I'm just a signpost. I show you the way, and you go there."

"So, what you're telling me here is that I never really needed to listen to you at all? You just tell me where to go and I go there?" the devotee asks.

"Yup." Sid answers, happy to be free of it all. "Well, nice chatting with you."

"Wait a minute" the disciple says "Does this mean I never really needed to honor and worship you at all?"

"Nope. All part of the path. See ya."

"Um... wait a minute. What about the food we've been

supplying you with for the last 40 years or so? We didn't need to do that either?"

"Well... no." Sid says, seeing the flaw in his escape. "Er, yes. I mean, you do need a signpost to point the way."

"But you said we don't need to listen to you."

"Well no. You do. You have to listen to me to know where you're going to. But that's it." Sid says.

"And after that you figure we don't really need to listen to you anymore... once we're on this path thingy?"

"Right. Once you're on the Path you can go on about things on your own and you don't need to listen to me anymore." Sid explained.

"So, we don't REALLY need to listen to you that much then?" the disciple asks.

"Unless I'm hungry." Sid says, and takes off to "meditate" alone in the woods.

The long and short of it is that Sid came up with this idea of private meditation that was supposedly the "true" path. This would be as opposed to all the other true paths he'd outlined in his Sutras over the years. (I feel tempted to point out here that all these tales of Sid's life might be total fiction made up long after he died. However, as we're studying religion I figure the possibility that it's all horse shit should be self-evident.)

Anyway, this whole master-versus-independent study thing was what created the split between the Mahayana's and the Theravada's. I look at it as a young versus old thing. It works like this:

The Mahayana's are the guys that followed Sid's teachings when he was young. Coincidentally, Mahayanists tend to be younger. They're the ones that are interested in learning how to master all creation, know all there is to know about the universe, solve the mysteries of life, and occasionally look good doing it. These are the martial artists, the Zen guys, etc.. All the Buddhist disciplines that require a person to do things or be somewhere to reach Enlightenment are generally Mahayana.

The Theravada's on the other hand just want to be left alone to "meditate". Basically it's a great way for older guys to slip away to the woods and nap under trees with no wife, kids or grandkids to bug them. If anyone happens along and catches them snoozing, they can then accuse the intruders of "interrupting their meditations." Of course, somewhere in all this they're supposed to find Enlightenment, but then again so are Kick Boxers. Personally, I prefer the snoozing old geezers that just want to be left alone.

From day one the Mahayana's and Theravadas each saw the other as corrupting the "true" message of the Buddha. To explain their unique message of truth and love the monks from each sect have painstakingly analyzed the teachings of the Buddha (Sid) to create intricate interpretations of the Buddha's teachings. These treatises form much of the depth and meaning of each sect, and give rise to the beauty and sanctity that each claim. Given the extreme importance of these treatises on the development of Buddhist thought and their impact on the Buddhist lifestyle we will, of course, forget they ever existed.

(Yeah, like you wanted to spend the next half hour reading what some monk 200 years ago thought about flowers.)

THAI A YELLOW RIBBON ROUND THE OLD OAK TREE...

Religion are little more than so many spiritual monopolies. ~Lord
Halifax

Before I get too far into this Thai Buddhism stuff I should explain that in the first three editions of this book I didn't cover the Thailand at all. I literally looked at it and said "Screw it... who's gonna know or care that I omitted the whole Thailand Buddhism stuff?" Of course, as these things go, I got a call from my agent who informed me he was in Thailand and had found a publisher who was interested in carrying the book there. I of course said great, panicked, and set to adding all this in so all you kind folks in Thailand who are now able to read this book will think I'd been all over Thai Buddhism all along. So Thailand and Cambodia...

Buddhism got to Thailand in about the third century BC. Apparently some Indian emperor named Ashoka sent two Theravada missionaries to the area. For the Thai readers out there, these Buddhist missionaries settled in Dvaravati, what's now called

Nakhon Pathom, west of Bangkok. (See... I do my research.)

Anyway, the area wasn't controlled by the Thais at the time. A group called the Mon were in charge back then. Much as I'd like to go into one of my famous bloodshed and gore tales here, the Thais didn't invade or kill anyone to take over. They just kinda sauntered in, settled down, and over generations the Mon faded and the Thais grew to power. Beginning to see why I omitted this?

Anyway, as near as I can figure the Thais that reached Thailand came in contact with Buddhism through the Mons. As the missionaries that went there were Theravadas, it was that form of Buddhism that became engrained in the society. So, when the Thais set to making their nation in the 13th century, they adopted Theravada as their state religion. By then of course most of the Theravadas had been wiped off the face of the planet by the Muslims, so they had to forget about India as a source for inspiration. About the only place that had Theravada monks alive and kicking in the 13thcentury was Sri Lanka, which is where the Thais went to get more info on how to set up a Theravada culture. The main difference here was that the Thais used the Theravada Pali scripts from Sri Lanka as doctrine as opposed to the Mahayana scripts done in Sanskrit that the rest of the Buddhist world was using back then. Don't worry... I don't expect anyone to care or even remember Pali scripts versus Sanskrit scripts, but I gotta throw this stuff in so the "real" theologians (read: eggheads) know that I actually did the research for this stuff.

King Ramkamhaeng[88] supposedly got a couple Sri Lankan monks to get the whole Thai Buddhist state thing going. I guess he figured that Thailand didn't have enough nothingness, he had to import it. Anyway, something about the King making Theravada Buddhism the only legal religion in the country suddenly inspired anyone who wasn't a Theravada to become one.

From here on in it all seems to follow the tracks of Catholicism. Church and State are intertwined (never a good idea) and a hell of a lot of the people's money goes into building ridiculously ornate temples for the people to go give their money in. Odd logic that.

We do a get a bit of horrid bloodshed in all this though, but not until 1767 when Burma of all places decides to invade Thailand. Awfully un-neighborly of them. Anyway, it was the standard blood, guts, murder, and wholesale destruction. A bunch of those damned

Pali scripts that I have to keep mentioning were burned and looted in the attack, and for about a year the nation fell to Burmese control.

This all gets kinda interesting through this part of it all. Burma holds control of the capital city, and Buddhism all but dies out for a couple months. Then, later the same year King Taksin makes a new capital city in Thonburi, then by King Rama I (1782-1809) moves the power base to Bangkok, the current capital of Thailand. Anyway, through all this Thailand regained its power, tossed off the Burmese, and carried on with a new capital city and a few less Pali scripts. Ok.. this really didn't affect Buddhism in Thailand at all, but it was the only really bloody story I knew about Thailand and I had to find something to toss in here to make it interesting.

The whole Theravada thing really got going when King Mongkut took the throne in 1851. The guy had been a Theravada monk for 27 years before he gave up that whole Nothingness concept to go off and become king. Unfortunately for Thailand this guy was a Buddhist zealot who figured none of the monasteries were quite strict enough. So much so that he created his own sect of the religion called Thammayut where the truly Enlightened could go off and torture themselves in sublimation and hard labor. (Not unlike Sid had done before he became Enlightened.)

According to the Thai Travel Guide I have sitting in front of me Thailand now has "a religious community of some 250,000 monks who reside at an estimated 27,000 temple monasteries throughout the country." Now, the population of Thailand is 61.4 million. As 250,000 of these are monks, this means one in every 245 people or so are monks. That's a hell of a lot of monks.

THE TUTTLE FACTOR

A thorn defends the rose, harming only those
who would steal the blossom. ~ Chinese proverb

(Note: The following contains excerpts of a conversation between myself and Master E. Tuttle, wherein I took no notes. For this reason, his responses are not verbatim. I am trusting in Tuttle's adherence to ahimsa, or non-violence, should I accidentally misquote him.)

Buddhist monks like to tell you about *ahimsa*, the doctrine of non-violence, and all the kindly loving stuff of Buddhism. The truth is, it was the Buddhists ability to kill that made them rich and accepted by the emperors. Which brings me around to the generic name of this military application of meditation: martial arts. The word "martial" means military. The martial arts were originally the arts perfected by Buddhists that created warriors.

Here we get to Sifu Tuttle, contemporary Buddhist sage and teacher. He's also a world class instructor in things like Tai Chi, Chi Gong, and a dozen other Buddhist disciplines.

Now, I'm 6'3", and about 250 pounds. He's about a foot shorter, and can throw me around like a rag doll. As with the military guys I was talking about, Tuttle uses a Buddhist mindset that's adopted a lot of Taoist ideals. In my never ending quest to understand religions, I sought out Sifu Tuttle and got his input on this whole martial arts as a tool of war concept. He disagreed vehemently.

So, to be fair (and because he could kill me) I'll give you the contemporary Buddhists ideas of martial arts as conveyed by Sifu Tuttle.

While he, and most modern Buddhists, do acknowledge that martial arts were used for war, he maintains that war was neither the reason for their invention nor the rationale behind them. He maintains that the martial arts were invented as a self-defense mechanism for Buddhist monks living in China and Japan during the feudal era. Since the concept of ahimsa restricted them from carrying weapons, these monks studied the animals to understand how a person could defend themselves in the most natural way.

It was, Tuttle assures me, a purely harmless and defensive invention designed to keep the monks safe during some pretty dangerous times.

"So, what about the guys chopping their own heads off? Or Ninjas, or any of the classic killing machines that fill Chinese and Japanese Buddhist lore?" I asked.

"They existed." says Tuttle. "But the theory is like any other power in life. It can be corrupted. Since it's a very powerful concept, the corruption of it is equally powerful."

"So you figure it was all based on peace and love and getting along even though it was a martial art?" I asked.

"Others call them martial arts. To the practitioner, Tai Chi or Bakwa are not "martial". It's the meditative aspect that has always been important. The sanzen [moving meditation] is merely the external image of a deeper transition; a deeper understanding of the energies around and within us." Eric explained.

"So it was never about war or killing?" I asked.

"No. There are those that have used it for these reasons, but it is NOT about violence. Most meditations would be absolutely useless as either defense or offense." Eric said, his hands unconsciously falling into the open-palmed stance that conveys peace.

"And you actually believe this crap?" I asked.

Eric's hands slowly closed over each other, a whiteness forming at the knuckles where his fingers met. He said nothing, and in his silence I came to understand two things. First, that he did believe with all his being that the intent of these arts was not and is not military in origin or ethic. And second, that it might not be a good idea to piss off a guy that could rip my heart out and show it to me before I died.

"I guess I'm convinced." I said.

"No you're not." Tuttle said, smiling a bit. "But it's ok. That's the path you're on."

"Oh." I replied, not exactly sure how to respond to that one. I had this odd sense as I left that he'd somehow one-upped me, though to be honest I have no idea where.

The Two Buddhisms

A man with a watch knows what time it is.

A man with two watches is never sure. ~ Segal's Law

I could go on and on about the intricacies of all the sects of Buddhism out there, but the dialogue with M. Tuttle pretty much explains the two sides of things. As with most religions, there is the esoteric, mystical side and the exoteric physical side. Tuttle, and masters like him, are entirely on the esoteric end of things.

I maintain that it was the killing part that made the money and popularity for Buddhism in China and Japan. Emperors don't tend to back things unless they can get something out of it, and the history books show that the various martial artists through the years were invaluable to the emperors in warfare. But, as Tuttle explains better than I could, there is a mystos to it all that's still about reaching Nirvana and being One with everything.

Of course, if you wander in to a martial arts studio you're not about to see any of the mystos. Tuttle explains that these studios are to Buddhism what televangelists are to Christianity. They can teach you things, including how to kill, but seldom if ever do they explain why the energies work the way they do or what the meditative foundation is for the actions they teach. They are the popularization of a deep and meaningful idea.

This inner search is the basis of a lot of Buddhism, including M. Tuttle's. While I don't pretend to understand a lot of it, I do recognize that there's a big difference between what is the traditional, almost Theravada idea of inner search and meditation and the newer "look this is cool and I can kill people" approach.

Which approach is more popular really depends on who you're talking to. The "this is cool" approach is definitely the louder, more obvious one, and perhaps I'd be more inclined to agree with Tuttle's ideas if I'd seen more of the inside of a Buddhist monastery and less of Superkicks for Kids. (I did ask Tuttle if it would be ok for me to visit a monastery with him some day. He just kind of looked at me and wandered away. Must not have heard the question.)

THE DALAI LAMA

Don't underestimate the value of doing nothing.

~Pooh's Little Instruction Book

I figure I have to cover the Dalai Lama. He's probably the best known Buddhist of all time, and if I don't put him in the book I'll get tons of e-mail saying how I overlooked the single most important man in the history of Buddhism. The guy has better PR managers than Bill Clinton.

The Dalai Lama was born in Tibet. And China. And Korea. Before that he was born in India and, some think, Atlantis. The guy gets around. The Dalai Lama you see on TV these days is one of those Bodhisattvas we talked about earlier; an Enlightened soul that has taken an oath never to enter into Nirvana until the last soul precedes him, so, he keeps coming back in a new body every time he dies to keep trying to lead the world to enlightenment. This latest incarnation has become something of a superstar, giving interviews and doing commercials for Amnesty International. I got to meet the guy when he came through Ottawa a couple years back. He's definitely charismatic. Smiles a lot, jokes around. Genuinely seems to be a nice guy, especially for someone his age. (Somewhere around 10,000 years old)

The role of the Dali Lama was established in the 16th century, when Buddhism was well entrenched in China and the Orient. For whatever reason, Altai Khan declared that the leader of the Tibetan monks was a genuine Bodhisattva, and ordered that everyone recognize this. (Altai Khan was Gangus Khan's semi-great grandson. He took on the last name Khan and as he was really good at killin' no one bothered to point out that he wasn't actually related to Gangus. Altai was only a "blood" relative of Gangus if you're measuring blood relativity by sheer volume spilled rather than the traditional genetic link. However, the guy that Altai recognized as a Bodhisattva coincidentally recognized that Altai was the reincarnation of Gangus Khan. Funny that.) Given Altai's reputation, everyone kinda said "Ok, no problem. We got a Bodhisattva in Tibet."

From that time to this the leader of the Tibetan monks has supposedly been the same guy in different bodies. Whenever the old guy dies, the monks travel around to find the body he was born into when he died. They look for an infant that was born 49 days after the old guy died (the amount of time it apparently takes a Bodhisattva to change bodies). In order to prove it's him, they take a bunch of toys and stuff that the old guy picked out, mix them in with a bunch of other toys, then set a bunch of kids loose in the room and wait. If the soul (atman) of the Bodhisattva is in one of the kids, that kid will pick out all the toys that the old Bodhisattva had chosen before he died. If they don't pick the right ones, then they're not him.

The current guy has made a lot of headlines politically because he was ousted by the Chinese in 1959. He's been in exile from Tibet because the state there no longer recognizes any religion. He's been on a quest to re-instate Tibetan Buddhism and get his place back as head of the faith, but it's not happening. This actually pays off for him though, since the whole world now knows who he is. If he hadn't been ousted he would have probably just stayed in Tibet and been yet another obscure Bodhisattva. As it is, he's welcomed almost everywhere and afforded more respect than most politicians or Hollywood celebrities.

Anyway, that's who the Dalai Lama is; a Bodhisattva that's been ousted from Tibet and is trying to re-instate Tibetan Buddhism while striving to save every living creature by enlightening all Creation to the fulfillment of Nirvana and the loss of self. When he has time in all this, he also does commercials for Amnesty International.

Nice guy though. I don't buy into the whole 10,000 years old bit, but he's a nice enough guy.

BUDDHISM: SUM UP

I'm going to speak my mind because I have nothing to lose. ~S. I. Hayakawa

That's the gist of Buddhism. The martial arts bit and the Dalai Lama are just examples of what we wind up with after Buddhism hit the Orient. The external and the internal. Killers or pacifists. You can pretty much go through the list of sects and divide them up into these categories.

Yet again, I am likely to wind up with a ton of people screaming at me that I didn't go into all the deep meaning of each sect of Buddhism, nor did I give proper credit to the many seers and thinkers that have added to the lore and practice of Buddhism in China and Japan. So sue me.

The real story in all this is in the life of Siddhartha Gautama (Sid) and what was said and done back in India. If you understand these roots, and the tie in with Hinduism and Vedism, you'll have a better understanding of it all than most modern Buddhists. The idea of all of it comes from Sid trying to find a way to get off the roller coaster of life, called Samsara, and get on to something that can give you eternal bliss instead of chasing after temporary pleasures that always fail you eventually. THAT'S what Sid was about. The

K'ung Fu and Karate studios you see nowadays are so far removed from this that the instructors are likely to never have heard of the Eight Fold Path or Siddhartha Gautama. (Though they might know the term Buddha, they wouldn't be able to put any other name on him or tell you anything about his life.)

Still, there are some Theravadas out there in places like Sri Lanka that still follow the original doctrine. Not many mind you, but some. The Mahayanists are generally too busy worshipping Sid to bother with what he had to say about personal enlightenment, but they don't see it that way. To them, they're just trying to get the best reincarnation they can on the assumption that they won't find enlightenment this lifetime anyway.

And that about covers it. Again, you can go off and read all the holy books (like the Sutra, the Vedas, etc.) if you want a better explanation of all the intricate meaningful crap. But you've got the basics of it, which is what I was striving for.

EPILOGUE

Doubt grows with knowledge. ~ Goethe

And so we reach the end of book one.

The idea here has not been to give you every detail of every religion there is. Instead, I've tried to give you a good working idea of who did what when and, where possible, why. I look at it as a self-defense manual for Sunday mornings when they leave the gates open at the churches. It's always best to hit these people with information about their own history. They hate that.

This book has covered Judaism, Christianity, Islam, Hinduism and Buddhism. Other peripheral faiths like Hellenism and Mithra found their way in out of necessity, but the idea here was to cover these five main faiths and how they got started. Hopefully amid the jokes you've figured out that there's a lot more to these faiths than meets the eye-and a lot more history and fact than they teach in Sunday school or your history class. You'd be amazed at the information that's available. As I write this, I have a stack of books here that takes up most of the desk, and this is only a fraction of the stuff I used. Just the thought of doing the bibliography is daunting to me.

At some point I will get the notes together for *The Heathen's Guide to Holidays*. (Apparently someone else already stole the name 'The Heathen's Guide to the Rapture. Good to know I'm worth stealing from.) The Heathen's Guide to Xmas has been out already, and will be out again each Xmas season. I'll also be doing cults, and a few other books. I'll get it all done eventually. Just keep an eye on www.heathensguide.com.

Anyway, hope you liked the book, and I'll see ya next time around.

Later,

Wm. J. Hopper,

Author@Heathensguide.com

BIBLIOGRAPHY

Bibliography n.; A list of books intended to illustrate that the author has read enough of other people's thoughts to think his own.

From the Stone Age to Christianity	Albright, W.F.
The Cross and the Sacred Shroom,	Allegro, A.
The City of God,	Augustine, St.
Buddhism,	B r a z i l l e r , George
A History of Israel,	Bright, John
Holy Bible, Constantine (ed.),	
Diamond Sutra,	G a u t a m a , Siddhartha
A History of Jews at the Time Of Jesus Glatzer, N.	
The Cartoon History of the Universe,	Gonick, Larry
The Gospel: Origin and Growth ,	Grant, F.
Contemporary Islam and the Challenge of History,	Haddad, Yvonne Yazbeck
Three Faiths – One God,	Hick, John/ Edmund S. Meltzer
Armageddon,	Jeffries, Grant
The Complete Josephus	Josephus
Early Christian Doctrine,	Kelly, J.
Humanist Anthology,	Knight, Margaret
Judaism	Kung, Hans
The Four Gospels and Revelations,	L a t t i m o r e , Richard
Medieval Thought: St.Augustine to Ockham,	Leff, Gordon
The Arabs in History	Lewis, B.

The Book of Mormon,	Joseph Smith
Beyond Good and Evil,	Nietzsche
The Gay Science,	Nietzsche
Islamic Mysticism,	Nicholson, R.
Adam, Eve and the Serpent,	Pagels, Elaine
The Gnostic Scriptures,	Pagels, Elaine
A Dictionary of Non-Christian Religions,	P a r r i n d e r , Geoffrey
Revue du Qumran	Periodical
The Glorious Qu'ran,(trans.)	P i c t h a l l , Marmaduke
Hinduism,	Renou, Louis
The Nag Hammandai Library (ed.)	R o b i n s o n , James M.
The Religious Experience of *Mankind,* *6ᵗʰ Edition,*	Smart, Ninian
Why I am Not a Christian	R u s s e l l , Bertrand
The Transcendent Unity of Religions,	S c h u a n , Fritchoff
Understanding the Dead Sea Scrolls	S h a n k s , Hershel
Atheism: The Case Against God,	S m i t h , George H.
Tao Te Ching,	Tsu, Lao
The Bible According to Mark Twain	Mark Twain,
Analects of Confucius,	Tzu, K'ung Fu
Babylonian Talmud,	Unknown
Bagavagita,	Unknown
Upanishads,	Unknown
The Vedas,	Unknown
Aid to Bible Understanding,	Watch Tower Bible and Tract

Society *(No, I'm not Kidding)*

Muhammed, Prophet and Statesman,   Watt,   W. Montgomery

A Criminal History of Mankind,   Wilson, Colin

WILL'S GLOSSARY OF TERMS

(Or, "Those Things That Everyone's Going Get Pissed Off With and Say I Misinterpreted")

Aaron: Born in Egypt as a slave, he was basically Moses' sidekick. Since Moses stuttered, Aaron did all the speaking for him. It was Aaron's fuck up on Mount Sinai that kept the people of Israel in the desert for an extra eighty years or so. While Moses was carving up the Ten Commandments, Aaron let the people worship another god, and commissioned the building of a golden calf—a symbol of Baal worship. Moses saws this, killed a bunch of them, then told the ones that survived that their kids can go on to the Promised Land but only after the "wicked generation" had all croaked. (Except Aaron, of course, who went on to found a successful line of priest called Aaronites. Go figure.)

Abraham: The leader of a group of nomads that settled in Goshen circa 1600 BC. He was from what's now Syria. It was his lineage that became the nation of Israel, and it's for this reason that he is known as "the father of all Jews."

Ahimsa: literally translates as "not killing." The idea here was that you shouldn't kill anything, even for food, because all life is on a path to enlightenment and killing would only create more karma for both you and your lunch.

Ahura Mazda: The god of Zoroastrianism , a Persian faith that was suspiciously similar to modern Christianity.

Allah: Arabic for Yahweh, or "I Am." The same god that Adam, Moses, Abraham, JC and the bunch talked with—same God, different language.

Al-Uzza: the second most important Bedouin deity in Mecca at the time of Mohammed, believed to have something to do with luck.

Anthropomorphize: *Anthro* means human. *Morpho* means to morph, or change. So to anthropomorphize something is to change it so as to make it ether human or appear human. To anthropomorphize a god is to make him or her look human.

Apostles' Creed: The creed by which books were accepted or rejected from the Bible at the Nicene Council. Also called the Nicene Creed.

Arhat: kind of a living saint that had reached satori but was still in his body so that he could teach before he leaves to Nirvana when he dies.

Arius: A Christian bishop and founder of a movement called Arians (not the same as the Aryan racist-types). He and Marcius were the only Gnostic influences at the Nicene Council. Both were beheaded.

Aryans: These are the white folks. Originally from the Ural plains of Russia, these guys moved out over the globe, killing pretty much anything that happened across their path.

Atman: Basically exactly like the Xian soul. It's uniquely human, and it's karma is entirely dependent on the actions of the human who possess it.

Avatar: An avatar (Sanskrit, literally "down-coming') is a manifestation of a god, sort of a mask the god wears to come down and deal with pesky humans. In India there are 330 million gods, (of which the old Vedic gods Agni and Soma were just two minor characters.) These 330 million are actually only avatars. Above all the small piddly incarnations or avatars of the gods, there are three prime manifestation of godliness. These are Brahma, Shiva, and Vishnu. Brahma, Shiva, and Vishnu are, in turn, avatars of the one true god or Godhead, known as the Brahman.

Bagavadgita: A really long, drawn out poetic epic that I highly recommend you never read. The plot sucks and frankly so do the characters, Krishna included. The implication of this story is pretty fundamental to the Hindu religion however. You see, what all this meant was that people need not and should not remove themselves from society in order to rid themselves of karma. Instead, they were to stay as good soldiers, wives, farmers, whatever, and work in the knowledge that they were fulfilling the role rather than creating karma.

Baha Ullah: *Farci* (Persian) for "The Glory of God". The assumed name of the founder of Baha'I. His real name was Mizra Hussein Ali, but in 1863 he declared himself to be the prophet that Ali Muhammed, the Bab, had foretold. He changed his name to Baha Ullah, as he felt this new name was more fitting of his role as prophet. Kind the same way Norma Jean changed her name to Marilyn—it was more marketable.

Bodhisatva: a Buddhist monk who reached full enlightenment and died, but made a noble promise never to go into Nirvana (even though he could) until every soul proceeds him. He reincarnates and comes back over and over again to help people achieve Nirvana. He's on an eternal quest to enlighten all existence. According to his oath, he will only enter Nirvana when the last soul precedes him.

Brahma: The third guy in the Hindu trinity. He kind of faded away after being invented. Basically he was just a basic representation of the Brahman, used to link Shiva and Vishnu into one character. A middle man for a theology that wanted all the gods connected into three gods, then those three linked into one god called Brahman.

Brahman: In Hinduism the higher god that you couldn't see or feel but had to worship. When the people asked where this Brahman was, the priests developed a neat catch phrase "Neti neti', or "Not this, not that' to explain that the Brahman was beyond human conception and had no human attributes. It merely "Is'".

Brahmin: In the Hindu caste system these guys are the priestly class (originated with the Vedics, the pre-Hindu religion.) They considered themselves to be the first class of people, second only to the gods. As the Kshatriya didn't care a hell of a lot about what they said, the Brahmin got away with this

Buddha: means "the Enlightened One." Enlightenment was; the realization that an individual self is an illusion and that we (and all existence) are more properly one big energy mass. When we give up on the idea of being an individual, we achieve Enlightenment.

Canaan: In Genesis 10:15-19, Noah went on a drunken diatribe about how he hated the people living in the area now known as Israel. He swore that his sons would rule the area and get rid of the Canaanites. Much later, Abraham (as a descendant of Noah) was promised this land when he was tripping through to Egypt. Moses, a few generations later, actually claimed the land (calling it the Promised Land, since it was promised to Abraham by Yahweh because of Noah's drunken curse on the people there). Jacob, Moses successor, was the guy who actually claimed Canaan for Israel by killing off the Canaanites that lived there.

Canon: Comes from the Hebrew word *qaneh*, which literally means "cane," as in a stick you might use to beat someone with. Adopted by Catholicism to refer to the laws of the Church set up to make sure you did exactly what you were told. You can guess what happened to those who didn't.

Confucianism: A system of how to get along in society that was invented in 500 BC China and everyone's been raving about ever since. It's basically a patriarchal and imperial system that lets you know who you serve and who should serve you. (The man serves the Emperor, the woman serves the man, the child serves the parent, etc., etc.)

Dead Sea Scrolls: Scrolls buried by Essenic monks circa 66 AD. These scrolls represented the holiest texts of all sects of Judaism and were hidden in Qumran to protect them from the Roman retaliation during the Jewish Revolt.

Diaspora: Greek for "dispersion." The Diaspora was the dispersion of the Jews throughout the world after the revolt in 66 AD bought an end to the Jewish homeland.

Diet of Worms: A diet is a mini-council of religious leaders. Worms was a city. Martin Luther was finally and eternally excommunicated from Catholicism in April of 1521 at the Diet of Worms.

Ecumenical: A word that derives from the Greek *oikoumene*, meaning "the inhabited world." An "ecumenical" council is a council made up of representatives from the whole of the inhabited world.

Eight Fold Path: A lot like a 12 step program, but with monks instead of sponsors and you don't get a six-week badge for sobriety. It's really just a "How to be a nice, passive monk that doesn't want anything" list. It demands things like "Right thinking" and "Right breathing" and all that. Pretty basic to Buddhism, but not relevant unless you want to buy into all this and forsake your "self" in favor of eternal nothingness.

Elohim: Divine beings that inhabited nature. Special rocks or oases were considered to be filled with the entity of a "god" (elohim). Elohim as used in the Torah and Bible is always in the plural form.

El-Shaddai: Hebrew for "god of the mountains" (later reinterpreted as "God Almighty"). The god/genie that Abraham had a deal with.

Eschatology: The study of "end of the world" stories and prophesies from all religions. Christians use to the word to refer to discussions of the second coming of Christ, the Apocalypse and the day I get dragged off to hell.

Essenes: A Jewish sect started by the remnants of another Jewish sect, the Hasidim, that had been obliterated circa 525 BC. Led by the Teacher of Righteousness, these guys believed in love, peace, and an apocalyptic war to end all wars. After nearly a millennium of preparing for said war, the Essenes were quickly and efficiently wiped off the face of the Earth by the Roman army in 70 AD.

Excommunication: As the word implies, it's the end of communication-specifically with the Roman Catholic Church- when you've done something bad, like writing this book. In the Middle Ages, excommunication could be considered synonymous with "ex-corporeal," or "ex-parrot."

Four Noble Truths:

1: Life is shit.

2: Life is shit because people keep wanting things that are just going to disappoint them.

3: Life would not be shit if you as an individual didn't have these cravings.

4: The only way to be free of your cravings and release yourself from Samara (the Wheel of life) is to follow the eight-fold path.

Gehenna: It translates as "pit of fire," in Greek "holocaust." It was originally a pit beneath or beside a home used for heating, and was also used occasionally (as was the case with Meshach and Abednego) to roast one's enemies. The idea of gehenna later evolved into the Judeo-Christian concept of hell.

Gnosticism: A popular polytheistic Christianity that's only vaguely mentioned in the Bible in Paul's letters. It comes from the Greek word gnosis, meaning "divine knowledge."

God: See "About the Author" at back of book.

    Gospel: Greek for "good news."

Grail: It's a cup used at the Last Supper: It's just a cup. That's it. No magic. No immortality. Just a plain old cup.

Hasidism: From a Hebrew word meaning "pious." A Jewish school of thought that was basically ripped off from Hinduism. The founder, Israel Baal Shem, created the idea of a pure and righteous man through whom the power of Yahweh could be channeled and experienced by those around him.

Herod the Great: The Herod that supposedly killed every male child under the age of three because he was told a new king was born was of a line of regional governors. He and his family had claimed a semi-kingship over Israel at the time of JC.

Hijrah: The Muslim era from 622 AD on. I means "The Migration," and refers to Mohammed's relocation from Taif to Medina. The Holy: The area in the Temple on the Mount (separated from the Most Holy by a blue cloth) where the Levite priests could see and read from the Torah.

Hinayana: or "smaller vehicles". To the Mahayanist the old fashioned personal enlightenment guys (the Theravadas) were considered oddballs, and are still referred to today as Hinayana, or "smaller vehicles". Ok, the language thing doesn't quite capture it, but that's a pretty big insult to the Theravadas in their own language.

Ialdoboath: "God of the Deaf "-the Gnostic creator god. An immature, childish god that did things like throw tantrums and kill everybody because they wouldn't love him. His garden of Eden was seen as a prison, a place where Ialdoboath could keep his creations as stupid, ignorant pets that would worship him blindly

Indulgences: Letters signed by the Pope and bought by Catholic sheep in the Middle Ages. They were basically "Get-Out-of-Hell-Free" cards. Islam: An Arabic word that translates as "submission," meaning submission to the will of God.

Israel: "Preservers With God." It's just a name hung on the descendants of Abraham to say, "Yeah, we're the guys that made a deal with the god/genie/deity guy on the mountain." Israel Baal Shem: See Hasidism.

Jehovah: The King James Version of the Bible translates "Yahweh" as being "Jehovah." Both words are translated from the same Hebrew word, but the KJ guys decided to be different. No real reason there. They just plain decided they wanted to write it out in English characters in a different way than everyone else did.

Jehovah's Witnesses: The original "millennium fever" guys. They're an American Christian sect started in Pittsburgh at the turn of the century by a guy named Charles Taze Russell. The adherents believe we are living in the end times and that both JC and the anti JC are on earth now, warming up for the final battle of Armageddon. Jesus: English version of Hebrew

Kabah: Similar to Rome's Hall of Gods, this was a shrine where each deity was represented. It was basically a cube with a whole bunch of icons and trinkets associated with the gods. It was built on top of the sacred Black Stone that still sits there. Since Mohammed, it has been converted to monotheism and represents only Allah.

Kabala: The mystic branch of Judaism. It is an esoteric philosophy that uses the standard books of Judaism (Torah, Talmud, Mishnas, etc.) but interprets them according to a book called the Zohar.

Karma: Literally translates from Sanskrit as "Doing"', as in "What are you doing with that gun?". In the Vedic tradition it referred to what people were *doing*. (i.e.: a Brahmin priest's Karma was sacrificing, a soldiers Karma was fighting.. You get the idea.) The idea of Karma had nothing to do with fate or doom or payback. More importantly, there is no real concept of Good' or Bad' karma. There was only karma, the doing of things.

Kshatriya: The Warrior class in the Hindu caste system. These are the guys directly responsible for offing the Indus Valley Civilization, and pretty much every other civilization they came across.

Labarum: a symbolic cross with JC's monogram. Manes: Roman ghosts honored in a form of ancestral worship. Moses

Mahayana: Means "Wide vehicle". A Buddhist belief system that a whole pantheon of Buddhas and Bodhisattvas could be worshipped and prayed to for help and guidance in getting to Nirvana. The name was picked because they felt that their idea of help from the Bodhisattvas allowed more people to reach Nirvana, or at least a better reincarnation. Of course, in order for them to help you you'd have to go to a temple and sacrifice accordingly to them, so the monks finally found a way to make a living.

Mendelson: Known as the first modern Jew. He was a philosopher from Westphalia. He basically looked at Orthodox Judaism, Kabala, and Hasidism, then shrugged his shoulders. As a fan of Immanuel Kant, he followed Kant's lead by reducing the faith to its base elements. From there, thought Mendelson, you can build on it any way you want and still be Jewish.

Messiah: Hebrew word meaning "anointed of God" (Christos in Greek). This is yet another one of those deep, mystic words that causes all kinds of fuzzy notions about things. To be "anointed" meant you were recognized as king. Saul, David, and Solomon were all messiahs, a.k.a. kings.

Mithras: The god of a popular Persian religion called Mithra. Mithras was very akin to Apollo, and, lie Jesus, was adopted into Emperor Constantine's vision of the world as being Apollo's alter-ego.

Mohenjodaro & Harrapa: Somewhere around 5,000 BC, Mohenjodaro and Harrapa in the Indus Valley were some of the few (if not the only) centers of human civilization on the planet. They had houses, public baths, that sort of thing. An easy going lot that farmed, tended to their families, and generally loved and honored all things. They weren't war-like, and had no ideas of conquest or domination. Instead, they lived quiet lives that genuinely reflected a willingness to get along and care for the people and land around them. Naturally then, they were slaughtered mercilessly and wiped off the face of the Earth.

Moksa (or *Moksha*): Sanskrit for liberation' or Freedom'. It's the Hindu equivalent of Nirvana. So Moksha is Nirvana.

Mystery Religion: Any religion that utilizes a ceremony wherein the adherents to "touch the Divine," as is supposed to happen with the Catholic Eucharist (people eat bread and wine that they believe is the transubstantiated body and blood of Jesus Christ). They're called "mystery religions" because they lay claim to "mystos," or hidden truths. Nephilim: A offspring of angels and humans mating.

Nirvana: Absence of Self or atman, wherein we give up all our karma (or personal actions) and cease to be individuals. We become One with all things, and finally find an eternal peace that isn't dependent on the physical world.

Numen: The Roman gods before Hellenism. Roughly the same idea as the Judaic version of the elohim. Pl., Numina.

Numerology: The study of (and belief in) a cosmic connection between numbers and mysticism. The belief that many deep and secret things can be revealed from seemingly innocent text if interpreted by applying various numerical codes.

Paulinian: Written by the apostle Paul. There's way too much of this stuff.

Pentateuch: The scholastic word that professors and theologians use to refer to the Torah.

Pharaoh: An Egyptian word meaning "king." Ramses, who ousted

Moses from Egypt, became a pharaoh when his father died and he ascended the throne.

Pharisees: A less political Judaic sect than the Sadducees, but way more religious. They believed in exact obedience to every word recorded in the Torah, no matter what. These guys are the rabbis and scribes, the ones you hear about who came out to chastise Jesus for not following "the Law."

Pogrom: Yiddish for "massacre," specifically the massacre of Jews in Europe in the Middle Ages.

Prana: In Vedic philosophy, living things have a quality of animation called the Prana. It was kind of what we might call a soul, but it wasn't really a personal being... just a force that inhabited and drove living stuff. Prana was from a central font of all Prana, called Nirvana.

Qu'ran: Arabic for "The Reading," meaning the reading of the silk scroll that the angel Gabriel presented to Mohammed. (Also spelt Koran, K'ran, and a thousand other ways.)

Rabbi(Or rebbe): It means "teacher" in Hebrew, and can be used to refer either to any person who teaches Judaism, or more specifically to the leader of a Jewish congregation who is qualified to instruct in Judaic law.

Rapture: An event supposed to occur just before JC comes back, where God will take 144,000 people he feels are just and kind and good and get them off the planet before the shit hits the fan.

Romulus and Remus: Two twin brothers who were abandoned at birth and raised by wolves until they were old enough to build the city of Rome.

Sadducees: A conservative sect of Judaism that abided by the "Law of the Prophets."

Samsara: The whole Wheel of Life thing. You're tied to the Wheel of Life by your desires, actions, and intentions. Both good intentions and bad intentions keep you coming back. Since both Hinduism and Buddhism see this as a bad thing, the idea of both religions is to free yourself from Samara by freeing yourself from all karma.

Sanatana Dharma: It's Sanskrit again. It means "Eternal Truth'. It was an extension of Vedism that was designed to create (sorry, "reveal') a higher god that you couldn't see or feel but had to worship. (I.E. Brahman)

Sangha: Originally a place that would be screened in before the rainy season and very carefully swept and cleaned so that no bugs would be there. Then, when the rains came, the monks could gather there where they could move about without killing anything. The Sanghas became temples in time as monks moved in and stayed there all year long. Besides, the Mahayana's needed a place for the people to give alms, in exchange for which they'd pray for the poor bastards who would never be enlightened.

Satori:Temporary enlightenment.

Shi'l: These are the guys that decided Abu Bahk was a jerk and rejected the line of caliphs, basically saying that the leadership of Islam should have been taken over by the descendants of Mohammed rather than democratically elected.

Shiva : First god in the Hindu Trinity, Shiva is the sustainer of all life, the source of all yogic power, the great and eternal meditative force in the universe, yada yada, you get the idea. Major guy in the Hindu pantheon. His devotees (yogis) smear themselves in ashes and sit around contemplating the temporary nature of the universe. Shiva was, actually I suppose IS, the god of the ascetic. The one you'd go to get in touch with your inner self and understand your place in the universe. All the hippies that traveled to India to Find themselves' during the sixties would have wound up in some form of Shiva worship.

Shudras: In the Hindu caste system they are the servant class. They're basically your average conquered people, considered low-life and generally abused.

Soma: The juice of a plant (perhaps asclepias acida) whose stalks were crushed and fermented then offered to the gods of ancient India.' *Source: A Dictionary of Non-Christian Religions, Geoffrey Parrinder, Hulton Press, 1981*

Sufism: From Sufi, an Arabic word for cheap cloth. Refers to the mystic branch of Islam.

Sunni: The most popular branch of Islam, whose origins follow the line of caliphs but do not acknowledge the Shi'l imams.

Synod at Jabna in 97 AD: A council where the Pharisees saw the chance to change Judaism into the faith they always wanted it to be by creating the Talmud.

Synoptic Gospels: Matthew, Mark, Luke, and John. They give the synopsis of Jesu's life, while all other biblical texts talk about stuff before and after he was on Earth.

Talmud: A book codifying all the rules and laws of Judaism. Basically reflects Pharisaical Judaism, with a heavy emphasis on legality and covenant.

Taoism: A belief in one all encompassing thing called the Tao (pronounced "Dow" as in Dow Jones Industrial). If you surrender yourself to the Tao and work within it your life is easy. If you work against the natural flow of energies by thinking and planning stuff out you're gonna have a hard time of it. It's where George Lucas stole the idea of The Force from.

The Ark of the Covenant: A Judaic artifact containing manna, the Rod of Aaron, a copy of the Ten Commandments and the Torah.

The Book of Mormon: A book translated from golden plates that were revealed to a man named Joseph Smith in upstate New York. They gave a dubious and uncorroborated account of the travels of the Lost Tribe of Israel across the Atlantic and into America.

The Copper Altar: The altar upon which a sacrifice was made in the Temple of David. The Altar Room was the Temple's antechamber— The first place you'd see as you came through the door.

The Hyksos: (Believed to translate as "Shepherd Kings.") are a bunch of guys that ruled Egypt for a time. No one knows who they were, but the name seems to suggest that they were from a nomadic tribe of herdsmen, not unlike Abraham's, that had managed to kill enough people to take control of the country. This nomadic heritage might explain how folks like Joseph and Abraham would have had connections with so powerful a political body as the Hyksos.

The Most Holy: a.k.a. The Holy Of Holies (Sanctum Sanctorum in Latin), was the chamber in Solomon's Temple where the Ark of the Covenant was kept.

The Upanishads: This is the book that killed Vedism. written as the first books to reflect this passing of old gods into new Gods; the tale of the higher ups taking over and leaving behind poor old Agni and Athurva , who all but died with the passing of Vedism

Theravada : Buddhist belief system Sid set up and it is centered on achieving personal enlightenment. It means "Way of the elders".

Torah : The first five books of the Bible-Genesis, Exodus, Leviticus, Numbers, and Deuteronomy. Supposedly written by Moses.

Vaisya : In the Hindu caste system these were the folks that actually did the work in the society. Merchants, farmers, that sort of thing.

Vedas : The Vedas are books. ("Veda" is actually the Sanskrit word for "knowledge", but when you refer to the Vedas you're talking about the books.) They're considered really holy and sacred, and are the foundation of almost all Eastern religious thought. Think of them as the Torah of the East. Collectively they form the back bone of both Hindu and Buddhist thought

Vedism Vedism, like early Judaism, is the launch pad for other belief systems. In the same way that the Mormons, Catholics, Muslims and Jehovah's Witnesses all started from Abraham 's deal with El-Shaddai, Hinduism and all the Buddhist sects derive from Vedism. It's objective--- getting rid of the self or atman to achieve eternal bliss--is standard fare in all eastern beliefs. It's the way you get to that stage that differs, which is how ya wind up getting all kinds of religions out of the same premise.

Vishnu: Second god in the Hindu trinity, Vishnu covers all the basic stuff that Shiva misses. Where Shiva does the ascetic trip, Vishnu is more about the external world of worship and ceremony. Basically Vishnu is the god for Hindus who would have grown up to be Born-again Christians had they been raised in America.

Yahweh : Hebrew for "I Am." The god Moses spoke with.

Yehoshua (pronounced "Jeshua" or "Joshua"). It was a common enough name at the time of JC, translating as "salvation of Yahweh." The Greek form of the word was Ieosous (Aye-E-oh-suse) which was translated into English as Jesus 'cause we just couldn't say it properly. In Hebrew it's the same name as "Joshua".

Yiddish: A "high" or "proper" German language, traditionally written and not spoken. It was adopted by Jews at a time when many of them were scribes.

Yogi and Yoga: Both words mean 'yoke', as in the thing you use to control oxen. It's a Control' or means' to achieve mystic stuff.

Zealots: A radical sect of Judaism that advocated open rebellion against Rome (and Herod whom they didn't recognize as king).

They were the "messianics," which means they wanted a real messiah (king) to take over.

Zion: The name of the "mountain (it's actually more of a big hill) that Jerusalem and Solomon's Temple sit on.

Zoroastrianism: Worship of Ahura Mazda, the ultimate god of Mithra.

End Notes

Judaism

(Endnotes)

1 Bible, Genesis 2, 10-14

2 Legend: The Genesis of Civilization Rohl, David M. Random House UK Distribution; November 24, 1998, ISBN: 071267747X

3 Smart, Ninian The Religious Experience of Mankind, p.284

4 Bible, Genesis12:5

5 A Dictionary of Non-Christian Religions, Parrinder, Geoffrey, p. 117.

6 Exodus 3:1-14

7 http://www.wsu.edu/~dee/MESO/CODE.HTM Wow... you actually looked for it. Good for you. Most people just pretend they're gonna look it up in the endnotes then forget all about it.

8 http://dictionary.reference.com/search?q=Pentateuch

9 Bible, Jonah 1:17

10 See:"The Queen of Sheba and Her Son Menyelek: The Kebra Nagast" E. A. Wallis Budge (Translator), E. A. Budge

11 1 Kings, iv.

12 Note that this figure was worked out in the first edition of this book, so the value is actually higher now. I could have worked out the new figures but I figured it would take too long and really all you cared about seeing were a whole bunch of zeros in a row to give the idea that it was a whole hell of a lot of money. Ok I am lazy.

13 1 Kings 6

14 2 Chronicles 34:33

15 2 Chronicles 36:23

16 The timeline of these Antiochus guys is confusing, so

I am putting the chronology here.

Antiochus I, 280-261 BCE

Antiochus II, 261-246 BCE

Antiochus the Great,

223-187 BCE

Antiochus IV Epiphanes,

175-164 BCE

Antiochus V, 163-162 BCE

Antiochus VII, 137-128 BCE

Antiochus VIII, 125-96 BCE

Antiochus IX, 95-95 BCE

Antiochus X 94-92 BCE

17   The main source for the Maccabees stuff are the First and Second Books of the Maccabees (found in some bibles but not all of them). You can also find them in Antiquities by Josephus.

18   Trust me, you don't care what happened with Antiochuses V through VII

19   You'll find a good copy of this resolution at http://www.yale.edu/lawweb/avalon/un/res181.htm

20   The Inalienable Rights of the Palestinian People (UN General Assembly Resolution 3236, 1974) http://student.cs.ucc.ie/cs1064/jabowen/IPSC/php/db.php?piwptype=article&id=527&journalID=0&href=http://domino.un.org/UNISPAL.NSF/9a798adbf322aff38525617b006d88d7/025974039acfb171852560de00548bbe?OpenDocument&Highlight=2,3236

21

Christianity

_____

See: http://www-personal.   umich.edu/~rtanter/

22   http://en.wikipedia.org/wiki/First_Intifada

23   http://www.palestinercs.org/crisistables/table_of_figures.htm

24   http://www.aljazeerah.info/News%20archives/2004%20News%20archives/Jan/27n/Hamas%20proposal%20of%2010year%20truce%20scorned.htm

25   http://www.cnn.com/2006/WORLD/meast/02/18/mideast.ap/index.html

26   James Strong, John R. Kohlenberger III, James A. Swanson, John R. Kohlenberge   Strong's Exhaustive Concordance of the Bible, The, Zondervan; Revised edition September 1, 2001, ISBN: 0310233437

27   Ibid.

28   Ibid.

29   Matthew 6:1-14

30   Matthew 21:23

31   Try these other events for proof of human endurance: MAN DIED FOR TWO HOURS: STILL LIVES — "Miracle" amazes doctors — ("Sunday Tribune" 27/3/60). HE DIED FOR 4 MINUTES — Man's heart stops but he lives on — ("Sunday Express" 23/7/61). DR. RETURNED FROM THE DEAD — ("Cape Argus" 4/5/61). THE COFFIN MOVED — Young man narrowly escaped being buried alive — ("Sunday Tribune" 13/5/62). BACK FROM THE DEAD — After being thought dead for 2 days — ("Post" 25/7/65). "CLINICALLY DEAD" — Toddler alive after hour-long revival battle —("Natal Mercury" 5/12/82). WAS HE DEAD OR ALIVE? — The dilemma facing transplant Doctors — ("Sunday Tribune" 17/7/83). SHAKEN AND STIRRED — Declared clinically dead "from too much Christmas liquor" — ("Daily News" 3/1/84).

32   "Essenes" is an English transliteration of the Greek Essenoi, which I earlier translated as "Monks with axes". Some etymologists believe the name comes from the Aramaic 'asen,' asayya, meaning "healers," Source: http://

mb-soft.com/believe/txo/essene.htm

33   The Catholic Encyclopedia http://www.newadvent.org/cathen/11049a.htm

34   Bible, Lev., iv, 3, I Kings 1:39 Oil was also used for Cyrus, king of Persia, Isaiah 45:1

35   That's another word I really love-anthropomorphized. It's really long and sounds cool. It's actually pretty simple. Anthro means man or humans for the politically correct out there. Morpho means, well, morph; to change something. So to anthropomorphize something is to change it in such a way as to make it either human or appear human

36   By the way, the word philosopher comes from "philo," for lover, and "sophia," for wisdom— so, philosophers are "lovers of wisdom".

37   Transubstantiation: the doctrine holding that the bread and wine of the Eucharist are transformed into the body and blood of Jesus, although their appearances remain the same. http://dictionary.reference.com/search?q=transubstantiation

38   Ok... I like M-dashes. —

39   Actually follow up on this one if you can. Go find The Complete Dead Sea Scrolls in English by Geza Vermes. Allen Lane Publishers; July 1997. ISBN: 0713991313. It is very worth the read.

40   Bible, Acts 9:4

41   His affliction is discussed in: I Cor. 2:1-5; II Cor. 11:23-29; Gal. 6:17; Phil. 1:30; II Tim. 1:11-12; 2:9; etc

42   For those who care, the modern word agnostic has the same root. "A" is a negative prefix in Greek, so agnostic means "not having divine knowledge" or "I dunno."

43   Colin Wilson, A Criminal History of Mankind, Eric Dobby Publishing ISBN: 1858820545 p.215

44   Ibid. p. 216

45   Reprinted her: http://www.newadvent.org/fathers/2819.htm

46   Myna, by the way, is in Turkey. And no, there was no mention of reindeer at the council.

47   For a much better overview of all this read Elaine Pagels' The Gnostic Scriptures. Vintage Press, ISBN: 0679724532

48   James M. Robinson The Nag Hammadi Library: A Translation of the Gnostic ScripturesHarperCollins Publishers ISBN: 0060669330

49   Ibid., The Apocalypse of Peter

50   Ibid.

51   Bible, 1 Corinthians 7:9

52   Polygamy references in the bible: Exodus 21:10, 2 Samuel 5:13; 1 Chronicles 3:1-9, 14:3, 1Kings 11:3, King Solomon 2 Chronicles 11:21, Deuteronomy 21:15

53   Rape: Deut.22: 25-27 Incest: 1Cor. 5:1 Bestiality: Lev. 20: 15 etc.

54   A good working report on the Muslin side of this story can be found at: http://www.jerusalemites.org/history_of_palestine/7.htm

55   Ok, another website, but some of them really are good references. Like this one if you want a good look at the Crusades and who did what when: http://www.medievalcrusades.com/

56   You can find copies of all of Calvin's works at: http://www.barnabasplace.com/CalvinWrks01.html

57   I am going to quote this one for you as it's just too good not to know: "And [the Lord] had caused the cursing to come upon then, yea, even a sore cursing, because of their iniquity. For behold, they had hardened their hearts against him, that they had become like unto a flint; wherefore, as they were white, and exceedingly fair and delightsome, that they might not be enticing unto them the Lord God did cause a skin of blackness to come upon them."

And thus saith the Lord God: I will cause that they shall be loathsome unto thy people, save they shall repent of their iniquities. And cursed shall be the seed of him that mixeth with their seed; for they shall be cursed even with the same cursing. And the Lord spake it, and it was done. (2 Nephi 5:21-23)

58 Kings 11:1-11, 2 Samuel 5:13, Exodus 21:10, 1 Kings 11:3, 2 Chronicles 11:2, Deuteronomy 21:15 (and for the Xians who think the Old Testament marriage laws do not apply to Xians...) Matthew 5:17-18 and especially Matthew 22:24-28

59 Doctrine and Covenants Section 89

60 Find and read: Steven Naifeh and Gregory White Simth, The Mormon Murders: A True Story of Greed, Forgery, Deceit, and Death Onyx Books; Reissue edition (June 1989) ASIN: 0451401522

61 Luke 22: 20:22-24

62 Charroux, France and Calcata, Italy are examples. Note though that the Vatican discourages this practice nowadays... they claim it encouraged "irreverent curiosity". Also, in 1983, thieves broke in and stole the 300 year-old jewel-encrusted foreskin from the reliquary in France. Fill in your own joke there. It's too easy.

63 I have to add this one in... In the 1400's Catherine of Sienna wrote about her "marriage" to Jesus in The Dialogue. According to her account, Jesus actually cut off his own foreskin of and his made it into a ring with which she was married to Him.

64

Islam

Smart, Ninian The Religious Experience of Mankind, p.290-292

65 Ibid., 291

66 Hadîth of the Prophet, Ibn Abî H.âtim in the introduction of al-Jarh. wa al-Ta`dîl (p. 22-23)

67 Holy Qur'aan 29:48

68 Bukhari Volume 1, Book 1, Number 3

69 Hafiz Ibn Hibban reported in al-Sahih (11/203/#4862)

70   Smart, Ninian The Religious Experience of Mankind, p.399

71   I really had to search to make sense of this. On the surface, it sounds like it's telling people it's okay to turn away from the faith. After speaking to an Islamic friend of mine, it was explained to me that, as with all Islamic literature, it loses a lot in the translation. Muslims believe the only true language for their scripture is Arabic, since that is what it was originally written in. Anyway, this line apparently means that those who want to turn away from Allah are hurting themselves, not Allah. Instead, they should be thankful that the prophet Mohammed was ever there to begin with, and Allah will reward those that are thankful.

72   "circa". I should explain that word... you see it all the time in academic papers and stuff. It's a Latin word that's often used in English by people who feel too uptight to say within a hundred years or so. It makes it sound like you know what you're talking about when you're really not sure. You see, when I say The caliphs did okay until the Umayyad Dynasty, circa 720 AD... I don't need to have a clue when the Umayyad Dynasty actually began. It could have been anywhere between 620A.D. and 820A.D. but because I said circa I'd still be right. See how cleverly scholars cover their ignorance?

73   Figure out the lineage there... it seems a tad close to me.

74   A Dictionary of Non-Christian Religions, Parrinder, Geoffrey, p. 133

75   Ibid p. 276

76   Ibid p. 153

77   A Dictionary of Non-Christian Religions, Parrinder, Geoffrey, p. 195

78   http://www.zackvision.com/weblog/archives/entry/000211.html

79   Louis Alexander Olivier De Corancez, Eric Tabet (Translator), Louis Alexandre De Corancez, Louis Alexandre Olivi Corancez History of the Wahabis (Founders of Saudi Arabia)

Garnet Pub Ltd; (September 1997) ISBN: 1859640362

80   A Dictionary of Non-Christian Religions, Parrinder, Geoffrey, p.268

81   See: http://www.geocities.com/onemansmind/hg/noi.html

Vedism/Hinduism

_____

82   This guy went to a farm and noticed a pig with a wooden leg hobbling about.

"Excuse me," the guy said to the farmer, "but why does that pig have a wooden leg?"

"Oh, it's like this, sir... one night a robber entered our household, tied all of us up, stole our jewelry and was about to escape when the pig came out of nowhere, attacked the robber and saved us all."

"Oh, I see," said guy said, "but I still don't understand. Why does the pig have a wooden leg?"

"Oh, it's like this, sir... There was a fire when we were all out at movies. The pig alerted our neighbors, ran around organizing a water bucket system, and helped the firemen put out the fire."

The guy was getting quite frustrated. "Listen, this is all very interesting, but I still don't get why the pig has a wooden leg. How did it get a wooden leg!?!"

"Oh, it's like this, sir..." the farmer said. "We used to have an old well. One day, our little daughter fell down the well. The pig jumped in, saved our girl, covered the well with planks and we never had that trouble again."

The guy then shouted, "I DON'T GET IT! WHY does that damn pig have a wooden leg?"

The farmer glared back at the man in indignation. "Well, " he said finally, "a pig like that you don't eat it all at once..."

83   A Dictionary of Non-Christian Religions, Parrinder, Geoffrey, p.34

84   Ibid p. 243

85   Ibid p. 35

86   Ibid 270

Buddhism

87   You can read the verbatim version of these truths at: Smart, Ninian The Religious Experience of Mankind, p.98-99

88   circa 1280-1300A.D

Printed in Great Britain
by Amazon

39874885R00165